Women Remember

Women Remember

An oral history

Anne Smith

R

ROUTLEDGE
London and New York

First published 1989 by Routledge
11 New Fetter Lane, London EC4P 4EE
29 West 35th Street, New York, NY 10001

Printed in Great Britain by
T. J. Press Ltd, Padstow, Cornwall

British Library Cataloguing in Publication Data
Smith, Anne
Women remember: an oral history
1. Great Britain. Women. Social life, history
I. Title
941'0088042

Library of Congress Cataloging in Publication Data
Smith, Anne
Women remember.
1. Women—Great Britain—Biography. 2. Aged women—
Great Britain—Biography. 3. Oral biography. I. Title.
CT3320.S65   1989   920.72'0941   89–5977

ISBN 0–415–03330–6

Contents

[Photos of the women as they are now by Vicky Wheeler]

Introduction

A few years ago a friend heard an item on a radio programme about a retreat for women in Sussex, where they could go to write or relax. We were both keen, and I agreed to go down for a week to try it out. I expected to find a semi-commercial version of the American yaddos, writers' retreats. What I did find was a sort of holiday-home for retired and mainly ancient Sussex gentlewomen.

I was enthralled and amused by these women's conversations, about how Kenya had gone to the dogs since it got its independence; playing cricket at school after the Great War; the shocking immorality of modern fiction – all in accents I had never heard before, and with a vocabulary in which echoes of Jane Austen seemed to mingle with Enid Blyton or the *Girls' Own Paper*. The ladies were all die-hard readers of the *Daily Telegraph*; they were socially confident, hearty, naive, and quite snobbish in a way that was amusing in its antiquity. Hardly a day passed without some hilarious comment. Watching a male body-builder in a fluid pose of rippling muscles on television, for instance, one of them exclaimed, 'He looks just like the X-ray of my colon!' One woman introduced herself to me with, 'I say, are you the new girl?'

I felt like some latter-day Rip Van Winkle who had slept backwards through time, and was constantly recalling these lines from Robert Lowell's *During Fever*:

> back in those settled years of World War One.
> Terrible that old life of decency
> without unseemly intimacy
> or quarrels, when the unemancipated woman
> still had her Freudian papa and maids!

Then one sunny morning in the garden I got into conversation with Phyllis, an eighty-six-year-old. We had not spoken before because Phyllis sat alone at meal-times, with her back to the rest of us. I asked her why and she explained that if she had company at meals she was inclined to talk far too much. I could not decide whether this was touching or ominous, but as we talked and I asked her about her life, I became fascinated.

Phyllis had been brought up like any middle-class Edwardian girl, but then her father had lost his money and suddenly she had her living to make. She had taught English and netball at a French convent school in the beginning, and eventually became a secretary–companion to a series of noblewomen who ranged from the eccentric to the downright autocratic. A spell in the Civil Service, during which she was secretary to a high-ranking Ghanaian minister, came in somewhere. The planned retirement had to be postponed after Phyllis gambled and lost all her savings on the Stock Exchange. She retired in her mid-seventies. For decades she had lived in a flat that was really a glorified cupboard in Shepherd's Market, spending her days in her club nearby, playing bridge.

Phyllis and I became fast friends, but very soon I discovered that she was dying, with cancer of the liver. I visited her in a hospice in Milton Keynes. She asked me to find out about a home for retired gentlefolk in Kensington. She could not stand the kindness of the hospice or, I think, this public way of dying. She was accustomed to being alone.

I went to see the home in Kensington. Inside the front door I encountered a purple-faced caricature of the crusty old colonel in a wheelchair. I asked him if he wanted any help and he responded with a snorting grunt of refusal, like a buffalo disturbed at a watering-hole. Other such ancient relics of both sexes were dotted around the sitting-room and the television-room, doing nothing at all so far as I could make out, but waiting to die. The matron was charming, the room was adequate. I reported to Phyllis and she arranged to move in.

As soon as she had moved to Kensington, Phyllis's condition deteriorated dramatically. Her hearing and her speech both faded; we communicated with notes. I sat by her in the early evenings, and what should have been a companionable silence was regularly punctuated by the eldritch shrieks and tormented groans of an old lady, a past president of the association that ran the home, wandering the corridor outside. Another old woman haunted the lift, trying to get out.

There was a commode in Phyllis's room, but she could not use it without assistance. One evening she asked me to ring for a nurse to help her. I rang and we waited for fifteen minutes, but no one came. I rang again. Another ten minutes passed. I went in search of a nurse. The shift was changing, I was told, but someone would come soon. I went back to Phyllis's room. When forty minutes had passed since I first rang for a nurse, I went back to the nurses' base. In the end, it had taken three-quarters of an hour for someone to come. How long it might have taken if I had not complained is anyone's guess. The whole experience made me think hard about what it says of our society, our civilization, that we can treat the elderly as we do.

Phyllis preferred moderate neglect to constant fussing. When she had been ill in the past she had only told her friends after she left hospital. I thought I saw in this what I have seen in other members of her generation, my grandmother's generation: courage and ferocious independence. I thought, somewhere the stories of these lives should be told, especially now, when the breakdown of family life means that few of us have ready access to our grandmothers while, paradoxically, the population of the elderly is booming. But as Simone de Beauvoir observed, 'Society looks upon old age as a kind of shameful secret that it is unseemly to mention' (*La Vieillesse*, 1970; English translation by Patrick O'Brian, Penguin, 1977). The number of grandmothers who will admit to being grandmothers is dwindling fast.

We shove our old folk away to vegetate in 'residential' homes (what is a home if it is not residential?), and in the process we deny ourselves the richest source of human history, the first-hand history of the human spirit, with the vital sense of continuity that comes with it. Without this intimate sense of continuity the history offered by the textbooks is quite meaningless, even irrelevant, and biographies of famous men and women only contribute to the destructive myth of the mass media, that the value or significance of any individual is directly related to the degree of fame or notoriety he or she manages to achieve. Now more than ever Gray's *Elegy* applies:

Let not ambition mock their useful toil
Their homely joys, and destiny obscure;
Nor grandeur hear with a disdainful smile,
The short and simple annals of the poor.

– if for 'poor' you read 'ordinary'.

The old cliché is true: there is no such being as an 'ordinary' person. One day I sat beside an old woman in the Botanical Gardens in Edinburgh. She was a retired postmistress, eighty-six years old. Hilda's father had been a gamekeeper on the Isle of Islay at the beginning of this century. She told me tales of how she and her brother used to go fishing at night in a rowing-boat with a blind fisherman; how her brothers knitted their own socks in the evenings when they were boys and how one, forced to retire through illness, now knitted socks for Oxfam that were very popular with the Aberdeenshire farmers; and about how Andrew Carnegie had donated little bookcases of the Victorian classics to all the schools in the Highlands. She told me, most memorably, about her first taste of a tomato, which she had expected to be a very superior sort of apple, and the shock she got, and how she had never eaten a tomato again from that day forward.

If life is interesting and worth living, then it follows that old folk who have lived long have a lot to offer succeeding generations. That was my first, simple reason for approaching the women in this book for their life-stories. The second was more high-flown and doomed to failure. I sought answers to the question, 'What is the meaning of life?' They did not come directly, but when I put together all my interviews, I began to think that the clue at least to the meaning of life, if there is a meaning, is implicit in the question itself; that we think to ask it at all. *Not* to ask seems to involve a conscious decision.

But the mildest generalization is impossible. I chose all but two of my interviewees almost at random, because any scientific, methodical, sociological approach would have betrayed my faith in the uniqueness of the individual. It would also have erected a barrier of pseudo-detachment between me and the women I interviewed, and I wanted to meet them woman to woman, human being to human being on equal terms. My own personality will have had an effect, for better or for worse, on what my interviewees chose to tell me, and how they told it.

Rebecca West once wrote to me: 'The Angel of Death is ransacking my brain, cancelling the memories to prepare me for death.' I did not question the accuracy or quality of the memories of the women I interviewed. I have no doubt – indeed I know – that their daughters would have given me quite a different picture, but anyway there was no way of checking it. Far more important to me than establishing whether an event or a relationship was as my interviewee described it, was what her description revealed of herself. I recognize the universal impulse to recreate one's life as a coherent fiction; I want to know how at the end of one's life one might look at it, for the reason given by Simone de Beauvoir: 'If we do not know what we are going to be, we cannot know what we are: let us recognize ourselves in this old man or that old woman.'

My curiosity was about women rather than men for that reason primarily – as a woman, I wanted to know the submerged history of women's feelings – but also because my grandmother was the greatest influence on my life and I wanted to know more about her generation, which seemed to me to have come to maturity at the interesting pivotal point between the Victorian world of repressed or 'redundant' women, and the world of the Flappers and the Bright Young Things. They were born with this century, and spent their formative years in a state of relative innocence, untainted by the two world wars that were to come, or by the knowledge that we ourselves could destroy the planet with nuclear weaponry in minutes, or even by the suspicion of one's own deeper motives that psychology inflicted upon us.

Having spoken to some of the women, I found myself wishing that I could also interview the men of the same generation. Without them the picture is at best incomplete and at worst distorted. What I did learn, by implication, was that the life of a man is at least as hard as the life of a woman.

I tried to avoid interpreting the characters of my interviewees because I thought that would be presumptuous, an insult to the women who were kind enough to give me so much of their time and were so patient with my insistent probing of their lives, and equally an insult to the reader, who is as qualified as I am to interpret or judge. I have been discreet where necessary, to avoid embarrassing the children and grandchildren of my subjects, but I have not left out anything that would significantly distort the self-portraits. Where it seemed that material which an interviewee would not allow me to include was vital to her revelation of herself, I dropped the interview. Once or twice I began to interview women whose life-stories had been sanitized or Disneyfied for them by their children, and I did not go on. It seemed to me that what might appear to be an indiscretion or flaw in the life or character of one woman must be offset by the different flaws and indiscretions in others and that the reader, taking them in aggregate, will, as I did, find that they offer a chastening perspective on the problems of trying to get by in this life, given one's character.

De Beauvoir said that old people are 'required to be a standing example of all the virtues. Above all they are called upon to display serenity: the world asserts that they possess it, and this assertion allows the world to ignore their unhappiness.' I found patience and resignation among the women who spoke to me, but as often as not these were the tactics of old age, weapons of a determination that could no longer express itself dynamically, rather than the signs of serenity. I found unhappiness too, but they had mostly learned to live with that. No one who reaches the age of eighty can possibly be surprised at the unhappiness of life. To ask them if they were happy was to invite a rebuke for crass naivety. Wilde's observation is only too true, 'Everyone is born a king and most people die in exile.'

Their children and grandchildren, my own generation, have questioned all the values my interviewees were brought up to believe in and rejected most of them, suppressing as best we can the uneasy suspicion that we may have thrown the baby out with the bathwater, while trying hard to ignore what we proved in the process, that morality is not absolute, it is a matter of fashion. The constant that keeps us going, as it kept our grandparents going, and has enabled us to laugh at the concept of ourselves as mere biological entities at the mercy of genetics and chemistry, is love – the love that is manifest in friendship and companionship; the love of individuals that radiates out to the whole. Love alone, or the possibility of love, is what makes life bearable, for it connects us to each other and to the source in the spirit.

That source is itself a mystery, and it seems that the longer you live the more mysterious it becomes. Each of my interviewees had her own theory about what makes us and the universe tick, and each one was vaguer than the last. Yet they would all have agreed with Jung, that 'the sole purpose of human existence is to kindle a light in the darkness of mere being'.

The most incontrovertible lesson I learned, or had confirmed for me in the course of these interviews, is one I had already had at my grandmother's knee and almost dismissed as a symptom of her Calvinism: that hard work and challenges are vital to the well-being of the race. Wealth is meaningless, an *ignis fatuus* that leads us away from the glorious hurly-burly of the struggle to survive. The satisfaction, in the end, is proportionate to the commitment. You do not find yourself on the analyst's couch or in the ashram of the guru. You find yourself in hard work; preferably work to survive, but if not that, then work with the purpose of making life better, richer, or just more tolerable for other people.

Listening to those 'unemancipated' women, with their Freudian papas and maids – to Bessie Brennan who worked hard all her days and is incapable of using the word 'sex' – I think there was a lot to be said for that old life of decency, that it produced women like these.

Alice (centre), with her sisters, Helen (left), and Francis (right),
Shanghai, 1901

Alice Berry-Hart

⇥ 1 ⇤

Alice Berry-Hart

'. . . constant changes and uncertainties gave to me, even
in childhood, a sense of the mutability and transience of
life. Since material things could not last, I grasped at
those which I could carry in my mind.'

*Alice Berry-Hart was born in Shanghai in 1896, fifth child in a family
of seven. Her parents were English missionaries, and she grew up in
China, with an interval of two years between the ages of ten and twelve
in the United States. She returned to America when she was eighteen
and supported herself while she worked for a degree in English from
Drake University, Iowa. After graduation she began teaching at the
English college in Shanghai, in her free time trying to make a career as
a writer. She became principal of the college very quickly, and married
a Scottish accountant in Malaya in 1926. They had three children,
lived in Malaya and Singapore, and moved to the West Indies during
the Second World War, returning to Britain before the war ended.
Alice taught English in a school in Liverpool, wrote for the*
Manchester Guardian *and* Blackwood's Magazine, *and broadcast on
radio. After her husband died in 1967 she went to live with her sister in
Falmouth. Her novel* Ching-a-Ring-a-Ring-Ching or Three Victorian
Sisters in Shanghai *was published in 1977, and a children's book,* To
School in the Spanish Main, *in 1953.*

Alice and I had written to each other for seven years before we
met. My first encounter with her was on the telephone. I had
just published the first issue of the *Literary Review* and she rang
to congratulate me on the magazine, but also to tick me off for
the explicit sex in a short story by William Boyd. She then sent
me one of her own stories. I thought it was good but rather
old-fashioned and weak at the end. We began to correspond
quite regularly, though I never did publish any of her work.

After I left the *Literary Review* she asked me if I would read a
children's story and a novel she had written long ago, and advise

her about publication. She offered to pay me for this at the professional rate, but I told her that I would be glad to read them just for pleasure.

I thought both books were good, but unlikely to attract a publisher because their themes and treatment were unfashionable – there was no post-Freudian psychology of character, nor any characters with modern occupations (or preoccupations): they had dated in the keeping. I told Alice this, and commented that it was a pity that publishers did not try to explore the market for readers who do not care for introspection, sex, and violence, but who do like a good story well told. By way of reply she sent me a Premium Bond for twenty-five pounds. If my number came up, she said, I could begin my own publishing house. She added that it was impossible for her to write about sex or violence.

She continued trying to publish her book:

About *Peggy*: I was writing articles for *Blackwood's Magazine* when I produced *Peggy*. I sent it to Douglas Blackwood who wrote to say that the Company had just decided to stop publishing Children's Books. He said, however, that I would have no difficulty in finding a publisher. You say that the present heir of Douglas does sometimes publish books. If you think that they would take *Peggy* by all means do ask them. I'd be delighted to see it in print.

If I had not been foolish years ago it might by now have been a success. It might even have been made into a film like *Mary Poppins* and the Dr. Dolittle books. I did send it to Scottish TV, and had a very kind reply: they would love to put it on, but lacked resources. They advised me to send it to London TV. Of course London sent it straight back to me.

Last week it came back from John Murray. They also don't publish books for children any more, but advise me to try Methuen or Hamish Hamilton. I won't do anything till I hear what your friends at *Blackwood's* say. (The people at John Murray's had 'read it with much interest'.)

Simultaneously, she was trying to get her novel into paperback and writing a memoir of her childhood. In her efforts with publishers Alice was as unrelenting as she was unsuccessful.

She finished writing her 'Childhood Memories' in 1984. I said I would try to find a publisher for it, but did not hold out much hope as it fell too far short of the ordinary book length. I sent it to all the publishers whom I thought might be interested, but without success. Meanwhile I tried to persuade Alice to expand what she had written, perhaps bringing it forward to her marriage. She took a lot of persuading because she really only wanted to write about her childhood days, which, she said, 'were the most beautiful of my life'.

Eventually she agreed to try, and began working at her typewriter every day in the garden hut she used as a study. Her sister's failing health held her back a great deal. Three or four years before, Dolly had had an accident – a Korean chest fell on her – and since then she had lost her powers of speech. Her health steadily failed from then, but Dolly was as stubbornly independent as Alice and could not be prevailed upon to take it seriously. Eventually Alice could no longer cope, and Dolly was taken into hospital. Although this relieved Alice's anxiety it did not give her much more time to write, for she made the journey across Falmouth every day (it involved changing buses) to visit her sister.

Not long afterwards Dolly died and Alice had to move into one council flat, then another. She was visited regularly by Mrs Yonge, a friend of both sisters. One evening, shortly after Mrs Yonge had left, Alice fell, breaking her hip and gashing her head. She couldn't reach her bell, and it was late in the night before she managed to attract a neighbour's attention by shouting.

In hospital Alice fought hard to be allowed to return to her flat. She was too successful, for she got home before she was really ready to cope alone. Soon after her return from hospital she fell again, wedging one leg behind a trunk and breaking the other hip. Fortunately Mrs Yonge was there: 'It was a complete splits', she told me later. (Alice never mentioned this in any of her letters; she never complained about anything.)

Mrs Yonge did not know how to extricate her. Alice was in shock and kept insisting, 'Leave me here! I'll be all right!' – she would not allow a doctor to be called. This went on for four hours, with Alice in terrible pain, trying to figure out how she could disentangle her leg from the trunk. Finally Mrs Yonge managed to pull her out. Alice fell asleep, and when she woke she let Mrs Yonge call the doctor.

After a third fall it became impossible to mend the broken hip, and Alice had to go into a residential home. When I saw her she was still determined that she would recover enough to cope on her own again, and she kept her flat, but after a while she had to give it up and resign herself to permanent residence in the home.

When I first met Alice I was struck by the bright benevolent intelligence in her eyes, and by her serenity. She gave no sign that she was less than perfectly content. Her great joy in life had been the outdoors, yet one little room with its tantalizing view over the Fal had become her everywhere. When she spoke to me about the times she had been taken out of the home, it was in a way that made the hearer share her pleasure, as if it were a present thing.

Interviewing her, I tried to understand her serenity. Although she was warm and direct, and put me at my ease straight away, I felt I could not get close to Alice; she eluded me. I could only see what she had decided I would see. Yet nothing was hidden. There just seemed to be none of the vulnerable places of self-doubt in her through which we reach and are reached for. Alice was completely self-contained, self-reliant, independent. I did not feel as if she held me at arm's length; I just felt that there was nothing personal in the rapport between us. Yet it was good to be with her.

On the surface Alice is perfectly English, as English as only a colonial missionary's child could be, born and brought up in exile. None the less I wondered whether the Chinese environment in which she grew up had had more influence on her than anything she learned more formally in the missionary enclave. Friends who have had nannies have shown that where the mother's role is split, with one woman assuming the formal responsibilities, as Alice's mother did, and another being in all the fundamental, physical day-to-day things responsible for the child, as her *amah* was, then the unconscious mind is informed by the attitudes, beliefs, and emotional responses of the nurturer rather than the manager.

Alice radiates goodness, and the stillness of Zen: 'If you do not get it from yourself where will you go for it?' She rarely let go of her purpose, but she could wait patiently for its fulfilment. She is not serene *because* of anything; she is serene.

Having received this image of her I thought it odd, and touching, when I came to her room too early one morning and had to wait while she put on some make-up. I thought I had uncovered a bit of plain, ordinary vanity, but it turned out that she has a scar on her lip which she was trained to hide.

She had hinted about it before, but when asked outright she would not discuss it. Then, when I returned next day, she told me a story about her parents' efforts to have the mark removed, and made me promise not to publish it. This still puzzles me, for the whole tale reflects no discredit on anyone, and the mark on Alice's lip is barely noticeable.

It was difficult to get Alice to talk about herself. She would much rather have talked about her grandchildren, of whom she is as proud as the most doting grandmother could be.

After months in the home, probably when she realized she was stuck there for good, Alice began to go off her food and turn night into day. She had always been a night person – most women who combine careers with motherhood have to be – but someone must have noticed, and taken it as a sign of disorientation. She was moved to another room, which has no view of the sea and which she shares with a somewhat cantankerous and very deaf fellow-nonagenarian, who begins to yell at her, 'Put that light out!' on the stroke of nine every night. Most of the day Alice sits in front of the television. All her personal effects have been put into storage.

I have interwoven what Alice told me with extracts from her unpublished manuscript, 'Childhood Memories'.

THE INTERVIEW

My father and mother had come out to China from England when they were in their twenties. When I was born, round about my mother's fortieth birthday, they spoke the Shanghai dialect as fluently as English.

My father belonged to the Disciples of Christ, who were a strict sort of Baptists. Before that, he was a captain in the Merchant Navy. Several of his near relations were in the Merchant Navy. He caught smallpox from Arab pilgrims in a ship on the Red Sea, and was put off in a rather dreadful small hospital. ...

[Alice used her father's experience as background for the missionary, Ben, in her novel: 'It was a stinking hole ... he was very ill. Off his head for days ... when he recovered consciousness he told me he had vowed to become a missionary.']

My father was so wrapped up in his missionary work. He preached so earnestly, with every muscle tense, acting out every dramatic part of the Bible teaching in so lifelike a way that the congregation was spellbound. He had places where he had a convert to hold the church together, and he used to go out and visit them. He was always off on his journeys.

My father travelled on foot through parts of China which were at that time little known, and wrote about the parts of the country which have lately been explored by modern methods and have astonished the world. He wrote some articles which were published by the Royal Geographical Society, and was made an FRGS.

One of his great achievements was the translation of *Monkey King*, which has since been retranslated. His translation was illustrated by Chinese artists whose pictures are beautiful. I have them still and it was always my intention to have them published with those original pictures. If I ever have the time and means to do this it will be done. ...

My parents were very much in love, and most happily married. My mother was a perfect wife of her time, always content to do what her husband wished. Both of my mother's sisters married missionaries, and followed her to China.

She took great interest in the 'Women and Work' group in her Chinese congregation and had classes several times a week teaching them the Romanized edition of the Chinese-language Bible. She had a long, padded gown made for church, but even so she suffered from the cold a great deal. I do not think father noticed it.

I was born in 1896. I had two sisters still to come and they came within the four years that remained of the century. My goodness, how my mother got through it I don't know! She wasn't the sort of person that should have had a large family anyway, because she wasn't at all domesticated.

I remember when we were in America – it was really dreadful because, you see, she had never had any *real* housekeeping, like the Americans had – the Americans are very hard workers; they bottled all their fruit and dried their apples ... apple-rings across the ceiling in the kitchen ... oh, they did *everything*, they were very hardworking.

My mother wasn't used to that, and I remember on her Silver Wedding Day, when the people in Shanghai who were my father's friends – not particularly missionaries but friends – all went together and got him a silver tea-set and he took a picture of himself in the garden of our missionary house with this tea-set, and when mother got it I remember for the first time in my life ever seeing my mother cry. She was washing up dishes and she had just had this letter with the photograph and she was weeping, and I'd never seen her weep before. It seemed such a dreadful thing to me. I didn't know what was the matter. But it was just that you see – there she was, washing dishes ... she missed him dreadfully.

The three of us girls at the end of the family were all born within four years, and were usually called by our Chinese nicknames: I was called Wu-Pao, or Fifth Precious One, my next sister Lu-Pao, or Sixth Precious, and the last Chi-Pao, Seventh Precious. It irked me to share babyhood with two younger ones. Much later my mother told me that I would try to push the next baby from her lap, saying in Chinese, 'Don't cuddle Sixth Precious! Cuddle me!'

My brother was the only son among so many daughters: dreadful – terribly spoilt. Everything he wanted he got you see. The rest of us had to fight for our wants. Anyway I didn't mind fighting for it. What I objected to when I was a very small girl was having to have the other two little ones follow me all the time, because the *amah* couldn't take care of us always, so I used to have to try to get away from them and hide myself in the shrubbery and then they would chase me and find me.

I think what I hated most in my life were the interminable wars in China. You know, there were always warlords fighting each other. Like when I went up to Peking to help my sister Dolly when her daughter was being born. All the terrible fighting that kept the doors being closed in Peking, and we could hardly ever get out of Peking. That was rather difficult, because I hate being shut in. . . . But I have so many happy things that I think of that I don't really remember any very unhappy things. At night now when I can't sleep I think about things I had done. For instance, the question of Queen Anne – now you know if you get yourself thinking about Queen Anne, how does she come in with James I – why did she come in as she did? It's very difficult to try to trace it out. I began to trace it out, and I thought, now how did that happen? I remembered seeing the house of Queen Anne near Lewes and thinking, 'This is one of the places I should know about more', and that's why the other night when I couldn't sleep I kept thinking about how she happened to be Queen Anne and – it was James I's son who died, wasn't it? – I was trying to get that out in my mind and I thought how dreadful, really, not to know exactly how these things happened. But all my books at that time were at my flat. Now I've got a lot of books here that I can look up things in, you know, and find out the truth about how these things happened. . . .

. . . Very early in my childhood consciousness I was aware of danger which might at any time intrude into our daily lives. Awakening suddenly one night, I found that I was not in bed, but on my *amah*'s lap in a rickshaw. It was the stopping of the vehicle and the sound of voices that woke me – standing up I looked back over the hood and saw a long procession of rickshaws which contained Mother and the rest of the seven children and luggage.

Our mission compound was isolated and remote from built-up areas. We were, in fact, displaced persons, a tiny minority which might at any time be wiped out. Not long after this whole families of missionaries were massacred, but this I did not know until years afterwards. That night was the first indication that the Boxers were beginning their uprising. The family were anxious about my mother's brother Tom, who was a doctor in Peking.

At the entrance of an alley near our school ragged country-folk who had fled to Shanghai used to gather to beg food from the throngs in the adjoining market. There we children saw one day a man in an attitude of exhaustion. His head was on his knees,

and around his neck was a placard offering for sale his three
children, who, poor little things, were playing with stones in the
dust at his feet. That forlorn immobility seemed to be the end of
all things. That anyone could rise from such despair to start life
anew seems incredible to westerners; yet they did so start again,
those unconquerable orientals. Any period of flood, or of
greedy warfare amongst outlaw generals resulted in such misery.
For weeks at a time father would be away from home administer-
ing relief to those who were without shelter or food. He would
come back exhausted, and his clothes would have to be burnt.
After those expeditions he said that every mouthful seemed to
choke him, so depressed was he by the sights he had seen.

He was walking one night towards a ferry where he hoped to
catch a house-boat. He had only an oil lantern, but when he
heard a child crying he went to find it and did so. When he
picked it up the feet dropped off. He had a blanket in his
bundle, and this he put around the child although he feared that
it would die. It survived, however. Esther, my parents called it,
after adopting it into our family. Her feet had been bound.
Because of the unusually cold weather they had frozen and
come off. She had therefore been taken some distance from the
village and thrown into a ditch. You will read her letters with
interest.

[Esther became headmistress of the Ware Memorial School –
named in memory of Alice's father. She wrote, through Alice's
sister Grace, in 1949: 'I have always remembered Alice. I know
you love father most and I have established a school in memory
of father to carry on his work to help the Chinese people....
Now I have been elected as the head of the district which I live
in and I am respected by all the people.... There is war and
famine everywhere which shows that Jesus is coming soon....
As to me I am healthy and strong and God has blessed me that I
am fatter than ever. I still drink salt water every morning. My
mind is still clear enough to be the school boss.']

... When I was very small I spent a period of illness in a mission
hospital some distance up the Yangtze. On my way home we
passed through the flooded areas around Wuhu where farmers
who had lost everything had made nests of mud and dried grass
on the higher ground and lived in them like rats. Old men with

wrinkled old wives on their backs, and young women with their naked children tied for warmth inside their own clothing crawled along the roads lifting their pitiful voices whenever a stranger passed by. I protected myself against the overwhelming horror which might have unnerved an older and stronger person by an assumption of callousness, which had its origin in my childish helplessness to deal with such situations, or to explain why God had allowed them. Mostly I was terrified by the troops of children with matted hair and filthy rags who were hustled along by rascals who had found or stolen them. At best they would be sold as household slaves. Had I not often heard from Eurasian children of Chinese 'slave girls' amongst their servants? Often these were bought out of pity by the Chinese wives of Europeans in such times of distress, and were treated like dependent relatives.

These constant changes and uncertainties gave to me, even in childhood, a sense of the mutability and transience of life. Since material things could not last, I grasped at those which I could carry in my mind: staring at a beautiful tree, or the shape of a mountain; going back and again to fix in my memory its perfection of shape or colouring, and to sniff those scents which, most vividly of all, brought back the reality which I craved....

... One day I was sitting on the garden wall gathering white roses from a climbing vine, when a group of women on their way to the cotton factory stopped and asked for flowers. I dropped a couple of blooms into each outstretched hand, and they thanked me and went off, putting the flowers into their hair with the cotton fuzz. I stared after them, forgetting to pick more, feeling my first conscious dislike of social conditions. We were so used to the horrible sights of Chinese beggars, professional as well as those who were the victims of misfortune, that it was not strange if we took human suffering for granted.

On holidays my sisters and I might go as far as Woosung, at the mouth of the Yangtze, and play all day amongst the ruins of the old forts. Or on wheelbarrows whose wooden wheels squeaked like tortured pigs we rode for miles through the flat country, bumping over stone bridges which spanned the creeks along which so much of the commerce of the countryside passed, our wheelbarrow man staggering behind a load of us balanced on either side of the shoulder-high central wheel.

When it was not possible to have so long a jaunt, we played in the fields near the compound, going in single file along footpaths between rows of bright green cabbages, or the yellow flowers of mustard. We played 'king of the castle' on the tops of graves, and sometimes our feet crashed through rotten wood, and we peered fearfully through to see the broken remains of bones which rats or dogs had already disturbed. Some of the coffins were left in temporary shelters, and some were covered with tiny whitewashed houses, with tiled roofs. The smell of the graveyard lay heavy over these fields which owed no small part of their fertility to the bodies decaying in them....

My father had a furlough in 1900 and we went to England for six months. Not long after our arrival I suddenly found that I could read.... I entered a magical world which has been my chief treasure all my life. My mother was seldom without a book in her hand, and like her I felt unsatisfied without one.... The first pages of the Chinese classics I learned in the missionary school are still in my memory.

... I remember the magic lantern shows at Sunday School in Shanghai. Our favourite was of a man in bed asleep with a great nightcap on, and a bushy beard. His jaw would drop and to our horrified delight a rat would slide up over the bed and enter his mouth which would then close, and if you wound fast enough a procession of rats ran up and were swallowed. Or, if you turned the machine the wrong way the man would disgorge them tail first. We never grew tired of it.

Mother racked her brain to clothe and feed necessitous families in the congregation. Once she took from the piano a strip of embroidery to make a Sunday suit for the infant son of one of the Christians. It was amazing what the Chinese women could do with their tiny, beautiful hands.

My father's salary was microscopic. Congregations of our sect in America used to send us large parcels of old clothes, some of which, of course, were of no use at all. Business friends of Mother who had daughters also gave her their outworn dresses. Out of these Mother and a 'sew-sew *amah*' used to make our clothes. Even as a small child I hated them: 'What was this made of?' I used to ask suspiciously. Not until I was earning my own living was I able to buy a new dress.

But food was very cheap when I was a small child in Shanghai. A person could live well in a private guest-house for a Shanghai dollar a day – about ten pence now. Our *amah* would take us to the temple. Holding tightly to her skirts we would push our way to the open space in front, to spend our coppers, if we could decide what to buy. There was an infinite variety of dainties exhibited in the booths and on the counters which had been set up. Hot chestnuts, water nuts peeled and stuck in rows on skewers, nuts shaped like the curving horns of water-buffalo, peanuts, salted melon seeds, sunflower seeds – an incredible assortment of nuts alone. There were also sugar-cane and fruits in their seasons, and exquisitely made animals of sugar. These last were displayed on a circular table over which a pointer swung. You paid your cash and swung the pointer. In theory, if it stopped at a sugar animal it was yours. If not, you had to be content with a small block of sugar which the man took out of a tin. In practice unless you were muscular enough to impress the man, or sufficiently loud of tongue to intimidate him, you were fobbed off with the small lump no matter if you were lucky enough to stop at the large animals. How we longed for them! There were cocks, dazzling white, with red sugar combs; pigs, ducks, and goats, and we chanced our coppers on them although we had the uncomfortable feeling that it might be gambling.

In our extreme youth the river in front of our mission compound at Yangtzepoo was our delight, and on its marshy edges we played endless games whilst our *amah*s sat on their small wooden stools mending our stockings or making shoes. We pulled the reeds, and played little wailing tunes through them for the benefit of the goats which cropped the weeds of the embankment. The children of the inspector of the neighbouring police station were the only other white children within miles, and our little group was allowed all kinds of privileges. The large and impressive lumber-yard which later grew up opposite our garden was a small place then, and at the end nearest us there was a sort of dumping ground for old launches and boilers and bits of broken-up shipping. What more could a child desire? We played 'follow-my-leader', crawling through boilers and pipes which left brown rust stains all over our pinafores; played 'house' and 'Noah's ark' inside the stranded launches, and climbed perilously up the sides of stacks of lumber. See-saws were to be had for the taking. The smell of sawdust, of river mud, and the hollow roar of our voices in the boilers and the wash of the waves against the bank whenever a steamer churned past in the river – all these things come back to me....

... The greatest joy of our lives was to travel down with the tender to meet a liner coming in from America or Europe.

... When I was in my teens I used to play the harmonium in my father's church. In those days, before gramophone and radio made western music familiar to eastern ears, I have seen Chinese look around in astonishment and then burst into screams of laughter when they first heard our hymn tunes.

I wanted to write. I didn't mind particularly what kind of thing. My father died when I went to America in the First World War, and that is why I had to work my way through four years at Drake University. I didn't mind this, as it was quite often done, but unlike the *au pairs* in English homes now I wasn't given any pocket-money. I was not treated badly you know. I was treated very well – I never had to justify my existence as an English person. They never tried to impress upon me that I was an alien.

Oh I had to work very hard! In the beginning I spent my Saturdays on housework, and very good training it was too. I have nothing to say against that. It was excellent training. I've never seen any housekeeper as good as that housekeeper who trained me. I'm very glad that I had that year with her.

My room was a small cupboard-like place behind the kitchen, although they had a very good guest-room. But I found out soon that I knew much more grammar than any of the American students. A great many students were trying to get into university but couldn't because they couldn't fulfil the entrance examinations. I found that I could teach them grammar much easier than working at housework in a house. So that's what I began to do. I left the house and taught grammar. I didn't have much money for it, but I had more than ever I would have found possible otherwise. It was sometimes a question of whether to buy a meal or a book.

I was ill with malaria at one time, and a girl who attended my classes told her mother that I was said to be ill, whereupon the mother came to the house where I was staying and took me home until I was better. After that, I lived with them because their daughter needed coaching, but I was in all respects one of the family. I was very happy with them. At my graduation Mrs Schmidt gave me a beautiful organdie dress for the graduation party.

I was at university when there was all the trouble about whether or not Darwin's theories should be taught. Of course, I had read *The Origin of Species*. I was called into the office of the head of the university. He said, 'Are you reading Darwin?' and I didn't say a thing. I just looked at him. He went on asking me question after question: did I believe in Darwinism? Did I believe in the fundamental word of Christ as explained in the scriptures? – and I never answered a word, not a word. Finally he got tired of asking me and I went away. I wasn't going to condemn myself. I didn't have to condemn myself according to the law.

The head of the Bible school said he'd read Darwin but didn't believe in him. They were going to dismiss him. He was frantic. He asked the students what he could do.

When I went back to China from university in America teaching seemed to be the only thing offered to me at the time. I did some work on a paper – articles about Christmas in Shanghai, and all sorts of things like that. I didn't write anything particularly interesting I don't think, but I did write some short stories.

I had an offer from an American newspaper to be on their staff, so to speak, but I found that meant all I was expected to do was to go to parties and all sorts of uninteresting things – never given anything interesting to write: always these social things that weren't interesting to me at all. And I was expected to emphasize the social part of it, you see. Undoubtedly because I was a woman. They wouldn't have given me anything important I don't think, no matter how – they just wouldn't suggest my writing except these women's things.

I don't like the women's pages in the *Telegraph* and others – I don't find them interesting at all. I try to read them sometimes but I just never succeed.

One thing I did for the *China Daily News* – they asked me if I would please write a play for children for Christmas. I set it just as if it was a world apart (not in Shanghai). I wrote this play and it was published and I was very pleased – I got quite a lot of money for it – it seemed a lot of money in those days anyhow. I had news from people in schools in inland China that they had put it on. It was called *The Christmas Visitors*.

I then began to write articles for the *Atlantic Monthly* and papers like that. I used to write for *Blackwood's* – about China of course – also the *Manchester Guardian*.

Anyhow, I did go on writing. I didn't just do my job in teaching, which was a very onerous one. I didn't want to teach, *ever*. I also used to write a column in the paper every week and I wrote stories. I always thought that I would escape into journalism, you see.

When the headmistress said to me, 'When you are in my seat here in the office . . . ,' I thought, my goodness me, what's going to happen to me?

I wanted to be a writer as soon as I could write, and that was very early. I used to write all kinds of little things. I was always writing something, as presumably plays, though I don't think I ever did write a very good play, but when I did write plays we used to perform them as a family – the younger ones – on our verandah in America for our neighbours. Funny to think of it now!

When I was teaching we had very long summer holidays, ten weeks, so we could do anything, come back to Europe and so on. I spent my summer holidays travelling in the Philippines and Borneo, Sumatra. . . .

Suddenly I was called to take the headmistress's place and there – oh dear – then my work really began. I had to do such a lot . . . all the work that a headmistress would now have a clerk to do. I was very well paid according to Shanghai – according to any woman. I think I was getting a thousand pounds a year. That was excellent for women at that time.

I travelled all over the place because I wanted to see as much as I could. It was very different in those days. I went to Formosa with a friend, when it was occupied by the Japanese.

It was the first time I think that girls could go without chaperones much. As a matter of fact, when we had house-parties – trips that we took in house-boats for weeks at a time – we always had a chaperone there, that is, a married woman who was the chaperone. She was always very welcome, you know. The strange thing is that nowadays everybody thinks because a girl is living by herself she must have some sort of lover or something. We never had that idea in my day. We never expected anybody to have such an idea. Sex before marriage was just not contemplated. I can't tell you why, but it just was not. . . . It was much easier to live in those days than it is now, I should think. Because if you have an idea that marriage is not before sex then you are at the mercy of a great many men who expect you not to be on your own if you don't want sex. They used to think that any girl who wasn't chaperoned, that's what they wanted. It's a matter of bodily strength. I can't explain to you why, but I've always had that belief.

I always had a lot of men friends. That sounds funny for a person who was born in my day, but you could have men friends in these days and not think any the worse. For instance, on Sundays a man or two would call up and say, 'Are you going for a walk today? May I go with you?' So I always had somebody like that, and my mother was always thinking that I was about to be engaged to somebody. She would like me to have been. Anyhow, I didn't bother about it, and the last man friend I had like that, my mother was sure I was going to be engaged to him. Suddenly I said no.

I think I thought I was in love once before my husband. Not in love as you would think 'in love', but sort of extravagantly . . . I don't know: I can't explain it, except that I do know why people go away like that if they have the same feeling that I had about this particular man. But I didn't have it for very long and we never did anything together or anything like that.

My mother always wanted us to go to parties. She'd say, 'So-and-so has been invited to this party. Are you going? Have you had an invitation?' If I had, she was very pleased. If not, she – I think – would have liked to see that I was invited. But I don't think she would go that far, because I had my own ideas.

I think that my marriage was made by the Holy Spirit. Because we were led into it. It was something that we were purposed to do, and we never had any difficulty about adjustments or anything like that. We were always – I think it must have been one of the happiest marriages I could imagine.

I met him several times in the East Indies before I got married. If you went to any Malayan port and went to, say, a club dance, you were sure to meet all the people that you had ever met before. So I met him several times, over four or five years. It was a wonderful way of being led into marriage, because you felt that you were. It was extraordinary. There was *never* any question.

We used to love to be together. At weekends we used to take the car as far as it would go up the forest in Malaya, and then go on foot, on rangers' footpaths.

We were married in Malaya in 1926, then went back to Shanghai for celebrations and parties, then went on honeymoon to Japan.

We landed at Kobe – or Nagasaki – we walked from there for about two days, staying at Japanese inns *en route*. We had a lovely time. Mind you, the Japanese at that time were always trying out their English. If they saw us coming they would tag on and speak to us in the few words that they knew. They wanted to learn English as cheaply as they could!

We walked up to a beautiful city that was full of temples and things ... I wish I could remember the name. We arrived in the course of time in Tokyo. In Tokyo we stayed at a missionary house my family had stayed at when we were in Japan *en route* for America. We went to see the Noh plays. We did so enjoy the acting – the strange thing was, you saw the man being pursued by his enemies, and he was running so fast but he didn't move an inch.

We went by train from Yokohama up to Gosenji, which was up in the mountains in the north, and we stayed in a beautiful inn which was all lacquer. In the morning they would bring us tea.

My husband had malaria and got a temperature and couldn't go walking with me. I went over the lacquer bridge up to Gosenji. It was simply beautiful. I could not make myself believe that I couldn't get Ralph up. I love walking and the road was so beautiful that I walked up myself.

I don't think he would have done that if I had been ill. He was a kinder person than I am, I think. We had a lovely time in Japan. I must say I *did* enjoy that honeymoon!

My mother-in-law was the world, the flesh, and the devil. She was a very beautiful woman and she didn't want her son to be married to anybody unless she had chosen the person. Dr Berry-Hart – my father-in-law: he was a gynaecologist – could have done so much more had she been less demanding. I don't think anybody liked her, especially her own family. She was always quarrelling with her own family, especially her sisters. They would say, 'Oh, she's stamped out on us now.'

One sister she couldn't get on with at all. The other moved down to England. She had such a nice family. She came to see me when Marian was born and she took her in her arms and she said, 'You know I *do* love children! I love my family – I would love to go through it again with my family, having these children again.' I thought, well, that's the only woman I've ever met who wanted to do that – actually to go through it again!

I was afraid that I wouldn't have any children. I didn't know why we shouldn't, because there was every reason for us to have one. We were not very young, you see.

In Singapore, when Gill was about to arrive in 1930, I woke my husband up and I said, 'I'm afraid I've had a show and I think we'd better be going along to the hospital.' He said 'Right-oh. Don't worry', you know, and he was more worried than I was. So he got the car out and as we were going along I said, 'Honestly, I don't know why they shouldn't do something more about the smell of the river. The river smell is dreadful', and he said, 'How you could think of a river smell when you're going along to have your first child, I *cannot* understand!'

When I got to the hospital there was somebody very important whose daughter was going to have a baby and I think the nurses had been told that she was diplomatic stock or something like that and so they left me with my old *amah*. They took me into the delivery room, and there was my dear *amah* who was such a blessing to me, and she said to me, 'Madam, baby going to arrive.' Just at the last minute, when I thought, my goodness what *am* I going to do?, the doctor came in. He had to use forceps but he gave me an anaesthetic and that was all right.

Gill was one of those children who was always awake. It's terrible for the parents, but it means that there's something very quick about the child. It's a good sign, if you know it – but I was just longing for sleep, almost out of my senses for lack of sleep, and if it hadn't been for my husband who was so kind . . . he used to take her on his shoulder and as long as she was there she was perfectly happy. He got her to sleep finally, but if it weren't for that I don't know what I would have done.

When I was in the West Indies and my son was going to be born . . . when I found out I was going to have a child it made all the difference in the world. Our leave was cancelled, because Hitler's war was just coming on. Luckily the doctor was one of my father-in-law's pupils in Edinburgh, so he was very pleased to have me. He said, 'Well I suppose you're taking your last chance to have another child.' I said, 'I *am*, but I didn't expect him to be born here.'

When the doctor said, 'You're having it at the last possible moment', I hadn't realized that I was having him at the last possible moment, but still it didn't make any difference to me. Age has never seemed very important to me. Now I'm ninety I don't feel ninety. I was fourty-four then.

I had a very difficult birth with my son because the midwife was terrified of my having the child without the doctor. The doctor had induced him to come early because he wanted to go on holiday. That was dreadful, you know, because having a child induced is not natural. If I had known I would never have consented to that.

I always enjoyed being a mother. I wish I had known more about childhood. My grandchildren have been a great source of comfort to me.

Ralph was a communications officer in the West Indies at the beginning of the war, but after a while he became ill. He had too much pressure on his brain, so he couldn't go on with his work. His superior was a very jealous man: I can't tell you how *cruel* he was. Even to think of him now – the cruel way he would speak to my husband, you know, and my husband wasn't the kind of man you could get any satisfaction being cruel to, because he would never respond in kind.

He recovered from his paralysis in four or five days. We came

back to England in convoy. And you can't think how it was to
have a sick husband and children the ages they were – three
children. I couldn't sleep at night at all. I couldn't sleep – the
whole ship was in darkness and I would walk up and down the
deck night after night until almost morning, thankful that the
children could sleep. Oh dear me, what a ... you would see the
lights of the convoy going up and down all the ships. It really
was the most frightening thing to be in convoy like that.

I sometimes – very often – go back to Shakespeare and get all
the words teased out for whole acts over two or three nights if I
can't sleep. The other night I went back to *Henry V* and went
through the 'muse' scene. After two or three nights I don't think
there's a word I missed out.

When we lived in Liverpool after the war, I used to write at dead
of night – *any* time I had. All my little Chinese stories. I was
broadcasting on 'Home in the Afternoon' or whatever it was
called. Mr Hill was at the head of the Manchester BBC at that
time, and he was so kind. He used to say, 'Let me know when
you've got anything to broadcast and I'll find time for it.'
   I always felt Britain was home. I loved it. When we were born
extraterritoriality was the law. We were registered at Somerset
House in London as if we were born in the UK. We always
spoke of Britain as home. I spent a lot of time in America. The
only thing that felt strange about Britain was I had to do my
own housework!
   When I was growing up, the Empire was everything. I think it
meant a great deal to people in those days to have an Empire ...
I think we did a great deal of good. For example, the people
who introduced education for Indian women were English. The
forests were another department of Empire that we treated well.
And we put railways in and we put schools of various kinds in,
especially women's schools and girls' schools. I think we did a
great deal of good in India. I don't think we did quite as much
good in South Africa.
   I think it was a sort of cult: you *must* get things for the
Empire; the Empire must come first.

Yes, I will tell you about my sisters if you like ... I don't believe in Freud at all – I'm not greatly attracted to these people you know ... what do you call them? Psychologists....

... My oldest sister, Lily, was a very kind, dear soul. She loved us children and didn't mind us at all, but my second sister, Grace, was a very different person. She couldn't bear children with running noses or anything like that – she just couldn't bear that sort of thing.

Lily was to have gone to university but she didn't because she had met an old school sweetheart of hers from childhood and she married him instead. Not a very good marriage, because he had very romantic ideas. He had never worked outside a firm in his life. He was an office-trained person, you see, and he thought it would be very romantic to go to Canada and buy a ranch and go around on horses and things like that. That was his idea. Of course, he was just plain foolish, but he had a Scottish grandmother who was ready to take on all his fancies. He was rather hopeless in his dreaming.

Within a year of their marriage in Shanghai my sister had a baby, and the grandmother took the family on. She realized, I think, that her grandson shouldn't go and try to buy a ranch in Canada, but she went with him, and it was the only thing that kept my sister alive, because my sister wouldn't have been able.

Within the next four years she had four children, and died in childbirth. Wasn't that sad? It was awful.

When we went to America first, my mother and the smallest sisters, we stopped at their little farmhouse and I heard my mother say to my father, 'What a poor little place for her to have lived in!' It was absolutely cut off from everything.

The Scottish grandmother was equal to everything. My sister was the kindest, sweetest-tempered person. She would always fit in with the grandmother. She would never try to oppose her or anything like that. Undoubtedly the grandmother ruled the roost – but it was a good thing she was there.

When we went back to Shanghai, leaving the oldest ones in America, we hadn't been back for more than a week when we got news that my sister had died in childbirth. My mother just went to pieces. She said, 'I knew it! I knew it!' and she fled into my father's study and we could hear them talking together and he praying with her. My little sister said to me, 'What did she mean by "I knew it"?'

... Where Lily lived, it was just forest and mountain. I remember walking out of the back door of their kitchen and going through long avenues of trees which had never been cut. These were primeval forests really. To me, there was something wonderful about them – these marvellous, long corridors between the trees, and, of course, I could have met all sorts of animals, I suppose. I never thought about that. I don't suppose the animals would have come so near the house. But anyhow, I thought they were one of the most wonderful things I had ever been in, those primeval woods.

Lily's husband and children and his grandmother came to live with my mother in China after she died.

I think Grace had a very good time in Shanghai. She was brought up by a very fine woman but very much an old maid who taught her as an old maid would in those days, and they were very strict – very strict Baptists. They called themselves the Disciples of Christ and they were very strict about everything. When she came back to Shanghai she wasn't quite so strict because she found herself invited to parties and things. She began to have a very nice life.

She taught French in the boys' part of the public school. The boys had a new school very shortly and they took her with them as a French mistress.

She didn't like the younger ones of the family very much. She was a lot older than us, of course. There were seventeen years between the oldest and the youngest of my sisters.

I think Grace was badly treated by somebody – I'm not sure because I had left Shanghai then. He didn't want to commit himself, I suppose, to marriage, but he had kept on walking her out. She went back to the old maid who had brought her up in America. It was a beautiful house. Grace bought it. She lived there all her life and never married.

Dolly's husband was the best chess player in the diplomatic corps in China, also the best bridge player. He was a lawyer, a very clever man.

Helen married an analytical chemist in Shanghai. She had one son and wanted a large family, but her husband did not want any more.

At the end of Hitler's war, when we were going back to England in convoy, she suddenly found she was going to have a child. I suppose she thought there was no need to have precautions at that time. She was forty-eight. She had another son. The unfortunate part of it was that he died. She built her life on the fact that she was going to have another child.

Life is funny – that that should have happened to her, one of the kindest and most beautiful-minded women. She taught French in a boys' school. It was very, very sad.

One of Helen's husband's sisters became a dentist and the other became a Roman Catholic. [*Laughs.*] He was a nice man and he always meant well. I think he was mixed up in his mind, with his Jewish father and his mother was a French Protestant. He became an Episcopalian. A person like Helen would be the only one who would be sweet enough and gentle enough to get on well with all of those people.

Frances always wanted to get married. She went to a college where my sister Dolly had been before, run by the Disciples of Christ. She couldn't take any exams or anything like that. They were very romantic these people, you know: they would say, 'Of course, you girls must think about marriage – you'll all get married.' Of course, she never did. But she always thought she might, so she was always sort of looking around, to see if she couldn't marry somebody, but unfortunately nobody wanted to marry her. Unfortunate, wasn't it? Sad. If she had been a kinder, gentler person . . . but she was always resenting the fact that she couldn't do as well as we could. That doesn't make a happy life at all. Towards the end of her life she began to realize that as a nurse she was very good, because people always liked to have her when they were ill. She really did know her job. It's a pity she didn't think more of herself and it. She went back to China because Helen went back. She was always pestering Helen, that was the difficulty. A person like that who doesn't like her own life, she spends her life living with other people and not being happily settled. My brother-in-law couldn't bear her.

She wasn't a very happy sort of person because most of us were teachers or writers or doctors or something, but she wasn't,

and the only thing she could do was get a position as an SRN –
but she did not qualify as a real nurse: she just couldn't take the
examinations. She just wasn't capable of that sort of thing.
What she wanted to do was what *we* were doing. She could not
bear to think that she was not doing as well as the rest of us, and
she was always very unhappy about it. Actually she got
reconciled. She was a very strict Christian – Episcopalian.

I'm not an atheist, but I believe in only one of the Trinity, the
Holy Spirit, the Lord and Giver of Life. I think in very many
cases the other two (God, Jesus) are idolatry. If you go to
Catholic countries you see the way they can't do anything but
. . . it must be idolatry. As for God, well, of course, there are so
many gods and in some parts of the psalms they speak about
'our God is the best god' or 'the strongest god' or something like
that – so God is a very common worship, any sort of worship.
But the Holy Spirit is a different matter. He is the Lord of Life.
Well, as long as there are human beings on earth I think there
must be a Holy Spirit to bring life.

Jesus said, 'Why call you me good? There is only one good
and that is God. But I will send you a companion – the
Comforter' – and so I have always taken that to mean that Jesus
didn't want to be worshipped. And I think that there were so
many people who believed in *a* god of some kind. Mostly they
were tribal gods.

I believe that all the things which have happened to me, which
have been good, like miracles, that is the Holy Spirit. One of the
things that happened to me was my marriage. I never would –
nobody would have predicted it – but it was as if we had been
'led'. No marriage could have been better, for either of us.

If the Holy Spirit has the running of your life, it's good. But if
you're trying to force something through, for instance when my
daughter-in-law wanted to marry my son instead of going to
university, I was a fool. I thought, she's stupid not to go to
university when she has a chance. But she had made up her
mind. I *could* not understand. I wanted to stop it if possible. I
should never have done that. That was stupid of me, to think
that I could plan somebody else's life. I have done stupid things
like that.

I know when it is the Holy Spirit because it goes right – it's the Comforter, as Jesus said. I know when the Holy Spirit comes to me, because I *feel*, I know it is, because it's nothing of my doing. You see what I mean? That is what I have brought myself to realize, that I mustn't try to run somebody else's life. If I'm worried what is happening, I hope it would be ... that my praying for the Holy Spirit to help in their lives *will* do something, because it's not myself that can do anything....

... I mustn't think too much about what I could do for my grandchildren. I must leave them; I can't impose myself upon them. It's difficult not to sometimes. Very difficult.

When it is fine I go out and sit in the garden. I feel as if I've been born again. You know, just to be outdoors, to be out of a hospital, to be out of any place. Just to sit there and feel the fresh air all around me.

What I want is to go on with my writing.

Erica Hunt

2

Erica Hunt

'How can I know myself when I have a different facet for
everyone with whom I come in contact?'

*Erica Hunt was born in 1898 at her parents' farm in Chirnside,
Berwickshire, the second of three children. She was educated privately
at St Andrews, trained as a teacher, then went to Edinburgh
University to study for an arts degree. After graduation in 1923 she
married a Presbyterian minister thirty years her senior and went to live
in Jamaica, where she had two children, a son and a daughter, and
taught at a boys' school. When her husband retired after the war they
came back to live in Chirnside. Erica took a lover thirty years her
junior, had a breakdown in which she attempted suicide, and was six
months in psychiatric hospital. Her husband died in 1964. She
collected the material for her successful* Chirnside Past and Present
*(1975), taught, broadcast on radio, and travelled round Europe and
Scandinavia with a rucksack. In the early 1980s she moved to a flat in
Edinburgh.*

Erica wrote to me out of the blue, care of the *Scotsman*, to
which I contributed a weekly column. A mutual friend whom
she had known since their university days had had to go into a
nursing home. 'The Lord is taking an unconscionably long time
in sending for Jean Mary Allen', she said. 'She would be far
happier in heaven. She is only conscious for fifteen minutes at a
time.'

I knew this to be true, for I had visited Jean Mary the
previous week. Incapacitated by a series of strokes, she sat
propped up in a chair, one of a row of old women in identical
chairs, ranged against the wall. A children's cartoon show
brayed its nonsense from the television, dominating the room
but ignored by everyone.

Jean Mary had been a librarian and a musician, a novelist
and a contributor to *Grove's Dictionary of Music*. Her first

experience of music came when as a child she had been
bedridden in her father's remote manse in rural Berwickshire.
To amuse her he had set up an Aeolian harp at her bedroom
window. She was captivated. In time she became a promising
violinist but made her career as a librarian on her father's
advice: 'You'll never make a living out of music.' Jean Mary was
a purist. She would not have a gramophone record in her house,
far less a television set.

'Because I am almost totally deaf I no longer visit her', Erica's
letter continued. 'I get so frustrated because she is inaudible.
Last time I just repeated a lecture I gave recently at Masson
Hall, on "Life Sixty Years Ago". She heard me and nodded
approval.' The picture of those two fine, deaf, eccentric old
Scotswomen striving against all the odds through the
cacophony of mumbling and snoring and Australian soap-
opera to share their passion for social history had a comic
dignity and cultural desperation that made me want to meet its
author.

Erica is a glorious mixture of reckless indiscretion,
casualness, and old-fashioned poker-backed formality. After I
met her she wrote to me, 'Jean Mary never got to know the real
me, as I acted a part.'

But then, Erica herself did not know the real Erica – 'How
can I know myself when I have a different facet for everyone
with whom I come in contact?' she demanded. She would never
entertain two of her friends together, for this reason. Yet when I
spoke to some of them at last, it seemed that they all knew the
same Erica.

Until two years ago, Erica lived alone in a ground-floor flat in
one of the douce residential streets of Edinburgh's Marchmont
area. She ate only fruit and hard-boiled eggs, because she did
not want to cook. An arterial condition gave her vertigo and to
stimulate her circulation she drank nine or ten cups of coffee in
the course of the day. She made them all in a single brewing in
the morning and laid them out on a tray in the kitchen. When
she was very dizzy, she drank brandy as well:

Very dear Anne
I am not compos mentis: VERTIGO. Yesterday I visited

Marjory Graham by cheap Handicab taxi. The driver was enthralled by my conversation and forgot to charge me. Marjory has a diabolical stair, it was a terrible ordeal to get up. I only managed by the grace of brandy.

No matter how bad she felt, Erica never passed up an opportunity to shock. 'My charming doctor is so sensible', she wrote. 'She ignores my complaints which makes me feel pusillanimous. For years I was taking 36 pills a day. She put me on *one* so I now no longer do involuntary shoplifting due to pill poisoning.'

From morning until dusk Erica would sit in her easy-chair by the window which overlooked the street, ready to converse with any passer-by who returned her greeting. Her friends visited her in the evenings, by request, for 'During the forenoons I am a zombie. My brain begins to clear about 4 p.m. and I am at my peak at midnight.' Her favourite topic of conversation, she claimed, was sex, and her favoured friends were male because, she said, she could 'talk about anything and everything with men – they are not prudish. My views on sex', she explained, 'are thought to be unorthodox by my genteel friends. My most intimate discussions are with my window-cleaner. He says he had no idea a woman could be so frank.'

Erica discovered men relatively late in life and went in for them enthusiastically ('They like being collected'). 'As I specialize in men', she wrote to me, 'I have laid down a cellar.' The men she collected were sober professional people: librarians, teachers, doctors, and clergymen. She relished what her own generation might have regarded as her wickedness, though for the most part it was wickedness at third remove. After forty years of marriage to a Calvinist minister, she had also discovered the fascination of sex:

> I am so lucky in my men friends ... One is persecuted by a brazen nymphomaniac who begs him to get on top of her. It is good to get involved in other people's amours. It takes my mind off my damnable disabilities.

In some ways she was a late developer – a Bright Young Thing of the twenties blooming out of her time. On one visit she greeted me with, 'Do you think it is quite *respectable* for a woman of my age to have orgasms? I had one in my sleep last night!' and went on to recount her dream.

The security of her great age ('One no longer has to mind one's p's and q's in one's eighties') made her free to be shocking about sex. But other repressions remained. When I visited her in a nursing home earlier this year I asked her if she had recovered from a bout of diarrhoea. I had to shout to make myself heard. The ward was empty, so I did not think I risked embarrassing her. 'Ssh! my dear', she exclaimed, horrified, 'I don't think diarrhoea is a *respectable* subject, is it?'

After she had persuaded someone to take her to a disco she commented, 'I cannot understand this reversion to the jungle!' in tones that Edith Evans might have envied.

Modern women intimidated her: 'I mix with some liberated women of about forty to whom I have to adjust as I am Victorian.' Partly that was true, but partly it was that if the Women's Movement succeeded, Erica would no longer be able to shock her visitors. She wrote to me once, 'I long to hear your remarks on being liberated. I've never been anything else because I am disreputably brazen. Ladies make me self-conscious. I avoid folk who refer to me as a lady.'

She told me that she once had a gypsy gardener who lived with fifteen brothers and sisters in a tiny cottage. 'This mother', she said, 'delivered herself on newspapers on the floor, never bothering the midwife. The bairns were bedded in boxes. Most never knew who the fathers were. *Why oh why*', she exploded in exasperation, '*are women so submissive about copulation?*'

One of her visitors was a nun of the Poor Clares: 'I can't resist teasing her as I have a ribald sense of humour. I ask who invented Purgatory and why did she do such a dotty thing as becoming a nun. For escapism? She patiently answers my havering letters but she chides me because I not only tolerate gays but like them.' At the same time she conducted an intense correspondence about homosexuality with a Calvinist minister in the Highlands. She took enormous pleasure in provoking his homophobia, although it did genuinely puzzle her.

Erica is full of such mischief. Her disreputable brazenness existed very much within inverted commas provided by the Scottish bourgeoisie. Excepting only one lapse, for which she almost paid with her life ('What is your attitude to suicide? I have tried it', she inserted casually in a letter), she managed to confine relationships with men to the verbal – cultural or intellectual conversation over the port, lasting into the wee small hours. In a perfectly paradoxical Scottish way, she combined the characteristics of the patroness of a French salon with the innocent heroine of a Barbara Pym novel, respectably hungry for the validation of male companionship.

She was ready for anything, impressionable as a child – 'Can we compare notes about smoking dope? What effect does it have on you?' Christopher Sykes's biography of Evelyn Waugh (she played with Waugh once or twice in childhood, but has no distinct recollections of him) inspired her: 'Evelyn Waugh got systematically drunk every night with companion at White's. Brilliant wit resulted from his tipple. As an experiment I made myself drunk on brandy. No sign of wit. It took three hours to sober up.'

When she became housebound, reading had to take the place of travel: 'I write in a hazy dream. I am in Greece with Maria Callas', she would write to me, or 'I have a crush on Laurens van der Post and through him on Jung'; 'Jimmy Boyle has made me reconciled to being housebound. At least I am not in a filthy cell'; 'I want *Greenvoe* as I have a crush on the author. He wrote to me'; and, tongue in cheek, 'WRVS has sent me *Washington Square* and about ten more of Henry James. I felt so exhausted that I retrieved *Alice in Wonderland* and savoured it with intense joy.'

Erica is typical of the educated women of her generation in that books were vital to her in a way that no single medium is to people of the present age: 'I've just had to stop to eat – a wicked waste of time. That "winged chariot" makes me feel so tense, as there is a vast number of books I MUST read before I am sent for.' Reading was a respectable, even a moral, activity, but it was also a life-line to a wider world. It provided women of Erica's class and time with the spiritual companionship and emotional sensibility they could rarely find within the subtle calibrations and rigid taboos of their immediate social circle.

Travel was another means of slipping the chains. It is plain that Erica loved her husband and enjoyed his companionship. It is equally plain that his death – he lived into his nineties – was a liberation for her. She never spoke of him to me by name. In some of her journals she refers to him only as 'Parson' or 'the Parson'. To me it was always, 'My husband – who was a Calvinist minister – ...' and it felt as if she were explaining her own identity rather than his; presenting the credentials of her respectability before she went on to say something shockingly frank ('If you never return it will make me wet my pants').

Erica's life seems to fall into two parts, Jamaica and after. The letters she wrote home during her early years in the West Indies show her to be blissfully happy ('Every prospect pleases and only the maid is vile') even allowing for the fact that those she has preserved were all written to her mother. In these letters her husband does not figure as the joyless Calvinist she somehow implied him to be later. I may have misinterpreted her, of course; it could be that there is a generation gap between us in our understanding of 'Calvinist': 'Last night and the night before it was midnight before we got to bed as Jim was singing out across the harbour to the full moon, Burns, Schumann, Brahms and the familiar old folk songs like "The Apple Blossom".' As they started out for a garden party, 'Jim looked me over and said I was too dowdy. While he sent me to change my stockings, he entirely re-trimmed my hat. ... Next he touched me up with a becoming daub of "Attar of Roses" on either cheek.' Their marriage seems to have a been a partnership of equals, which is all the more surprising given the difference in their ages. Erica had problems with the feeding of her infant son. He cried all day. She wrote to her mother: 'My milk does not agree with him at all. Jim says he is not surprised that infanticide is common among women and wonders that fathers are not guilty of it.' She and she alone chose their car, and was in complete charge of it. She crowed to her mother, 'Ah! I am so happy! You can't feel such a grand tiger in your new coat as I do in my new car!'.

She also enjoyed motherhood. In journal after journal, letter after letter, she details minutely every phase of her children's development and their achievements, especially her daughter's. The first serious break in her life seems to come when she had to send her daughter – 'the apple of my eye' – to school in Britain. Shortly after the birth she had written, 'no children of ours must be educated in this sinful land', though she never so much as hints how Jamaica was more sinful than Scotland.

War broke out and the rift between mother and daughter inevitably widened, never to be healed. In 1945, when Erica and her husband returned to Berwickshire, he was in his late seventies and she was forty-seven. Her children had grown away from her; her husband was an old man; postwar Scotland was a grim place after the 'paradise' of Jamaica. But Erica, as her photos show, was still in her prime. She had run a school, chaired committees, managed a cook and housemaid, and enjoyed the social status of her class in the colonies. Overnight she became the useless wife of a retired clergyman, not at all well-off, in a tiny country village, fending for herself.

No doubt these were factors that contributed to her indiscreet passion for the young student, and had as much to do with her breakdown as the affair itself. But this can only be speculation, for I could never persuade Erica to tell me the humdrum details, the accumulation of trivial causes, in her life.

I wondered too what sort of liberation it was for her when her husband died. For many women the disruption of decades of companionship leaves them disoriented. They live in a twilight zone, going through the motions as if their husbands were still there, only temporarily invisible: lonely, incomplete women, marking the empty time. Or they go a little crazy in their unsought freedom. Suddenly they have no one to consider but themselves, and anything is possible.

If you have no one to consider but yourself, it means you are not really important to anyone but yourself, and that is rather a frightening kind of freedom. It takes courage to restructure your life, to find new meanings and purposes. Erica had this courage.

Her freedom excited her. But when she wandered the world it was as the somewhat 'dotty' but essentially respectable widow of the Calvinist minister. Although she was proud to be known by chance companions as 'the Hippy Granny', her journals show her to be much more in tune with Mary Kingsley than Jack Kerouac.

The letters she sent from abroad are masterpieces of the form, starting with wry comments from the SS *Vienna* coming home from Berlin in 1919 – 'It's most unfortunate that I am too infantile to manage alone' – and culminating in her description of a Saga tour of Yugoslavia sixty years later. She begins this: 'I am very ill and weak. This may be my last chance to write as

God may send for me any time and I am ready to go.' The day before she left Edinburgh she had been 'hit by a radiator', and from death's door she comments, 'I looked so repulsive no fellow Sagaist could be expected to share a bedroom with a lady who had a tartan face.'

She embarked on the Saga holiday with some trepidation: 'I had had misgivings about my "group" as 4 years ago a Saga brochure came with rows of inane looking nitwits on the cover grinning fatuously and eating ice-cream cones.' In the end she was singing the praises of the travel company and of Yugoslavia. The ironic humour is still to the fore none the less: 'There is no lovelier place in which to die. I would leap into Eternity quietly and would give no trouble, only a quiet Jugoslavian funeral which I am sure they would be good at as they are so efficient in every way.'

In Malta she broke her ankle and lay for weeks in a bed without sheets in a primitive hospital ward run by a holy terror of a nursing sister:

> Sister Manuela looks like Ignatius Loyola ... she deserves to be burnt at the stake for she is a vicious monster of evil and cruelty. I got desperate and my only means to escape was to attempt suicide. My plaster is so heavy I could not succeed in throwing myself over a balcony but my attempt fairly shook them.

It is difficult to know if this was a genuine suicide bid (Erica claims, 'I was not quite right in the head for a while in Malta') or a violent protest. Another incident in the same episode makes it even harder to believe she could have been entirely in earnest: 'The priest came on the dot of 6 a.m. to celebrate Mass. I wanted extreme unction but as a heretic I could not qualify.' In the end she had to resort to cunning and stealth to procure the basic comforts: 'I never can get that obscene thing a bed pan when I want one so I have become wily. I hide one inside my bed. In desperation I have to sleep with it.'

She got her friends to send her chewing-gum to stave off the hunger pangs, for she was given no food between noon and 8 p.m., and toilet-paper, for the hospital did not provide any. She also asked her friends to keep her letters so that she could use the material in the lectures she always gave about her travels on her return. She was seventy-nine at this time.

Whatever her tribulations, Erica's spirit never dimmed. 'I have been for a week in the Infirmary in the Euthanasia Ward' (another broken ankle). 'My fellow patients are all mental and look like corpses. They cry loudly all night long.' She loathed the central heating: 'No wonder the 80-year-olds look like 100 as they are being roasted.' At that time she was still based in Chirnside: 'I don't look forward at all to adjusting to my rural rut at the end of the month. My spur to complete recovery is the prospect of a week in London with the endearing homosexuals.' For in Chirnside, she complained, 'the topics never varied – Knitting, Rheumatism, Recipes, Cost of Living'.

Erica looked at life, and herself, with an open-mindedness that seemed to stop short just this side of chaos. But though this seems to place her very much in the second half of the twentieth century, vestiges of the old Calvinism still clung. From her Maltese bed of pain she wrote, 'I have the John Knox feeling that this ordeal is my retribution for having been indulged too much.' Again, she wrote to me once, 'My nose has never stopped running since I wrote you that snide letter. So this is my punishment. I have to stuff cotton wool up my nostrils.' She believed in God still, but not the stern Calvinist God worshipped by her husband.

When I first knew Erica she told me that for want of companionship she was 'forced to make a pal of God'. She always had a fresh example to relate of the wonderful benefits of this special relationship: 'It was the day on which I expected the WRVS Book Ladies. They brought me 4 books. God sent them back in the late afternoon with 26 books!' In another letter she announced, 'God is playing pranks with me. You may think me naive but I feel He is my pal and yesterday I heard Him laugh.'

She had run out of the ruled paper she used to write her letters. So she prayed: '"Dear God send me some more ruled paper." I had to go out to the gate. There on the pavement, quite loose, lay 6 exercise books of pristine paper like this.... God makes it so snappy in answering my prayers!'

Another instance of divine intervention came after she was robbed. Her front door unlocked, Erica lay in bed dozing. It was 2 a.m. Suddenly she awoke to find a young man standing at the foot of her bed. 'Is there something I can do for you?' she enquired politely, mistaking him for one of her visitors, and he fled, taking with him most of the jewellery she had inherited from her mother. A few weeks – and prayers – later, a man was arrested with Erica's jewels in his possession, and they were returned to her.

She confessed in a letter:

I am greedy in what I pray for. Never in my life have I drunk Coca Cola. I asked Philip for one when we visited the Burrell Collection but they had none. Somehow I've never put C.C. on my grocery list. I shall leave it to the Management [God]. Once He actually sent me a lipstick but :t was too flamboyant.

In the same breath, without lifting her pen from the page, she went on:

The Devil used to fill me with apprehension. I got morbid at the prospect of being sent to another geriatric ward. They are hellish and I've been a patient in 7. Now I sincerely believe that I am a privileged part of the Management. He will give me a safe conduct to the Elysian Fields. He won't let me decay in another geriatric hell. I am enjoying this stage of transition in our civilization and I want to see how things develop. I find life so thrilling I want i0 more years but not if I have senile dementia. But He may want me to come next week and make the angels laugh.

Her arterial problems got worse, till she was practically bedridden. Even then, she managed to draw sexual confidences from the middle-aged man who would come in response to her bleeper, but eventually I had a letter from her in hospital. Her legs were paralysed and she was depressed.

I visited her in the convalescent home and recorded the interview below. She was tired, confused, and deeply disappointed in God. Now she is in a nursing home, physically better but subdued. She can no longer read, or write letters. She calls the staff her 'daffodils', because of their yellow overalls, and they call her 'Doll' – 'C'mon Doll, we'll get you up . . .'. The last words of the last letter Erica wrote to me were, 'It's time I kicked the bucket. Except for making people laugh I am useless.'

THE INTERVIEW

I was born on March 4th 1898, in my parents' home, the farm at Chirnside. My father's family had been farmers in that district for generations – right back to 1400. I had a younger sister and there was also a brother.

My mother's father was brought up in a cottage in Leadhills. He typified the Scottish student of those days: he went with his Bible and his bag of oatmeal to Glasgow University. He became a millionaire – started with practically nothing. He was very, very brainy, and he was taken up by various influential professors. Through his patron he was introduced to a Scottish family who had tremendous copper-mines in Norway. (He's had twenty grandchildren, but I'm the only one who got there, to the Hardangar Fjord.)

His predecessor went out to Chile, and Grandfather took over the mine, and felt he needed a wife. The predecessor's wife had had a confinement, and she had a girl from the Lofoten Islands to help her. When Grandfather suggested that she might find one of her sisters, she asked for an assortment to be sent from Lofoten. They all came, and the one that he chose was Fridrikke (it sounds a harsh and ugly name, but I have inherited it and so have a lot of the grandchildren). So my mother was half Scottish and half Norwegian.

None of the sisters would have refused my Grandfather, because a good, promising, and very clever Scotsman was a treasure to find in that remote part of Norway.

They didn't live very long in that place. As soon as they had a child ... This kind of thing was never mentioned, but when I went up to the Hardangar Fjord, and I asked people about my ancestry – the first sister, my Aunt Maggie, was illegitimate – the local padre said to me, 'Well you see we have these dark, dark months of winter, and there's really nothing to do – they just get into bed with each other. It passes the time.'

Fridrikke was fair and very lovely. She had fifteen children and then just died. She had them in very quick succession.

When the family started, Grandfather saw it was quite

impossible to stay in this isolated place – it was so dark in that valley. In the summer you only had the sun for two or three hours a day. Very dark and very depressing. And there was no proper education. Grandfather had to leave this job. Another British firm offered him another mine in the middle of Germany, in Hessen, and the rest of the family were born there.

Each time he had a new baby he built a new room, so he ended up with an enormous house and a huge garden.

When my grandmother died, my grandfather always meant to settle back in Leadhills, but he'd put all his daughters in different boarding-schools and he took a great interest in their education and upbringing, and he never got away from Germany. So during the war ...

I found any amount of letters my mother had written to her favourite sister, Bella. They described life on a Scottish farm during the 1914 war. I got them translated and sent copies to the various cousins. It was an eye-opener to me how beautifully my mother could express herself. You see her native language really was German.

She had a dreadful time in the war because the village, of course, made up terrible lies about her and she was persecuted and terribly unhappy.

One of Fridrikke's sons, Charlie, wanted to study mining and he was coming to Edinburgh to do that. He was living in Spence Street, and next door there was a family called Blackadder. He became very friendly with them. They had a beautiful niece who used to come to Edinburgh quite often. She would dance all night – she went on horseback to dances with her good clothes bundled behind – and was rather spoilt, because she was witty and clever and handsome. So – you see, Charles fell in love with Isabel, and they were married in this country. Therefore my father got to know all those people who looked like Germans but weren't Germans – they were really Scotch. My father met Charles's sister, and fell in love with her.

My father farmed 600 acres, mixed arable.

When we were children we wore thick woollen combinations, thick black knitted stockings, and suspenders going up to our bodice; when we were very young we had sailor suits made of rather rough serge. We wore clogs quite a lot, for the mud.

My mother had a lot of money, and when she married Dad, she doubled the size of the house. But the maids had just 'doon the gairden' for the toilet – they had little seats with two holes at the bottom of the garden.

My mother was a very good organist. She did a lot to help run the village. She started the soup-kitchen for the school. She was a very good, bossy person.

When she was having her second child, she decided to go back to her father's house in Germany. She arranged for a substitute farmer to run the farm for a year. My poor darling Dad was sent to the Institute Tilly in Marburg to learn German. I found his exercise book with that *ghastly* script you know. She told him he must learn conversational German, and there is a pathetic letter from him, after Rosemary was born, saying, 'Dear Anna, when can I come and see the new baby?' She answered, 'John, you must remember your promise. You promised to stick to your work. Stay where you are and *learn German!*' Just imagine! . . . she had the mailed fist in the velvet glove. Dad should have been studying *agriculture*, not highbrow culture.

After a year living like that he just hated the Germans more than ever!

My mother was very keen on the Suffrage Movement. We would go around doing propaganda with her. They paved the way for me going to university.

Women always had their lips locked. They always had to be respectable and mind their p's and q's. Now they can express themselves. I'm profoundly grateful that I was born when I was and not a hundred years before.

My mother was snobbish and on my father's farm I was not allowed to play with the workers' bairns. I wish I'd gone to Duns High School. I was sent to a snobby school – St Leonard's in St Andrews – and what is now Nunraw Abbey was the home of the girl who slept next to me in the dormitory. She invited me for the half-term weekend. I was waiting for her to come to the train. I had my bag packed ready to go. She came downstairs with a face like thunder, holding a letter. She said, 'My mother has just discovered that your father is only a farmer, so she can't have you under our roof. Goodbye!' And I said, 'Elspeth, if you were a boy you would have a black eye!' That gave me an awful inferiority complex all through my schooling. But now the farmers are the aristocracy of the Borders!

I was always very homesick at school. None of the staff were motherly. They were, I thought, rather brusque people, always finding fault. I really was unhappy. The rules were terribly strict. I was fond of music and I used to work hard at practising on the piano, but we had to go out on these miserably cold East Cliffs to play cricket. My hands were black and blue.

Everything was cold at St Leonard's. When we'd been out, we came back and were supposed to strip. They had a sitz-bath under the bed. We had to pull that out and have a bath. That was a kind of regulation at that period. My mother had a cold bath every morning, summer and winter.

My mother was very, very *green*. She wasn't a worldly person. Anybody else who had been reading the newspapers at that time knew the war was coming any minute. She sent me all alone at the age of sixteen to Berlin to do a cram course in German. I got there, I went to the Institute Tilly. It was an Australian who ran it. They'd never had a girl with her hair down her neck. They had a lot of military people – officers and opera-singers and people like that – because they did teach German very quickly.

I had no sooner arrived than war was declared. Well the Tillys had no money – they were bankrupt. Mr Tilly had been spending all his money on buying beautiful furniture and beautiful ornaments and pictures, but he hadn't saved anything. He must have had about fifty students there, but we had no money and we had no food.

Now ... one of his daughters was going to take me out to hear the Kaiser give a speech from the town hall, so when we were there mixing with all these people, she brought up a man and his wife. She said, 'This is a bank director retired, Schossenberg. They have a lovely house.' Well they were greatly concerned about me. I could hardly stand up. I was starving. They said, 'You must come and stay with us', and I was only too glad. They took a great fancy to me and they gave me such a marvellous time. We never seemed to be in bed till about midnight.

I had lived a very genteel life. I had never been to operas and things like that. We went to the most wonderful theatres and operas, and yachting on the Wannsee and I was having the time of my life. I said to the Schossenbergs, 'You know, I have cousins in Norway. Couldn't I get a boat over to Norway?' They said, 'No, no, no. There will be a submarine and you will be drowned. Stay with us till the war is over. It will be over by Christmas, it's all right.'

It used to amuse me to hear these Germans discussing where they would spend their holidays – Eastbourne or Brighton.

In the end the British government and the German government decided to exchange females. I was with the first lot of females that were sent over....

... I am so glad that we don't have our mouths padlocked now, because I *really* knew nothing about sex. The son-in-law of the Schossenbergs, who had married an opera-singer – I could never go to any Charlie Chaplin films because his face was the duplicate of Charlie Chaplin's, it gave me the creeps. What was an ignorant girl to do when she discovered this man had crawled along the floor ... I was leaning against the piano, listening to his wife doing her opera, when all of a sudden I found his hand in a place where it had no right to be. And a night or two after – I had no lock on my bedroom door – I was appalled to find him walking into the room, so I beat it. There was another daughter down the road, not too far away, and I ran with bare feet and just a dressing-gown in the night to get away.

Nowadays if anything like that had happened a girl could tell her mother and get comfort, and a little advice on how to face similar cases – concupiscent men. I didn't dare mention it to my mother. The funny thing is, when I got back to St Leonard's the headmistress had written to my mother that she was very vexed to hear that I was caught in Berlin: 'Erica is not a very worldly-wise young woman. I pray for her welfare.'

My friends at school crowded round to commiserate with me, and I think they recoiled in amazement because I said, 'Oh, I didn't want to come back here! I had the time of my life!' They took me out every evening. They spoiled me – it was marvellous. They gave me gold bracelets and things like that. I really *did* have a fine time with the Germans. They always called me 'the poor little foreigner'. It was unusual to find an English schoolgirl in Berlin.

... I was all in a turmoil yesterday. I never mentioned that I had had teacher training when I left St Leonard's. I went to the House of Education, a very cranky place in Ambleside and got my certificate there. I got a very nice job in Haslemere – very rich family, the children didn't need to pass exams so sometimes the headmistress would say we'd have no lessons that day, we'd go out and do a Shakespeare play. We did *The Tempest* that way. I was very happy, but I was too ignorant. I found that I didn't know enough to teach, so I just thought I'd go to Edinburgh University and learn a bit more.

... I came to Edinburgh University. I had had a distant relation who was Professor of Scottish History. He came from Galloway and he was very handsome and very musical, and the girls in his classes *swooned* whenever he came in. When I first got to Edinburgh I was put as a boarder in his wife's house. Cousin Jane was always going in for politics and she neglected her husband. He used to take me through the Pentland Hills and he used to spend his holidays with us at Chirnside.

I wasn't very good at knowing how to manage men and I knew very little about sex ... I was terribly, terribly green. But my mother felt kind of proud that this distinguished and well-known professor had taken such an interest in me. He took me to orchestral concerts and so on. I didn't know what to do, because I couldn't do any work. I was just knocked flat, falling in love. It was his beautiful voice. He sang wonderful songs and I used to sit and adore him.

I would meet very interesting people. They had an 'At Home' every Sunday, and all kinds of distinguished people came, and one time there was a man who was introduced to me as 'Colonel Hunt'. He spoke about going to British Honduras. He'd had a church there for a good many years. He said, 'You know, I had a parish as big as *Wales*, and I felt, "Nobody has ever trodden on this soil before except the Almighty".' (I've been to British Honduras, and I don't know how he *stuck* it; but that man would have been happy anywhere: he had a wonderful disposition.)

He'd been a colonel in the war you see. I thought he'd have a good position in life, lots of wherewithal, but one day he took me to the National Gallery. We were in the Raeburn Room and he asked me to marry him. He said, 'But I have nothing to give you.' I thought he meant a bunch of red roses or a box of chocolates, but he meant that he had practically no money. It was quite true – he had nothing. He had given it all away. His sisters each got several thousand pounds from him because he thought, now, he was far too old to marry, so they got it. . . .

AS: What made him want to marry you, suddenly?

EH: [Huffily] I'm a very desirable person. Since that I've had lots of offers.

. . . That was typical of him. He was very unworldly and not very practical. But he used to take me out in the Pentlands every Saturday. I had been entangled with the Professor of Scottish History, you see, and I didn't know how to get free of that. So I said to this clergyman, 'You are the last straw. I'm just clutching at you, because I can't do any work. I'll never get my degree.'

He said he'd take the other man's place. And do you know what the wife of the other man said? She wrote to my mother and said, 'Erica has been like a steam-roller over my husband's heart. For heaven's sake tell her not to leave us.' Well, it was so silly, but I just felt it was quite impossible to go back to the first one – I wouldn't get anywhere, so . . . he was getting no younger, and I never got my four years of work, and I've regretted it ever since. I think one can sacrifice too much for a man. Because in order not to delay the marriage, to get married earlier, I did all that work in three years. I had no social life at all; I never met any other people. It was just a terrible grind. I think I should have gone on taking the four years.

We were never officially engaged, because my family wouldn't hear of it. I had only fallen in love with a very sainted man, but I was treated as if I had been a criminal, and ostracized. I was told not to see him for a whole year. But I couldn't do that. So, strange to say, we were very happily married.

His father had a gentleman's clothing department in Perth. They had been very poor. There were five brothers and two sisters. They had all to earn, they had practically nothing. When my mother asked me about the man I wanted to marry, she said, 'Tell me about his family and his background. Who is he?' I didn't like to say he was the penniless son of a tailor. I just said, 'Oh he's in the church . . .'. She didn't ask for any details, but I gave a brazen lie.

Our marriage in the village was the first that had been celebrated there for many, many years. We led the fashion, not to be married in the manse, but to go to church.

So we went out to Jamaica in 1923. I had an awful voyage. Being of a religious disposition, I thought when I was going out there I should choose the very cheapest boat of the whole fleet, but she really nearly sunk, and I arrived so ill in Jamaica I couldn't stand up.

Now, these are the kind of things that I say that are indiscreet. I was put to bed at once. It was a Scottish doctor, and the congregation were terribly concerned about me, because he told them 'Mrs Hunt is suffering from a miscarriage.' I used to say, 'I don't know anything about miscarriages, but I don't *feel* as if I've had a miscarriage – can I get out of bed?' 'Oh, stay where you are – don't move, don't move!' It was rather a comedown for the doctor and I changed to another one, because my miscarriage turned out to be bleeding piles. [*Laughs.*]

My husband had gone to Jamaica early. I found I was pregnant and had to stay at home to sew all the little outfits.

My husband was so nervous ... we spent the first night of our honeymoon in Perth at the Salutation Hotel – he couldn't face it, so he sat there smoking a cigarette. No, he thought that anything sexual was sinful. His family were *poisonously* narrow. He'd been brought up that way – terribly narrow, very Calvinistic. Thank goodness we've got liberated now!

Well, it meant that after twenty-five years of practical abstinence, I had a violent affair with a much younger man, a student who lodged with us when we came back to Scotland. I had a letter from him yesterday. It was too difficult to live with my husband and the other one, who was as much to me as my husband, so I found it quite unbearable, and I thought the only way to solve this terrible situation is to take all the sleeping pills in the house. So I committed suicide.

It was the first time I had the chance to enjoy sex. My husband was so Calvinistic – he just felt it was something you should be ashamed of. I knew I was missing something but I felt it was worthwhile missing it because I was really very fond of him.

When my husband saw me never waking up – I'd been sound asleep for two days and three nights and he never noticed the bottle was empty, lying beside me – he called in the doctor, and when I recovered I was in Dingleton Asylum in Melrose. I was there for six months.

I was torn to pieces because I loved them both equally. The other man was an orphan. He'd had a very unhappy upbringing. He just idolized me, because I provided him with all the things . . . I can't resist teaching and I taught him a lot of literature, and about art and things like that. I'd been the only woman in his life and I still get a passionate love letter from him. My lover would dig an acre of garden. He would do anything to help me. My dear husband always disappeared behind the *Scotsman*; I never saw his face.

There was I, married to a man thirty years older, and in love with a man thirty years younger. I don't think anybody else can have been that extraordinary. The situation is quite unique. . . .

While I lived in Chirnside I hadn't a car. I went out walking every afternoon. For thirty years I had been all over that district. I knew people in every house. I thought nobody would ever have such an intricate knowledge of this place, so I'd better record it. I'm very glad I did it. They knew who I was; they knew I was a bit dotty but nicely dotty. It was after my husband died.

My house there was cold so I just hibernated in bed till the spring came again. I got to know the Chirnsiders. Sex and drink preoccupied their minds, but there was a prudish lack of frankness. Sex was furtive and the villagers were too embarrassed to talk about contraceptives. There was an embarrassment about illegitimates too. A man told me how he dug a hole and buried an unwelcome baby. We had a backstreet abortionist. My gardener had two sisters living with the same man. One of them murdered her child. The great thing was to be respectable.

. . . My husband and I had been very happy. We shared everything. We read the same books, went to the same plays . . . every night I used to play good songs for him. He'd never been able to study music because they were too poor. He did it all by ear, but he could improvise beautifully.

In my marriage I had to wear the breeks. I had to. He was very easy-going and never had any strong opinions about where to go or what to do. But he was so good-natured, we always got on very amicably. Nobody could have quarrelled with him.

It seems rather odd, because I had three nieces who married millionaires, and I married a poor Presbyterian parson who never got more than four hundred pounds a year, and I think that on the whole I had the happiest life. Money doesn't bring any spiritual satisfaction. Spiritual satisfaction comes with self-confidence, a well-balanced spirit, and a well-stored mind. I feel it's of tremendous importance in life to have something inside – I need it now you see, I need something now from the days when I took life seriously and studied, and all my travels.

I think I'd better mention the children. I wanted five girls and a boy: I've always been very fond of little girls. But we thought with this distance in age, we'd better stop at two, so we did. We had a girl and a boy.

I had the most *awful* maternity nurse. She never would do anything for me. She said, 'I'm resting for the event. I must store up strength for the event.' I couldn't stand this. There was a hospital not very far away, and I had my Model T Ford, so I flung all my luggage into the car because I felt things were starting, and I told the woman, 'I'll pay you for your three weeks but I don't want you ever to come near me again.' I drove myself round to the hospital and had the baby with no trouble. How I wish I could have had five!

I heard a little splash, and I thought it was the doctor washing his hands, and he said, 'Oh my word, you've got a beautiful boy!' I never realized that I'd given birth. As easy as that. The second birth was very easy too. I could breed like a rabbit. It's a kind of waste that I didn't get the chance.

My daughter took up social work out in Mauritius, after her degree, and my son went into the RAF.

... The world is going round and round in my head. I couldn't sleep last night because I was far too indiscreet. One reason that I am such a wreck today is that I had a disturbed night. I had nightmares about what I said to you. I shouldn't have talked so much about sex. My daughter would be horrified. I know you're in a muddle because I haven't got my chronology right. ...

I took an honours degree in history and got married and went to Jamaica. I was just a housewife and a parson's wife. I had a

Model T Ford, but my husband never learned to drive a car so I did a lot of chauffeuring for him. We were blissfully happy. Eventually I ran a schoolie. I took only white children, so I had my pick. Every five years we got leave to come home.

I went to the biggest boys' school in Jamaica, but I had my children first. Look, I say things that should never be said in public but I think they're very interesting. Things have changed more in the last eighty years than they have in eight hundred. The boys liked me because I always made them laugh, so I was very popular. But there was one class – I used to get in a panic when I had to go to it, because I was too green and there wasn't a soul I could have referred to in Jamaica. No doctor, no minister, nobody who could tell me exactly what was happening. Every time I went to this class, in the middle of the class a boy of about fourteen got up and exposed himself. His father was the head of the prison. I went to the headmaster and said, 'What am I to do? Should I take that as something nasty, or has he got a diseased brain, does he need psychiatric treatment?'

The headmaster was terribly embarrassed and he said, 'I'll think it over', but on the following Monday he had the whole school round the playground, and this boy was brought to the middle, and publicly thrashed. I left under a cloud. At speech-day at the end of the summer term, the fact that I'd done a lot of hard work – my husband used to help me with the corrections, he was a great help – I thought it was unfair that my name was never mentioned. They must have thought that there was something *sinister* about it. You see nowadays no woman would ever have been in that predicament. I didn't know what he was doing.

AS: Even though you were a married woman?

EH: [*Lady Bracknellish*] Well that makes no difference – my husband never went in for pastimes like that!

I immediately got another job, in the training college for men teachers. I loved it there. In Jamaica teaching was a joy because they were all so anxious to learn and to get a good education. I never had any trouble with discipline.

I sometimes did naughty things. It might amuse you. I used to look at those advertisements in the local paper, 'Wanting to

meet somebody'. This was somebody from the north coast who
wanted to meet a girl who was very fair, and who was musical,
and who was born under Taurus, and who had some experience.
So – I never told anyone, because even my husband would have
been shocked. I answered it, and I said, 'I am so fair that
although my name is Heather my friends all call me Lily – You
ask about experience: I have several kinds of experience. What
kind were you thinking about? I was born under Taurus ...'. It
was quite a long letter I wrote anyhow.

The answer *amazed* me. This was one of my pupils from the
training college. [*Laughs.*] Well, life is never dull. This is the first
time that I've really been thoroughly bored and I don't know
what to do.

When I left St Leonard's they didn't have the wide choice that
you can have now – you can be an engineer, computer specialist,
and so on. We had three choices: you could be a nurse or a
secretary or a teacher.

I liked teaching and the Jamaican servants were excellent.
When I came back to Scotland I couldn't manage. In the village
there was a mill, and all the women got a good wage there, so
there was nobody to help me. It sent me back to the asylum. I
phoned Dingleton and said, 'If you can't come and fetch me
tomorrow I'll commit suicide.' Because I had hardly gone to
bed. The house had been rewired and the whole place was full of
these little bits of dust, and it just made me feel quite demented.
So back I went. It was very lonely when we came back to
Chirnside, because all my school-friends were English.

The asylums were dreadful when I was first there. I was put in
a very cold room, in the winter. Every time anybody got up it
was, 'Sit down this *minute*! Don't dare to move.' They never
ever told me I could get out again if I asked: I thought I was
there for life. A doctor saw I was reading the life of Nelson, and
he thought I couldn't be so mad, and he arranged for me to get
out. But when I got out my memory had completely gone. I
didn't know where to go when I got off the bus, and my
husband hadn't come to meet me – I was lost. When I came into
my house I didn't recognize the furniture or anything. I told
Winifred Rushforth how much electric shock treatment I had
had and she was *horrified*. I wish we had more psychiatry when
I was young – it tries to get to the bottom of things. ...

I've been three times in the asylum. The third time I went invited by them because I've always done a lot of public speaking, to organizations like the church guilds, so now they had found a more enlightening way of treating lunatics – visiting their homes and that kind of thing – they asked me to go round and do propaganda for them. Most of the people in every audience that I addressed had some relations who were mental.

... My sister Rosemary, my mother would never admit it, but she had schizophrenia. She got a scholarship to go to Girton, and she was taken up by Quiller-Couch. She took the place of his wife and was hostess. When I came back to Chirnside, I found a box of the most *amazing* letters from Rosemary to my mother, always asking for money but telling about the VIPs whom she met in Quiller-Couch's dining-room. He rather spoilt her. Her head was a bit turned – she never bothered to work at all. She didn't pass her exams, she just had a good time there.

She married Prince Urach of ... my brain won't work. She was very popular, very witty and clever and beautiful. She had expressive purple eyes.

When she left Cambridge she couldn't stick at any job, and Mama always did what she asked. She gave her money, so she was always moving around, she never got settled. She was a good artist. A famous London paper employed her to go two or three times a week to interview people, people like Chaliapin – but his interview consisted of nothing but violence and kisses, so it wasn't suitable to print. It was a good job but she was always restless.

She did a lot of dancing. She went to RADA to learn to be an actress, and she worked for Fagin in Oxford, and had a very good part in a play called *And So To Bed*, but she never bothered to learn her lines in any other plays, so she never got engagements. One of her Cambridge friends wrote to me at this time and said Rosemary had an awful way of helping herself to other people's property and of sawning on them.

When she was in Norway with our cousins she met this Prince Urach of Bertenberg and he fell frantically in love with her. He was engaged to an aristocrat in Spain and he had seven brothers who were all in the Mercedes-Benz business, but Urach thought he was an artist. He was no good, but he got his Mama to pay for an exhibition in London. He only sold one picture and it was a very poor one.

I don't think Rosemary loved him at all, but she was very pleased to become a princess. She was writing for the *Saturday Review* and two or three important papers. She became quite well-known.

They had a child, Gabrielle ... I would so love to tell you, because it's amazing, the story of Rosemary's life, but my head is empty.... She didn't like to bother to bring up the baby, she got away with everything. She determined to go to Hollywood and get on the movies. So she left the child in Florence with the father. She went to my brother's house at Los Angeles. They didn't know the symptoms of schizophrenia. Ian was to meet her at the terminus, but she got out a few stations before. When he found her she said, 'You must not tell anybody who I am – just call me Little Annie Rooney.'

My two nieces were thrilled to be having this princess, but when they met her outside the bungalow she just waved them aside, 'Go away little girls – go away!' She came into the living-room and shook her head in disapproval at the pictures. She turned every picture with its face to the wall, and then without telling my brother or his wife anything, she lay down like Madame Récamier, with bare feet. In came some Dutch aristocrat who manicured her toes for her, and she paid no attention to her hostess.

She didn't get the job. She was rather sawning on Del and Ian, and they couldn't get rid of her. When my mother arrived in Florence, Rosemary was there. She had a cold, cold heart. She never loved any of her suitors, but she wanted the prestige of being a princess. ...

... Rosemary should have come home to Chirnside, and Mama would have looked after the child, but she wanted glamorous people and a lot of glitter. She never wrote a letter without asking for a cheque. She was always moving from hotel to hotel and place to place. Urach meanwhile was at the Sino-Japanese War ...

Now I'm all muddled, but I do remember that Rosemary's madness got so awful ... when her husband was away, he was writing for the press about this war, and Rosemary was determined to stop the war, so she went to the Emperor's

Palace, and there were two sentries with guns, and she seized
their rifles and she blipped them over the head and walked past
them and tried to get to the Crown Prince – she was trying to
drown the Crown Prince in Tokyo. Then when she couldn't get
the Crown Prince she tried to drown her baby.

Our Norwegian cousins wrote to Urach and said he must
come and attend to her because she was quite mad. They put her
in an asylum there. What happened to the baby I don't know,
but Mama ... I remember we were home on leave, and Mama
said to my husband that she'd met a woman who would have
looked after Rosemary. She wanted to take her to Russia, and
she said the smell of the pine trees and nature would cure her
mind. My husband said, 'She sounds like an adventuress. Don't
trust Rosemary to her.' But Mama did; gave her a lot of money
and paid for her ticket to Norway. All that woman wanted was
to meet a man in Russia – they never saw her again.

They got Rosemary back. When Urach came back from the
war he found Rosemary throwing all the furniture out of the
house and crowds around. She was quite mad, you see. They
put her on a boat with two mental nurses, but Rosemary was
very majestic and she said in her princely way when they got to
Marseilles, 'You can leave me here now. Go ashore and don't
come back.' So she arrived in London alone and went straight
to Miss Ramsden and asked for a large cheque. She said, 'I have
to go and see Hitler.' So she went to his office in Berlin and
demanded to see him, but he wasn't in the mood. She said she
would wait and she seized a glass inkstand and cut her wrists.
She was staying at the Hotel Adlon in Berlin, the very Ritzy
hotel, and Mama paying for everything.

Mama went down to Miss Ramsden's house to bring
Rosemary to Chirnside. She would disappear when the dark
came on, and Mama would have an awful time searching the
river for Rosemary's corpse. One time she was found in a
mansion house quite near us – people we didn't know at all. She
was stark naked except for a fur coat and I think Mama found it
so difficult, and she felt Urach should take some responsibility
for Rosemary. She thought we weren't grand enough to put him
up at Chirnside, so she took the best suite in Berwick's foremost
hotel and I just couldn't speak to him because he was such a
bore. He never mentioned Rosemary and he wasn't going to do

anything about looking after her. He just had a nice quiet holiday on his own account. Mama was very disappointed.

Miss Ramsden looked after Rosemary's daughter. She adopted her legally.

At Lasswade Mama's cousin thought it would be a good thing to invite Rosemary from London to meet Gabrielle, her baby, who was there. Idiots – they stayed upstairs and they left Rosemary alone downstairs with Gabrielle, and they heard awful shrieks. We don't know whether Rosemary attacked the child, but when she saw these people coming in she jumped out of the window through the glass and the end of her nose came off. It was found and it was eventually sewn on again. For two nights and a day she was completely lost. All the police in the Lothians and Borders were looking for her. It would have been better if she'd never been found, and it broke Mama's heart.

Mama just had to decide to put Rosemary into the asylum. It was a private ward. I think it cost Mama her life, because she only had one maid in the house, Alice, and Alice stayed summer and winter. Every week Mama went to the asylum to see Rosemary, and sometimes Rosemary was heavily sedated and couldn't speak to her, and Mama got into an awful state.

Much later I had to go to the head of the asylum and I said, my niece had married the Lord Mayor's son and her father-in-law wanted to know if Rosemary's condition was hereditary, and the head of the asylum said, 'If it had been my son I would have moved heaven and earth not to let that marriage take place.'

Miss Ramsden had a lovely house in an estate near Haslemere. I'd come back from Jamaica and I thought I'd better go and see her and Rosemary's daughter as I was in London. Miss Ramsden was the niece of the Earl of Somerset I think. I thought it was Urach who had come out to meet me, and gave him a warm kiss and said it was nice to see him, and he was very embarrassed because he was only the butler!

We had a terrible lunch, a little wine and a pheasant. The conversation was very stiff, and Urach said nothing of any interest. I said, 'I would like to see my little niece – may I see the baby?' Rosemary said, 'We don't show the baby to strangers.' She called a taxi for me.

Rosemary was twenty-seven years in the asylum. I often used to think I should write down what I knew of Rosemary's life.

I'll tell you about my brother, because it's rather extraordinary. He was terribly spoiled! He ran away from St Mary's in Melrose and he got expelled from Loretto. I never found out why till I got to Malta just a few years ago. One of his school friends used to come and help us with the harvest. He said Ian was perfectly dreadful. He would put on drag, and he got out on the roof of Loretto, and would spend the night with girls and dancing. . . .

. . . My father bred horses and was very famous as a horseman. He went to Olympia and won many prizes for his horsemanship, and of course he was determined that his only son must carry on the farm. But he overdid it. He talked farming morning, noon, and night, and Ian was only interested in motorbikes and cars. When he was sent to the College of Agriculture in Edinburgh he just couldn't stand it any more. So when he was given the wages to pay the farm-workers, he pocketed the lot and went down to Liverpool, meaning to go to the States. Well he's never been back. My mother put detectives in all the ports down the west side of Britain and he was caught and brought home.

The same day that he was brought back – he was the conquering hero and admired and made a lot of – *I* had come with my fiancé, and because he was the same age as my father (he was thirty years older than me) I was looked on as a kind of *criminal*.

Well, Ian lived in sin with a woman with a streak of South American. She had very black hair and flashing black eyes. Ian worked on the railways. There were strikes and he would go to these places to act as a stop-gap. This woman – her name was Idela – her mother had met Ian, and I think she thought this would be a wonderful thing for Idela if she could find somebody who could earn steadily – a good well-set-up Scotsman. (Incidentally, when I went over to see them in Los Angeles, I didn't remember what my brother looked like. I was sitting waiting at the airport with both my children, and I got a bit worried when he wasn't there, so I went to the telephone, and the man who had been sitting behind me heard me say the name 'Blackadder'. . . that was Ian, that was my brother! I said, 'Good heavens Ian, when you went to Loretto you never had that broad Scots accent – what is all this about?' He said, 'It's good business. In the USA Scotland stands for solid worth. So I put on the accent and it paid.')

When his daughters were about twelve and fourteen, and my two were the same age, we went over to spend a week or two with them. Here comes the interesting thing about genes: the oldest daughter was the image of my grandmother – a pure Norwegian blonde. Ian would have nothing to do with horses or riding. Ruth was born with a craze for horses. She went in for all those rodeos and competitions. She became the champion cowgirl of California. ...

The difference between this generation and ours – we were never body-conscious. One nurse told me yesterday that she spent ten pounds on a bottle of scent! Why does it matter so much? I've never used anything but eau de cologne, you see. My husband didn't even like that. I asked him why and he said, 'Because it always reminds me of a death-bed.' But this generation are preoccupied with what they look like and their figures and their weight and everything. We just never thought about these things, which I think perhaps was more wholesome in a way.

The important thing in life is making friendships, and loving people. When I came to Edinburgh first, I was in a ground-floor flat. I used to sit at my window and wave to people passing. I started knowing nobody, but I kept a visitors' book and quite a good cellar and I was amazed to see that in no time I'd had about 130 visitors. They came to discuss sex with me because I'm safe. I don't think they always liked what I said. I know I shock people, but I get shocked myself, because so many of these girls, living all round in the flats, said to me, 'Oh yes, we want to have babies, but we'll never get married.' They said, 'You look around – a husband just expects a wife to do everything for him while he just relaxes and enjoys life, and I'm not going to be treated like a slave that way.' They laugh when I say, 'When you get to retirement age you're going to feel lonely, and that is the time when one appreciates a husband most, to share old age.'

Does the modern girl just do what her friends are doing? Do they all just conform? I wouldn't like my daughter experimenting with sex – they get a soiled attitude.

What the modern girl doesn't seem to realize is that marriage entails getting down to brass tacks. I think they go far too lightheartedly into marriage. They just think if it doesn't work they'll try somebody else. How many young people try very hard to get to *know* each other? I think the secret of a good marriage is *sharing*. I think they often don't discuss the really important and deep things of life. They're shallow.

In friendships with men I value their – I think they're not so volatile as women: they're steadier. Somehow or other I've been let down by several women friends. I don't trust them, they're not loyal to each other. The men are much more loyal. My education is chiefly due to the men who have influenced me. They've given me a broader outlook. Some women are very petty and narrow.

Before I left Chirnside I used to stay at the YWCA in Edinburgh, for it was very cheap – far cheaper than living at home. I was the Queen of 7 Bruntsfield Crescent – the Youth Hostel – I used to go there too. I had a bunk perpetually reserved for me near the window. I shared with twenty-nine virgins. The BBC paid me nine pounds a minute to talk on 'Youth Hostelling for Grandmothers'.

During the Edinburgh Festival I went into the rehearsals at the Usher Hall on crutches. I had broken my ankles (I've broken them so often, I don't know how I did it that time). They were so sorry for me, they couldn't turn me out, so having once made the entrée I always got in.

The man who looked after the hall knew I was keen on going to rehearsal and I loved opera. He said I should go at 2 p.m. to the King's Theatre, for they were rehearsing *Don Giovanni*. So I didn't go back to the YWCA to cook my sausages, I just went straight there. It was André Previn. He was at the door and he said, 'Not this time Mrs Hunt. There's a very temperamental soprano coming from the United States. She would have fits if there were somebody in the auditorium. Some other time.'

I pretended to go away but I didn't. I just went round the corner and said, 'Oh God, let me in – I want to hear this rehearsal.' And He said, 'Lie on your face in box number three. No one will know that you're hidden but me.' So as I knew my way in at the back ... I found this heavy door with 'No Admittance' in red paint. I pushed my way in, and really it was an extraordinary experience, to be lying on the floor all the time, to hear the whole thing and not seeing anybody. Nobody knew I'd been there.

I went to a rehearsal. Previn was playing Chopin. Fischer-Dieskau came in and sang the whole of *Winterreise*. It inspired me; it was wonderful. . . . You need somebody outside yourself. I'm going through a dreadful phase of being disillusioned. I'm wallowing in misery and self-pity. . . .

We'll always be speculating about the meaning of life. None of us will ever know.

•

Enid with her son

Enid Shears

⇢ 3 ⇠

Enid Shears

'I think I could have created a world that was easier in a
lot of respects.'

*Enid Shears was born in Newcastle in 1900. Her father was Scottish, a
Congregationalist minister who moved to the Unitarian church; her
mother was Devon born and bred. Enid had one older brother. She
was educated at tiny private schools in Pendleton and Bristol, and at
Redland and Wallasey High Schools. When she was eighteen her
father became a minister at George's Chapel, Exeter, and Enid began
work as a secretary with Devon County Council there. She married in
1931 and had one son. At forty she became a lay preacher in the
Unitarian church. For many years she took an active part in church
life, and contributed letters and poetry to the Unitarian church
magazine, the* Inquirer, *and to* Faith and Freedom. *She left the church
when she was in her seventies. Enid published one pamphlet of poems,*
Soliloquy, *in 1970.*

I came to know Enid through a young cartoonist friend from
Exeter who wrote to me in 1985 that she had met an interesting
old lady in the Milkmaid cafeteria there. Enid, she said, was
someone you could really talk to and argue with about the
important questions without having to go all round the houses
with the usual social small-talk. Since Enid went regularly, twice
a week, to the Milkmaid my friend could always find her when
she felt like having a good conversation, and their friendship,
though they only ever met in the cafeteria, grew.

My friend said that Enid was independent to the point of
bloody-mindedness. She would not have a cup of coffee bought
for her; she would never accept a cigarette. She loved to argue,
and to provoke impossible debates beginning with such
contentions as, say, that there is no such thing as a masterpiece
in art, there are only paintings that in the opinion of other people
– not Enid – are masterpieces. Her mission was not so much to

initiate metaphysical discussion of the basic assumptions as to question the consensus of opinion on everything upon which there is a consensus of opinion.

I met her briefly in the Milkmaid in 1985 and we began to correspond. In the beginning the main topic was free will. Enid argued that we are absolutely determined in everything we think and do by our genes: we have no freedom at all. She was not quite open-minded in argument, but rather determined to prove her own thesis against all comers. When discussion was exhausted neither side was much further forward, and she would shrug it off with, 'But of course, the whole subject would make a book in itself and then never settle it, like so many other arguments.'

There seemed to be something immature about Enid in this, something much more reminiscent of the student debater than the seeker after truth. Her constant questioning, especially about the nature of God, had never led her on any pilgrimage. She had a mild obsession with the question of the existence and divinity of Jesus. The scrapbook of her published pieces, which she gave me, is full of letters to the *Inquirer* on this subject. The philosophers she had read, she told me, were 'The Huxleys, William Gerhardi, J. B. Priestley and Shaw in the Prefaces'. She later added, 'I do have a smattering of Schopenhauer, and A. J. Ayer is my pin-up.'

The key to understanding this side of Enid seems to be in the dominant personality of her father, whom she idolized. She wrote to me once, 'I have always seemed to land myself with friends who were more gifted than I was, as well as a father and brother who also were.' When Enid was ten years old her father fell under the spell of the New Theology and became a Unitarian. Then when she was fourteen, at the outbreak of the First World War, her beloved brother was imprisoned in Dartmoor for being a conscientious objector.

She gave me the obituaries of her father, stained with rust from the paper-clip holding them together. One spoke of 'his noble Dantesque head, explosive eloquence and rich humour', and went on, 'He could, of course, be indiscreet to put it mildly, but it was a great joy to know such a wholehearted great soul.' Another spoke of his spiritual power, and yet another described him as 'A man who never failed to speak the truth as he found it.... A man of fearlessness and courage in championing unpopular causes ... always an original thinker ... undoubtedly a born poet ... he often confessed to having long shed or discarded the theology of college or books ... an unrepentant Christian pacifist.'

Enid had some of his writings published in the *Inquirer* in a series after his death. Reading them, it could have been her own voice I heard. 'I like this world. I like the things I don't like in it. I like them because it is possible for me to dislike them.... It's nice to be hated – it gives you such a sense of your importance.'

In an interview with her local paper she stated flatly, 'I am usually in a minority of one on most issues.' It did not seem to have occurred to her that the sphere she lived in may have been too small, or the wrong one for her. After our first long talk she wrote to me, 'I can't remember ever having a five-hour talking exchange with anyone in which there was entire agreement on all counts, except for the world-shattering one as to the pronunciation of the world "controversy"', and added, characteristically, 'though I suppose wars have been started on even less'.

That made me wonder why Enid had not sought to widen her circle to include more who were like-minded, who might have drawn her thinking on.

All her married life she lived next door to her parents. She needed the security of routine, of being surrounded by conventional people. I did not have the courage to ask her about this directly, and half-supposed that it had more to do with the way her generation grew up than with any deep psychological fear anyway. Then she wrote to me:

> it isn't what I have learned that counts so much as the spice of variety supplied by human associations which have come my way, starting with my father and brother, both of whom, in their similar and dissimilar ways, acted as yardsticks for my evaluation of all subsequent members of the male sex! Some of them fell sadly short, some of them put up a pretty good imitation and were fine as companions for the sort of moor-walking wide-open-space life I loved but whom I couldn't see as lifelong partners reducible to necessities such as settling bills. I suppose their main attraction was that they kept me off the ground and into the rarer air of creativeness.

In the end I married someone exactly the opposite of them all – a down-to-earth local government officer, brilliant at administration as to housing, water supplies etc., and absolutely the right material for a successful, feet on the ground marriage. The others mostly did the same – married eminently suitable ladies with degrees and the social flair necessary for their academic stations in life – and, as an escape from our thus highly commendable and respectable, if ordinary, domestic lives, we again sought each other on many occasions for that departure from the normal, and even pleasant, routine of our daily lives into the upper air we were wont to sigh for. No harm done. We remained strictly loyal to our respective spouses.

Nothing in Enid's adult life matched up to her girlhood and adolescence, and no men matched up to her father and brother, that much was plain. Yet her division of the male sex into solid marriageable types and high-flown intellectual companions is curious, and more curious still is her description of her relationship with them after they had all married. Why could she not just say, 'We continued to be friends'? A letter she wrote to me after I had interviewed her revised the picture:

It seems necessary to say that I could have offered several, sometimes opposite, views on every subject which arose, but usually I plumped for one out of those many as if there were no alternatives, particularly, I recall, on the subject of my marriage! I said I married my husband as a last resort. True, in some respects, because I may have thought he was, but I could have added that, though my approach to religion, politics and other matters requiring rational thought, may be cool and calculated, I have been a soft, silly romantic where men are concerned. If there had not been also physical attraction and a shared interest in a number of ways, nothing would have got me to the registry office! As it happened, while it was not so apparent when I married him, the sort of personality I looked for in a man developed in my husband through the years and, added to the interesting career he made for himself, it made me glad that I had reluctantly taken the plunge. We had arguments, of course ...

The romantic fantasies of Enid's adolescence persisted through the rest of her life, and it was perhaps the ever-present sense of a lost Eden that accounts for the bitterness of disillusionment that ran as an undercurrent through her conversation. Yet her bitterness was part of her charm, for it was the wry bitterness of a thinker, and it provided the foundation for her self-deprecating humour. She would deflate a grand statement that seemed to hover alarmingly close to pomposity by illustrating it with a trivial incident, as when she went on after her 'minority of one' claim to say, 'I believe in comfort rather than convention (being the first female in Exeter to go without stockings in the early 1920s because I was too hot in them).'

Somewhere along the line Enid had been brought to believe that the plain common sense that she possessed in full measure was inferior to the high flights of rhetorical fancy of her father and her brother. Her father's writings seem now to be self-indulgent – 'And I love the silence of that inner chamber of vision when I stand upright in defiant adoration and gaze upon the burning beauty of holiness.' For Enid this was creativity of the highest order; a splendid, high-flown gift given only to a few men. The belief sapped her faith in her own gifts. Most of her poetry is either prose put into lines or comic doggerel. If her father and brother had not had the writing bug, I doubt whether Enid would have tried so hard herself in that direction.

As her admiration for her father blocked her development as an individual, in another way it blocked her thinking. In Enid the notorious Caledonian antisyzygy, the antithetical-mindedness demonstrated in her father's 'defiant adoration' – his 'I like things I don't like' in the world – became a bad habit, a mental tic or trick that operated automatically and often made her seem simply thrawn. She rejected the great in literature and art to champion the mediocre, whom she regarded as the underdogs, and introduced an anthology of her favourite pieces with a plea for 'recognition of those whose name didn't happen to be Jesus or George Bernard Shaw or Gladstone, but who have offered the world, to my mind, equally valuable pointers to this business of living and what it's all about'. The anthology is in a notebook, possibly intended for publication. It includes such pieces as C. D. B. Ellis's 'Pro Vita Mea':

My life has been the common lot,
Love, pleasure, sorrow, God knows what
Now it is time for me to die
And I am sorry, God knows why.

I'll sleep, with all the rest of men,
Perhaps to waken, God knows when,
And in His presence make my bow
And Apologia – God knows how.

Perhaps the only form the natural rebellion against such a father as hers could take was to prize the humdrum, everyday journeymen in the arts, but there was also genuine appreciation and fellow-feeling there. I think Enid had been too impressed by the demand that significance be found in everything.

Yet she was genuine. She lived up to her principles of 'honesty rather than history, truth rather than tradition, originality, even ignorance, rather than orthodoxy, and doubt rather than dogmatism'. In the circles in which she moved, first as a minister's daughter, then as wife of the Clerk of the Water Board, in genteel conservative Exeter, this cannot have been easy and it must have been lonely. She prefaced the pamphlet of her poems, *Soliloquy* (which she published herself), with: 'It is possible they may not be read, in which case I am talking to myself and the title of the book will be as appropriate as I expect it to be.'

Her son came to take the place of her father and her brother in her life. She wrote to me, 'Colin went the way of all the male members of my family – did his own thing regardless of attempts to lead them in living–earning directions.' He restores and hires vintage buses. After his divorce he returned to live with his mother, and it was plain that Enid doted on him: the happiest my friend had ever seen her was the day Enid had succeeded in buying Colin a pair of the sandals he liked cheaply in the market in Exeter. Colin is not a man of many words, like her father and brother; he is extremely reserved. As far as I could gather Enid seemed to have little or nothing to do with her grandchildren. She never spoke of them voluntarily.

Housework did not agitate Enid. She lived in shabby comfort. Her husband had designed their bungalow soon after their marriage, and I doubt whether it had had any decoration since his death, or even before that. Enid held to Quentin Crisp's maxim that after seven years no more dust will collect in an untended house. One of the walls of her bedroom was covered in mould. Everything was for Colin, and cigarettes were the only luxury she allowed herself. She even drew her own Christmas cards.

One day at the beginning of last year Enid's friend Win visited her and was shocked to see how ill Enid was. She was struggling just to get about the house. Win called the social services and Enid was promptly taken into hospital, where cancer was diagnosed. My friend got a little notelet from her, shakily written, apologizing for the long silence and explaining baldly that she was in hospital with cancer.

When my friend visited her, Enid, now unable to walk or eat solid food and looking extremely fragile, leaned forward with an effort and confided seriously, 'I'm not trying to put this on, you know.' She had refused to entertain the visiting clergyman – 'I told him I wasn't interested. I don't want any of that. Of course, he was rather taken aback, but there you are.'

Asked about visitors she said, 'There's one person I'd really like to see, my mother. Oh, she was marvellous! If you had a problem, she was there for you.' She was relishing two memories. The first and dearest was her holiday with her brother in the Lake District, described in the interview – coming back to a good meal and a warm fire after a long day's walking in rough weather. The second was an incident during the Second World War, when she had a team of plasterers repairing her bungalow. Her husband had somehow got hold of a joint of sirloin steak, and Enid baked a pie and made them all sit down to share it. The plasterers were amazed and delighted that anyone should show this generosity when meat was so scarce. Enid said, 'Yes, *that* was something good I did ...'. And then, 'I wish we were having this conversation in the Milkmaid. Have you been there? I don't suppose they miss me? Do they know I'm not there?' Later she said, 'I know it's very wicked of me, but it's my one consolation that everybody's going to end like this.' She insisted on being allowed to go home to die.

A week after her return home she died. Her friend Win said, 'Enid met her death with dignity; she held her dignity to the end.' I thought of the first line of her poem, 'Immortality': 'Our little life is rounded by ... who knows?' She had stipulated in her will that a particular Unitarian preacher, a woman, should take her funeral service, and that two of her poems should be read out.

THE INTERVIEW

I was born in 1900. Before the First World War the world was a lovely secure, serene place. Everybody was happy; nobody knew about all these dreadful things that were going to happen. But that was because I was young. I didn't know all the nasty things that were going on then.

My parents were Unitarians. I think that's where I got a lot of my liking and knowledge of poetry from, because you don't always have to read the Bible for the lessons in the Unitarian church, you can read anything that anybody's contributed that makes some sort of sense of the whole scheme of things. My father used to read from anybody who did so, and I think that's where I got my liking for poetry from, or possibly from a teacher at Wallasey High School who put us on to Keats's 'Ode to a Nightingale'. From then on I really liked it. They can keep things like *The Canterbury Tales* or whatever, all these ancient things. I don't understand them: I don't know what they're aiming at. Rupert Brooke's my favourite, I suppose ... 'Dust'. And Matthew Arnold's 'Self-Dependence'. In my worst moods when I was young – gosh! – when I thought who am I, what am I, am I going the right way and ... and 'Self-Dependence' is absolutely lovely. I've got two books there and I filled them up with poems I like. Tagore for instance. W. N. P. Barbellion – I've got all three of his. All Bernard Shaw's, mostly for the Prefaces. *Saint Joan* was one of his best plays because she finishes up with 'When will the world be ready to receive thy Saints?' as well as her arguments with the Bishop of Beauvais and the Count.

Barrie's *Mary Rose* is my favourite play and I love Henry Williamson's *The Pathway* – they're all marked like blazes, all down the margins. I like Rosamond Lehmann's *Dusty Answer* because life is a dusty answer. My absolute favourite novel is Countess von Arnheim's *Fräulein Schmidt and Mr Anstruther*. J. B. Priestley – he was marvellous! I've tried *War and Peace* –

absolutely hopeless! I couldn't get through it. My brother said I must read it because it's most important. But those Russians ... they were too long. I went to see the film of *War and Peace* instead. But then they had a reputation, didn't they, these Russian novels, for being, oh, absolutely terrific – tremendous amount of meaning in them. I didn't understand it; my brother did but I didn't. I didn't know what they were getting at.

I don't always take everybody else's opinion as to what is good – like these masterpieces. Somebody says that the *Mona Lisa* was a masterpiece. Well, who decides what is a masterpiece in painting? I might not agree – this business of authority ... somebody comes along and says so-and-so is an authority on something.

My father was born in Bishop's Stortford. He died in 1957 aged eighty-seven. He was one of my favourite men. You can't describe him unless you met him. People either hated him – they used to walk out of church when he was preaching a sermon that they disagreed with – they either hated him and *violently* disagreed with him, or else they agreed with him. He had about half a dozen what I call disciples, who knew what he was talking about. His basis for religious belief was the same as Jesus's: 'I and the father are one; before Abraham was, I am' – not Jesus's: 'I am'; everybody's 'I am', everybody's got an 'I am'. That's the other thing in the *Faith and Freedom* thing that I wrote about. It's the sort of theme. He insisted that Jesus didn't mean that you had to go through Him to get to God and I don't think Jesus meant that at all. 'I am' is the way, *anybody's* 'I am', it's the only thing we know, isn't it? You don't know anything else for certain. It's the one subjective truth we know. And that's what he based all his sermons on, when everyone else was basing it on the person and the authority of Jesus and so on. Mind you, Jesus used a lot of phrases that were convenient to borrow, but you only understand Jesus if you think the same way yourself. You can't understand anybody unless you've thought it out yourself first. ...

My father was really wonderful. He preached sermons like nobody else has ever preached. He was in the Congregational church for about six years and then discovered that he just couldn't believe it at all, so he decided to become a Unitarian, which is a free pulpit. You can say what you like in the Unitarian church. But all the same, Unitarians weren't to his liking because he was different from all the others. Half of them were orthodox.

He wrote a book called *A Possible God*. I've got a few copies up in the roof and I can't find them. And that was something quite different. I liked him because he was different from anything else I've ever heard. And my goodness, I wish he were still around. He'd have something to say about the present state of the world! He was a pacifist. He was called 'the crazy crank of Liverpool' because he was a pacifist during the First World War. Seems to me it's the only way to save the world now, to be a pacifist. The alternative is to blow it up! I can't see what else. There's not much else in between.

My brother was in prison during the First World War. He was a conscientious objector. They asked what his religion was. He said he was a Fraserian – not meaning that he was following his father but meaning that he had his own religion. He was in Wormwood Scrubs, then he was in Dartmoor for the duration of the war, amongst a wonderful load of intellectuals. They were marvellous! But they were regarded as the scum of the earth at the time ... they just had to follow their beliefs, whatever they were.

I don't know where anyone got the idea from that morality started with Jesus. It's this idea Jesus introduced things as though he was an authority: I don't agree with that at all ... I think he just discovered something and put shape to it. Do you call the Inquisition a moral institution? If I'd been threatened by the rack or the thumbscrew I'd have become a Catholic straight away – I'd give in. It's just like we said in the First World War, if the Germans invaded us, it's like butter: the more it is spread, the thinner it gets. We might influence them: it could be a two-way thing. ... I think if there was one ruler in the whole world things might be better.

Mother was an Okehampton person. She had a very interesting father who practically built Okehampton and he almost invented the dynamo. He installed electricity in several places in Devon early this century, including Lynton and Lynmouth. He was an engineer.

She met my father when he came to preach at the Congregational church in Okehampton and she married him. She was a wonderful person in all sorts of ways, but we crossed so many times; we clashed in all sorts of ways. In other ways, if you were feeling down or worried about anything, she was marvellous; she was a good philosopher and sometimes she could put my father's ideas into words better than he could, on the hop. Yes ... but, oh goodness, we had terrible rows. She didn't understand me like my father did. She attributed motives to me that didn't exist. My brother was more like her.

My parents had helluva rows sometimes. I remember my mother, we were staying at Llangollen at the time, she said she wanted to go down and throw herself in the canal because they had a row. But mostly they were ... they were happy. They say if your parents have rows it affects you, but I don't think it did. I think these Dunmow Flitch people are absolutely boring – any two people are bound to disagree over some things.

I had a lovely childhood. We all did things together, the four of us. My father's first church was Newcastle, where I was born. Then he went to Pendleton in Manchester – still Congregationalist. Then he went to Bristol – still Congregationalist – then he gave up Congregationalism and went to Pembroke Chapel in Liverpool, where there was a free pulpit, and he turned officially Unitarian. He came to Exeter in 1918 and stayed here for the rest of his life, about thirty-four years. Two sermons a Sunday and I've got all the sermons up in the roof. I don't know what to do with them. A lot of them are printed. And somebody left me in his will a bound book of his printed sermons, and like a mug I gave it to somebody. I didn't know what to do with it, my son wouldn't be interested. And I wish I hadn't because I think the library would have liked it in Exeter.

I always liked moving. I always liked the change. I used to keep moving my bedroom round, putting my bed in different places. I can't do it now because there's a storage heater in there and I can't put the bed in that particular place, but I always liked changing round. I don't so much now. I like staying put now.

As a child we had lovely holidays. My father used to go around looking for remote places, for example in North Wales – we used to go there. We went to Lowestoft, we went to Buck's

Mills in North Devon. They were lovely holidays because everything came alive when my father went there. He'd lay on concerts and that sort of thing, with his own poems and verses, odd bits like:

> Jack and Jill went up the hill
> To buy a postage stamp;
> The postmistress said it wouldn't stick
> Unless you make it damp.

– that sort of thing. We always took some members of the congregation with us. We always took the same cottage at Buck's Mills. We used to rent it. They didn't have much money at all, but it was quite cheap. We always used to take some friends of my brother's or mine wherever we went. We did things together until my brother and I were old enough to spread ourselves then we went our own ways. . . .

We had a very good childhood. We were never disciplined. My father wrote an article once about 'Bringing Up Children' and he said he always waited until we saw the need for doing a thing and then we did it. We were never forced to do it. He didn't believe in compulsion at *all*. One of his sermons was on conscription, and what he said about conscription is nobody's business. Somehow he never managed to get run in by the police for what really was sedition in these days, during the war. He generally quoted the Bible, which he was perfectly entitled to do, and that made it all right. They couldn't arrest him for quoting the Bible. Oh, he was a marvellous man!

They could only afford to have two children because there was no Child Allowance then. He never earned more than three hundred and fifty pounds a year. It was enough to live on. We had to have a maid – five shillings a week – because my mother was involved in the church business so much – she had to have a maid to look after us. I grew very fond of these maids . . . five shillings a week and they were very happy.

Mother used to have 'At Homes' and that sort of thing. She used to take part in the dramatics – oh, she had a lot to do, one way and another, going round visiting people. . . .

One thing they believed in was education. My brother went to Bristol Grammar School. They had to pay in those days, although my brother got a scholarship. I didn't. I didn't even sit for one. Then he went to Liverpool University. Got his inter-BSc then got thrown out because he was a conscientious objector, and they wouldn't have him back. Then he got a job at Rowntrees because they were pacifists. It was a very good job but he, like *all* the men in my family, wanted to be independent and do his own thing. He wanted to write, so he left. Oh, he had about ten different jobs, of *all* kinds.

A lot of people write, even with ordinary parents who couldn't put two words together. There's no accounting for where it comes from. We were all inclined to write. My brother wrote – got articles in the then *Manchester Guardian*. He wanted to earn his living by writing but he found he couldn't. We all got the writing bug. I don't know why.

This is the sort of menfolk in my family. Not my husband. He was very respectable and conventional. He'd do all the right things. But my son's the same. He did his own thing. He had a good job in the tax office. He left that. He wanted to pioneer this bus preservation business. It's been highly successful. I suppose it's all pioneering in a way, isn't it, to do something that other people don't do? You must stand out against the status quo sometimes. This was the point of Bronowski's lectures wasn't it, on 'The Ascent of Man'?

I wrote to Bronowski about one point I wanted to take up with him. I had a very nice letter back, enclosing a printed copy of one of his lectures, and the gist of that was, that it's the rebels who keep evolution going. It's the people who go out of step who alter the course of things. Otherwise, I suppose, if the amoeba hadn't come out of the slime we'd still be in the slime. It's always the rebels who keep it going, keep it on the move.

I've always had response from people. I like the people who go against the stream somehow or other. I do it myself, I mean. My father never took his authority from anyone else, except on things like medicine and that sort of thing. That's what's really wrong ... everything, *everything* in life people go so much by authority. We're all regimented now. We stand in the bus queue – we obey the traffic lights. I think if somebody up aloft could look down and see us waiting – going forward – waiting – crossing – going back – oh dear ... the pattern of life is getting more regimented, isn't it?

If you're in society you've got to conform over nonessentials, haven't you? You can't be a square peg in a round hole *all* the time. And I don't mind conceding to the most idiotic things sometimes.

I asked a Baptist once what's the difference between the Baptist belief and Church of England beliefs. She said, 'Oh, we believe in *total* immersion!' What's the difference, my word!

I had two letters in the *Sunday Times* about a series they had about 'The Mystery of Life'. All the top people were writing about it and I had a massive correspondence from all sorts of people, including the Archbishop of York. He signed himself 'Michael Ebor' so I wrote to him 'Michael Ebor Esquire'. You see I don't know these church things. You've got to be the odd man out to get anywhere in this world.

In Pendleton when I was five or six years old, I went to Miss Mackintosh's little school, at the end of the road. When we went to Bristol I went to Miss Cockrell's school, another kindergarten. Eventually I went to Redland High School. I was made to find my own way there, I was always early for everything, the first person there. I didn't know which classroom to go to and I sat in what turned out to be the Sixth Form.

I was good at all the things you had to think out and not the things you had to remember. I was brilliant at mathematics and not at history. I was moderate at English. I'm not boasting, it's just that I've got that kind of mind. We moved to Liverpool; I went to Wallasey High School when I was twelve. Somebody ran a college for the daughters of gentlemen, so I could get there for nothing as a pupil teacher. I went there at fifteen, for a year, to finish me off like! I was supposed to take charge of some of the younger children and look after the dormitories. I had a bed in the corner of a huge dormitory and some of the children piled in on my bed in the morning. I was hopeless at keeping them in order.

They were daughters of rich merchants in Manchester most of them. I made some wonderful friendships there too. They were all sorts, all kinds, all rich. I went there, my mother made all my clothes, and the first thing I said on my first night there was, 'Oh, excuse my dressing-gown.' I was so ashamed of a home-made dressing-gown when they'd got all those elaborate things, bought things. My God, everything of mine was home-made! I thought, I'll never get away with it. It didn't matter in the end. They took me for me not my clothes. That was a lovely year.

You know my brother was in prison. That was another thing I didn't like to say. That was a terrible crime in those days. I suppose it got out that my brother was there. I didn't let it out but somebody must have done. I had a friend there who was horrified that I'd got a brother who was a conscientious objector. She later turned Quaker, and she was seeing my arguments in the end. I enjoyed school mainly for the friends I made.

My brother's education at Bristol Grammar School was rather different from mine – more classical. He was quite a brilliant scholar and I always felt the poor relation intellectually. I was always trying to keep up with him, but it was good for me to keep on trying to catch up with him.

I was reading silly old trashy novels like Elinor Glyn's and he was always at me to read good books, so I read them, but I couldn't understand them like he could. I did later on, and in the end I think I overtook him for reading. But always everything he did I had to try. He organized a concert party in Rowntrees; I had to organize a concert party. We once had a holiday in the Lakes over Easter and that was good for me too, because we stayed in a little cottage over in Seathwaite and we walked all day and every day over the mountains – up Scafell in a blizzard – and in the evening he'd read. We'd sit by a lovely roaring fire in this cottage and he'd read to me from one of the current books of Charles Morgan. I probably didn't understand it but it was lovely to sit there and hear it read. But all the way back to Keswick – we had to walk to Keswick to catch the train to York – he gave me a lecture. I was absolutely *weeping* when we got to the station because I'd been so downed for my choice of reading. I must not read these trashy novels. But I was a romantic and I had to read them, didn't I?

I always found conversation difficult with him because he was so much above me. I thought, oh, whatever I say is going to be stupid and idiotic. It got easier as we got older. He gradually acknowledged that I had a bit of a brain. He even sometimes said, 'I wish I could write poetry like you do', and that lifted me up a little, made me more confident, so that when I was with him I could talk to him.

My adolescence was lovely because I didn't know what all this getting together, all this *lovely* feeling, was in aid of. I didn't know it at all. Consequently it was a sort of . . . out of this world sort of thing. It wasn't connected with anything physical at all, although the physical must have been there. But – oh thank heaven – my mother used to say, 'You were once a seed under my heart', or something or other. It horrified me; it embarrassed me so much, I didn't want to know. I wouldn't let her tell me the facts of life. I wouldn't let her discuss the subject. I couldn't bear the subject. It's no use telling me that people are taking risks by not knowing. You know yourself. You find it out yourself. I found what it was with one of my boyfriends, I suppose. I discovered what was going on. You add two and two together and find out. I didn't have to be told. It's no excuse to say you haven't been told. No excuse at all.

Nowadays they thrust it on all these poor children. They miss out on all this lovely period when you don't know why. It's forced on them so early; they make such a physical thing out of it. Surely there's something else a little bit better than the physical aspect of any relationship. It's quite true, as someone said – 'Where do you come from baby dear? – I come from everywhere out of here.' We all come from everywhere.

Adolescence was a lovely time, largely because we didn't know anything about sex at all. It wasn't reduced to the biological thing it is now. I didn't know anything about it whatever and it was a wonderful period. One of the poems that influenced me most – my father used it as one of the readings in the church – was a sort of romantic dream world that I lived in at the time. It was lovely. I had my down moments but that poem expresses exactly what I felt:

> The still blue silence of dusk in the woods of sleep,
> Pale stardust trembling over the shoreless night,
> The flowers of foam on the halcyon breast of the deep,
> And the call of the hills, and the road, and the wind's delight:
> The tender beacons of primrose waking the moon
> Through whispering boughs unveiled –
> To these I was born.

My husband used to say I was always chasing the infinite. He was only joking, but it was quite true. I was.... I used that poem when I took a Unitarian service, and I made alterations from the original, because it didn't apply.

I made lots of mistakes in my life. When I first worked in the Devon County Council office they said, 'Take a letter to the County Surveyor', and I addressed it to the Countess of Ayr – well, who wouldn't? I didn't know about these things. It started 'Dear Sir' so I must have been absolutely dim.

I knew all the answers when I was eighteen so I didn't ask a lot of questions. I hoped for enough money to live on – that was one of my major worries, that I'd never have enough to live on, because my parents were always hard-up and I always thought money was very difficult to come by. I even worried when I got married how I would be able to afford enough cutlery. This sort of thing worried me. I'm forever grateful now that things have worked out, that I've got enough to live on. I haven't got too much; I've got enough, I wouldn't want more than that.

The worst time of my life was when I had a sort of nervous breakdown. I was looking ahead to the time when my mum wouldn't be there. I thought, what would the world be like without my mother? I was between twenty and thirty at the time. I just thought, gosh, I'm going to be all alone in the world! My mother lived on thirty years after that, but I looked ahead to the time, thinking, of course, that I would be totally dependent on her, like I was then. I mean I couldn't see ...

... I had a horrible feeling of the isolation of life, the sort of loneliness of it. I had a horrible time then, but my mother was absolutely marvellous. She gave me all the right answers. I was off work for a few weeks and that frightened me even more. Supposing I lost my job and I didn't have any money? But it was a physical thing rather than a mental thing – it was something going on in my mind, a depressant or something. I hated to hear other people laugh and smile – I thought, what can anybody be happy about in this life? It didn't last long but, oh gosh, I wouldn't like to go through that again!

Doesn't everybody who's sensitive have some sort of black period in their life when everything seems cloudy and desperate and ... I suppose everybody feels suicidal at some point or other when problems become so much you can't solve them, or think you can't. There are times when you can't see any daylight at all. Because I could have lived here when my mother died, I had already got my own circle of friends, but it didn't seem to count at the time. I thought, the whole world will go when my mother goes.

My husband and I worked in the same office. I was in the Devon County Council, so was he. He was my last resort. Everybody else had had somebody but I just couldn't marry and I thought nobody else was likely to ask me to marry. It worked very well really. We were different. He was brought up Church of England and had to go to church three times on a Sunday, but he didn't believe in it all. He gave it up quite easily. He wasn't anything. He didn't go in for that kind of thing. He believed in practical things.

I think he married me because I appealed to him physically, I suppose, and because I was one of the staff who had made a sort of name for myself in all sorts of ways, writing in the staff journal and organizing the concert party and organizing various things. I was secretary to the clerk to Devon County Council, as well as the accountant.

I didn't want to get married at all as a matter of fact. I just didn't want to. Partly because I couldn't find anybody I thought I could live with for the rest of my life. Partly because I was scared stiff of having children and I thought I might have one, which I did. I got married really for security, to someone who was possible to live with. That's all you can say about it. I just wanted somebody to keep me, I suppose ... is that what it was? Don't ask me – that's one of life's questions that I've never answered. I wasn't a career person. I didn't want to go on having to earn my own living forever. I just preferred somebody else to look after me.

I just had to suddenly decide – I just had to make myself decide to get married so – he bought two or three licences but we didn't take them up. I just had to make myself decide to do it. So eventually we got married on a special licence, in the Registry Office. I wasn't going to be married by my father. I'd have laughed; I couldn't take it seriously at all. And we just went away for the night and came back to the office in the morning. About three months later we went to Cornwall and had a honeymoon. I suppose everybody thought I had to get married, but I wasn't pregnant. In those days you couldn't risk that at all, that's what disciplined you about sex, because you couldn't *risk* it: there were no contraceptives. You went as far as you could without taking risks.

I didn't want children. It was getting on towards the Second World War – about 1934. I still didn't think it was a world to bring children into. I wouldn't from choice, no. In fact, that's why I was scared stiff about getting married. I was scared stiff of the physical process of having a child. I'm not a hero at all. I hate physical pain. At least I hated the prospect of it. No, I didn't think it was the right sort of world to bring children into. I still don't. But then there is always the hope that one of them will come along with the answer to the evils of the world.

AS: Why did you get pregnant?
ES Oh, that was my husband's doing. Well, we sort of agreed. He knew I didn't want one but I suppose – we didn't have contraceptives in those days and he just didn't withdraw in time, or whatever it was. I don't know what happened. I just left it to him to take avoiding action.
AS: Why didn't you have more in that case?
ES: I don't know why. I suppose he was more careful, but it must have been pretty hard on him.

The birth was quite all right – it was the apprehension of it. I used to lie in the bath and think, well, how the hell is all this going to come out without an awful, terrible screaming pain? But it didn't work out like that. They put me out.

... It's a horrible way, I think, of procreation, all this awful, you know trying to get a wide thing out of a narrow passage. It's quite an impossible thing. I'd have thought up something better for that I think.

AS: Was your husband in love with you?
ES: Well, he said so.
AS: Did you tell him you were in love with him?
ES: I suppose I went through all the motions.

But I mean, I had known what being passionately in love was before, and this wasn't up to *that* kind of thing. And then my parents didn't like him, of course, because he was totally different from anything they'd hoped for for me – the sort of person I was drawn to weren't the sort of people you would marry. They wouldn't have made good husbands. They made good husbands to the wives they chose. I don't think you should marry the people you are in love with. It's too risky. One or other of you might fall out of love, then I imagine it gets desperate. But I never lost all the people I didn't marry. They married other people and . . . I suppose *something* in marriage is missing that you can get from somebody else – there's bound to be really, isn't there? You can't get everything you want in one person.

I'd got my yardsticks in my brother and father and I couldn't find anybody anywhere nearly up to them, so I settled for something a long way down. It was practical. It worked out quite well.

The first argument I had with my husband . . . he used to polish his shoes with one brush and my father always polished his shoes with *two* brushes. He put polish on one and brushed it off with the other, and I thought it was a real crime to do your shoes with one brush. We had a row. It was so trivial. It didn't matter in the slightest degree. But because my father didn't do it, it was wrong for my husband to do it.

He had funny little ways – *eating* habits. He used to swallow a mouthful of tea and swill his mouth round with it. I didn't like that and I had to say something. You're bound to. I mean, he had all sorts of little ways that I didn't think were right. I probably had ways that he didn't think were right, too. So we had words, yes, we had *quite* a lot of rows. It's no use letting it fester, is it? Another row we had . . . he joined the Freemasons to get on, to get promotion, and that sort of thing, but I went for him before we were married and I said, 'No, for godsake don't go in for it.' But when we were married I found that he was officially one. He was progressing up the scale in it and he got all his little aprons and things. Oh, we had a hell of a row! I said, 'You *can't*, I'm not going to live with you. You should have told me about all this before. I can't live with anybody who goes in for these childish things.' In the end I think I talked him out of it. I don't think he ever went again, much against his will, but he should have stuck to it if he really believed in it. Really I think he got on through doing some good work himself. He brought water to I don't know how many villages in Devon that had never had it before. North Devon Water Board, he ran that, you see. When it was first inaugurated he helped get the Bill through Parliament, the House of Lords, and so on. I think he really did something for Devon. He was a good administrator, he really was.

On the whole I think men get the best of it, though I don't know. I think I'm quite glad I was born who and what I was, but then I've been lucky; I've had all sorts of opportunities and all sorts of aims that I've been able to achieve, they're all modest aims and I've been able to fulfil most of them. A lot of people don't get that chance.

I've always had an interest in life. Everybody's got to have a purpose in life to keep going. It's no use if you're just aimlessly drifting around. But then, what's *my* purpose in life for goodness' sake? It seems to be planted on me. It turned out that I had a son. My purpose has got to be to keep his interests at heart; to keep my husband reasonably fed and comforted and happy. What is your purpose as a son or a daughter? To keep your parents happy? I don't know. Don't ask me! I just don't know. Just to go on enjoying myself in my own way without ruining other people's lives? I don't know.

Life hasn't been a struggle really. There've always been enough compensations to get me through – but mind you, I can still worry about my son. It's funny, you worry about your own son. Even taking him to the dentist. I could take anybody else's son to the dentist and it wouldn't matter at all – you don't bat an eyelid. There is something in a blood relationship that does that. It's almost worse him being unhappy than being unhappy yourself. He very rarely is.

I had my own ideas about my son. I was going to bring him up in the way I was brought up, with no particular discipline, but he was so damned obstinate over the things he had to do, absolutely had to do – it was a battle every blooming time: he wouldn't do it. Now I can see the advantage it was to have a child who's determined to do what he wants to do and go his own way. He was unmouldable. I hate to compel anybody else.

I didn't like children. Of course, people like that are *much* worse when they have them, they go absolutely soppy over them. Everything that he felt, I felt and still do. I made the worst mother in the world, I think, because I could always see his

point of view. The sort of things I objected to in my mother I try
not to do with him. It would have been less complicated without
a child, but when you've got one, damn it all, you get so bloody
fond of them.

No, I don't like the system at all. I don't like the system of
people growing up as a family and then the elder ones have to
go off – I don't like that. I think I could have created a world
that was easier in lots of respects. But then the answer they
always give to that is, 'Well, you can't know happiness unless
you know sorrow.' I don't believe that.

After I was married I went back to work several times to help
out. I was glad to earn a bit of extra money. But I wasn't the
sort of self-dependent person who could have been happy being
single. I think I depend on other people quite a lot, for practical
things mostly. I don't depend on them for thinking. I think I just
wanted somebody else to get the money. I'd do the work. It was
just a change of occupation: when you get married you get paid
your housekeeping, when you're in a job you get paid a salary –
it's just a change of occupation for a different return.

I didn't miss my husband when he died because some other
man came along and I was pretty well stuck on him and he was
just absolutely marvellous. He took my mind off the whole
thing. He took me for days out on Dartmoor ... we had a most
glorious time, and it eased it. I did miss Reg for a time.

I heard quite a lot about the Suffragettes. I thought they were a
bit cranky. And I don't know what it's done for women to have
a vote. I don't know that it makes a lot of difference. Are they
any better at voting than teenagers? Even when I have got a vote
I don't know who to vote for – there's no party that's got what *I*
want. ...

I've always been interested in sex, ever since I can remember. In
other people's anatomy, ever since I was tiny. People say all
those girls get so shocked when they get their first experience –
somebody rapes them or something – I mean, I loved it. School,
my brothers' friends used to come along and try exploring. It
never put me off at all. I think I liked it. I've always liked it. If
you're fond of anybody then you don't mind how close you get
to them. Somehow it goes with physical contact in some form or

other. You don't want this chalk line, beyond which you mustn't go. I don't see anything wrong with physical contact at all. Except I really draw the line at these homosexuals who insist on everybody recognizing them. What they do in their own private sexual life is their affair. We had a lot to do with the Campaign for Homosexual Equality because one of our ministers let them have use of our lecture hall in church for a time. They stuck up their posters all round the wall so that if we used it for anything else it simply wasn't applicable. They went into the church. They moved the cushions out of the pews, and placed them all upstairs in the gallery. They were an absolute nuisance – they made a mess of the place. It wasn't suitable and quite a lot of people left the church because of it.

Oh, they can do what they like! I suppose all of us have got a part ... you start off usually if you're at college in amongst your own kind, like boys in a preparatory school, they get together in a mild sort of way. I don't like the *business* they make of it now.

... I think men are worse than women. I think when they get older they get a little bit peculiar about sex – it's horrible isn't it? It's much more imperative for men than it is for women, I think. As they get older they do all sorts of untold things to have it. But I didn't know *incest* went on. It's quite a nasty practice these days. I think there's such a thing; like a religious mania, there's sex mania, I suppose. It takes control of them and they've got no control over it. But I can't understand anybody being a blood relation having that sort of desire at all. You don't have – it doesn't exist. I don't know *why* it doesn't – that's a queer thing. It just doesn't. Isn't that what happened with Oedipus and his mother? I wouldn't have thought it was necessary.

I'm not shy about anything. I've never been a prude. Why are people so fussy about ... there's always a chalk line somewhere. They wear these bikinis that are merely just a band but they've got to wear them. I wouldn't care if I was nude – I wouldn't care at all. I think that's what keeps sex going, that everybody's got a little bit covered. I hate restrictions of any kind.

I never taught my son – nobody ever told him about sex. He never asked. *I* never asked. I imagined he was like me. I found it a terribly embarrassing subject with my parents.

I don't think it ever really goes. You always feel responsive to the male, whatever your age. I often have erotic dreams. But then you're ageless in your dreams. Just being a woman. They're always even better than life – larger than life. But you mustn't admit to things like that. ...

... Where do dreams come from? I do an awful lot of swimming in my dreams, in very warm water. Or I'm flying – never very high off the earth. If you counted up the number of aspects of life, how many would there be – it's just one huge conglomeration of experiences of all kinds.

The most important thing in life is human relationships, as long as you don't get so involved that they rule you. I think there's *nothing* nicer than being in love, quite honestly. I don't think there's a more wonderful experience in life than that. Doesn't matter whether it's returned or not. What it does for you is it makes you creative; it makes you ride on air. Oh, I've been in love lots of times in my life. Looking back, I wonder how the hell I ever fell in love with a Conservative and a Church of England organist. I don't know how I ever did it. But I did.

A lot depends on appearances – what they look like. I've had friends who made most unlikely matches, and they've lasted. When one died the other died, because they couldn't live without them. I could never understand it either way.

You couldn't write a book about yourself, not completely, could you? Every second counts, doesn't it? I mean, every second of your life something's going on that you could write about.

I've changed my handwriting about fifty times. I could copy anybody's handwriting. I was heading for being a criminal at one time. I think most children have to be criminals. I stole something once, a pencil-sharpener. I wanted one and I hadn't got one. I stole it and I came home with it and didn't it give me a conscience! Next time I went there I secreted it back again. I used to take the money out of the collection plate when it came round and keep it and put it back again next week.

There is no absolute morality, is there? I mean, the Ten Commandments aren't morality – half of them don't apply. And how do you order somebody to 'honour your parents'? You either do or don't honour your parents. You can't order people to love. That's why the Ten Commandments seem to me to be ridiculous. They're asking the impossible. Some parents are not honour-worthy. That's the whole point. And I don't covet my neighbour's ox or his ass: she hasn't got one. I don't covet her microwave either.

As a lay preacher I took several services over the years. I was an organist for about thirty years. I wouldn't go to church now if you paid me. I don't even agree with what my father said now. I don't think anybody can know about God to preach about 'Him'. It took me until I was forty to get the nerve to preach – I suppose to think I'd got anything to say that was worth listening to.

I don't know what a Christian is. I don't want to be called a Christian necessarily. Jesus himself was the only person who knew what He was talking about. The only person who really understands what they mean is the person who says it himself. Why Jesus? I mean, all sorts of other people have said all sorts of wise things – why has He got the monopoly?

I don't know what Jesus would make of all these bishops' enthronements and such things. I don't know what He would make of the Christian religion. It's all political – the Pope ... it's just as bad ideology as Russian communism is ... but we've got to try to have systems, because you can't live in chaos. I bought a book once, because I liked the title. It's called *The Margins of Chaos* and I thought it was such a lovely title.... The World – nature certainly *has* got order. I don't think man was a good invention, on the whole.

I think tolerance is a virtue. They say we should be tolerant of other people's religions, but if you've rejected the whole caboodle, why should I be tolerant of something I've discarded? Some religions are totally contradictory. They can't both be right. You've got to be intolerant of some things. I'm not tolerant at all. I'm totally intolerant of the things I'm intolerant of. There's hypocrisy the whole way along.

Oh, these Greeks had something – it's a legacy that really we couldn't do without. Not that we need them, for we could think out some of the things they thought out for ourselves.

Writing is just an imperative. If I get an idea in my head, somehow I've got to put it down. I suppose that's what every writer does. They've got to write and nobody can explain why. My lack of success as a writer is due to the fact that I don't research.

I've written 'em all – I've written plays, teenage plays they used to do at church. I've written one one-act play for grown-ups. I've written music: I've published an *introit*, a vesper, and two songs. I've tried most things. I've written lots and lots of articles. Mostly they get published in our *Inquirer*, which I like the title of. That's what Unitarianism is, it's an enquiring religion. I wrote an article, 'Opium of the People', which is what religions are. Usually the Unitarian paper takes whatever I write. That's not why I do it. You don't write to get noticed at all. You write because you have to. God knows where inspiration comes from. I can be at the kitchen sink and think of a line and then I've got to do something with it. You can't waste an idea. You've got to do something with it, and I suppose writing's one way of doing something about it. If you get an idea for an atom bomb you've got to do something about it. You've got to make the atom bomb. I don't like waste of any kind.

Yes, absolutely, I've had a happy life. Rich, full – I mean, everybody's life seems like that, doesn't it?

↠ 4 ↞

Miss X

'One was hoping one would do the right thing.'

Miss X was born in Worcestershire, in 1902. Her father was a solicitor and her mother came from an Anglo-Irish family; she had a brother and a sister. Her mother died in 1906, a year after Miss X's brother was born. At the age of seven Miss X went to a private school as a day-girl. She left in 1920 and kept house for her father, as she had done from the age of twelve. From 1925 to 1932 she taught needlework at her old school. Her father died in 1929.

Miss X played an active part in the Guide movement and for many years she did voluntary service in the St John's Ambulance Brigade. During the Second World War she worked full-time for St John's and was for a while in charge of an eye hospital. After the war she continued to work for St John's and for the Guides, and became more involved with the Women's Institute. She wrote a camping manual in 1950. She is now almost completely blind, and lives in a nursing home in Surrey.

When I asked a friend with some vaguely aristocratic connections if she could find me an upper-class octogenarian, she introduced me to her cousin. The cousin wrote to me that she thought it good that there should be a record of the way her class and generation lived, and that she herself had been trying to put together a history of sorts for her great-nephews and great-nieces.

I expected to find little scraps of notes and the odd document, but when I arrived to interview her, there on her bed was album after album of photos, letters, and papers. She was working on a huge family tree that went back to the sixteenth century. The albums – among others, there were two devoted to her Guide work; two relating to her work for St John's, and many containing family photographs – were in scrupulous chronological order. And there were lists: lists of her prizes from the

Women's Institute for needlework, of the posts she had held in all her voluntary organizations ... hers was the perfectly documented life.

Although she is almost blind, Miss X knew the photos in her albums by heart. She knew the position of every photo, and the position of every person on every photo. She knew every member of all the branches of the family; the colonels in the Indian Army, Masters of Hounds, parsons, and squires.

I do not think this showed any insecurity about her identity, but rather a continuation of the ideals of kinship and service which have shaped her life. The Guides, the Ambulance Service, the Women's Institute meant 'the feeling of helping people in need'. Letters from Lady Baden-Powell and other leading lights in the conservative tradition of voluntary service were cherished as testimonials to this. At the same time, the family, she continually stressed, was the most important factor in her world.

As I interviewed her I was increasingly and uncomfortably aware of the barriers of class. It seemed to me that she had led a life as sheltered as that of any Victorian spinster of good family. Once she mentioned to me as if it were an astonishing fact that the family of one of the workers on her grandfather's estate slept five or six to a room. I pointed out that this still happens, and remarked that some of my mother's neighbour's children slept five to a bed, under coats. I do not think it was coincidence that afterwards she took to showing me out by the tradesman's entrance, or that she was the only person I interviewed who offered me no hospitality in any form.

We covered a lot of family history pretty quickly, and greatly to my confusion, before we got to Miss X's own story. Because she would not talk about her private life and feelings, I at first hesitated to include her here, but on rereading my transcript I felt that there is a certain eloquence in her reticence, and that the reticence itself demonstrates so much about a particular world and time.

I sent Miss X a copy of her interview. She wrote almost by return to say that it was far too personal to print. I asked her to cut out the parts that might embarrass her, so that I could see whether what was left had sufficient interest. Back came the interview completely gutted, reduced to about a tenth of its length, with a letter saying: 'I am not willing to have my private thoughts and feelings published.' She did not say that she had changed her mind since I had interviewed her; presumably she thought that the hours we spent on her personal thoughts and feelings, and in her relating stories about her family, were merely the social context for the real stuff, a history of her careers in various charitable organizations. In the end she agreed to let me use the material, provided she remained anonymous. While I feel that this is out of harmony with the spirit of the book, it seemed that the desire for anonymity from someone who has led such a blameless life is in itself a valuable extra dimension to Miss X's account of herself, and I made the compromise.

THE INTERVIEW

My father was one of six sons and four daughters. Grandfather was a parson, one of eight sons and five daughters. My great-grandfather shot with Edward VII.

My mother died after she'd been married five and a half years. I was three and a half when she died. My mother was a wonderful needlewoman. She made all our things – embroidered them all. My brother was a year and a bit old when my mother died.

My mother's parents were in the Indian Mutiny. At the age of nineteen my grandmother met her future husband, who was on leave from India. My grandmother, who was born and brought up in Ireland, was the only child and very much looked after. Her mother died when she was young, but she had never gone without a maid or anything else.

She went out to India. In those days you had to go all round the Cape, because this was before the Suez Canal was made. There was a lot of trouble going on in India then, and her husband had to rejoin his regiment. He had had a year's leave, as they used to do then. It took the ship three months to get to India. He was in one of the newer, iron-clad ships. It had a wooden lining and it had engines, but it had still got its sails and so on. Apparently the captain of the ship and the contractor had done some hanky-panky. The army used to charter vessels to move the troops about; they didn't have transport ships. The captain had signed that he had taken on so much coal, but they hadn't. They had a very bad voyage and they ran out of fuel, so they had to use the sails. After they had been at sea for five months they had the most terrible storm and all the masts were broken. They had to put the troops to hacking out wood from the sides for use in the boilers.

In the middle of all this my grandmother's baby arrived. There was only one other woman on the ship, a sergeant's wife, and a very young army doctor. A fortnight later they landed at Madras to be told the Mutiny had broken out. My grandfather had to go immediately to rejoin his regiment. So there was my grandmother, not yet twenty, with a fortnight-old baby, never having even walked across the road alone in Dublin in her life without a maid, alone in India. ...

She was sent with some natives in a litter up to a hill station near Madras, and it was a two-day journey, through the jungle, and the second day suddenly these men put down the litter, and disappeared. She couldn't do anything except just stay there, with the baby. After about two hours they came creeping back again. They couldn't speak any English, she couldn't speak any Tamil or whatever it was in that part of India, but they managed to say 'Man-eater' – they had seen a man-eating tiger. Apparently they'd not been far off, but they'd shinned up the trees. Somehow the tiger hadn't got wind of the baby.

She was one of only two English women to survive the Mutiny, but she never would speak of it afterwards, and they didn't have any more family until – he was invalided in the Mutiny and he left India seven years later – until then.

When they came back they found the estate had gone to nothing. So after she was widowed my grandmother had to bring up five sons and three daughters on a minute pension from the Indian Army. So although my mother was a very gentle, warm-hearted Irish girl, at the same time she must have had a practical strain, from the experience of her upbringing in these circumstances.

The only memory I have of my mother was of her sitting in a low chair nursing my baby brother, and she was wearing a red velvet dress. She was ill for a year before she died.

I was very close to my father. He was over forty when he married, you see. Oh yes, from the time when I was a very small child he used to come and play in the nursery – play 'bears' with us, and all the rest of it, you know. He was a very human person. He would take us out for walks and show us all the birds and flowers. He never seemed to be in a hurry. He was always full of interest and patience, and he helped us in anything we wanted to do. He would take out his carpentry tools and make us anything we wanted. He could do anything. He was good with his hands. I think all people used to be in the country in those days.

There were some people who believed children should be seen and not heard, but they were Victorian – we'd got into the Edwardian era by then.

Because we didn't have a mother my father was so caring and thoughtful. He was very understanding. Everybody tried to suggest he should get married again, but he had absolutely no intention of getting married again. They were absolutely devoted. It was so sad the marriage lasted such a short time. I think my father had been a very eligible bachelor – a lot of people had done their best, but without success. It was very much a love match for both of them.

One had very simple beliefs as a child. I went to church and that was the right thing to do, and Sunday was a special day, but there were never any restrictions nor anything imposed on us. My father was a very simple-minded man in many ways. Caring was the sort of thing that came very high to him. I don't think he ever thought about his own behaviour, but he knew instinctively what was the right thing and what wasn't. If we did wrong we were told so, but we were neither preached at nor were we punished. There wasn't this awful business of recrimination or disappointment. It was simply: 'Now you understand and that won't happen again.' He would explain with great patience. Like snatching a toy from another child, shall we say. It wasn't that you were naughty or greedy, but that that was going to give great pain and distress to somebody else, and would you have liked that pain or distress given to you? He would just say, 'Just think about it and I'll trust you'll never do it again.' And you didn't.

My father used to read to me. He had a very beautiful reading voice. He was very fond of Walter Scott. He was very clever in reading out all the very long descriptions. He didn't like

Dickens. He said Dickens had never described a gentleman in his life; he said he was not giving a fair picture, he was only stressing certain deprivations and disadvantages. Thackeray, Trollope – not the Brontës, they were not a man's book, and I was brought up rather on a man's lines ... anything to do with nature or animals. There was a beautiful book called *The Story of a Red Deer* which was written by Fortescue, who was George V's librarian, Lord Fortescue. Then books written by Lord Grey of Falloden, about birds. My father only ever chose books which had beautiful English, very good descriptive qualities, and about things he thought we should be interested in. Not so much about people and problems. I loved reading books like *Children of the New Forest, Treasure Island*, Henty. We always had four books to read as a holiday task, and they were all what was known as 'classics'. That took a bit of reading because they were two years ahead of our age.

Children had nursery times, and times with their parents then. The average mother spent a great deal of time and thought with the children. I think the natural motherhood instinct was very much more highly developed then. A girl was a daughter at home after either her governess left or her education finished. She did all the at-home things. ...

My brother and I were devoted to each other. He was younger than I was. But he was away at school all the time. We were given twopence a week pocket-money. The village shop was half a mile away. It was kept by a dear old lady. We discovered that if we bought a pennyworth of sweets, acid drops say, we got nine, but if we bought a farthing's worth we got three, so if we bought four farthing's worth we got twelve! We discovered that at a very early age. That was our great joy.

We used to go for a week in the Easter holidays to Tenby with our nanny. In the summer we went to Colwyn Bay with our nanny, and very often our cook–housekeeper came too. I remember the greatest thrill was listening to the Red Boys – the pierrot troupe – on the sands. We were allowed to bathe. I had an old-fashioned bathing-dress with long sleeves; it came right down to my ankles with elastic and a mob-cap. We even had bathing-machines: you got in at one side and the horse pulled you into the water, and you came out the other side. The old lady who had the bathing-machine would dip you in the water and hold you up while you swam with water-wings. All that was put a stop to in 1914 because of the war. We loved climbing trees, and we had bicycles. It was much freer in those days.

My sister was always an invalid, and she died when she was young. There was an accident when she was born; it was an instrument birth; and so she was paralysed. In those days they didn't know how to manage these things. Unfortunately the doctor was drunk when he arrived, so that was that – it was a terrible tragedy.

I was rather a fragile child. I had a governess for six weeks before I went to school. I knew pothooks and things – just my alphabet. On my first day at school I wouldn't let my nanny go with me. I didn't realize that there were two entrances, one for the girls and one the main entrance proper. I went to the main entrance and found I couldn't reach the bell – it was a pull-out bell. I had to stand on the foot-scraper. The door was opened by a very stern-looking elderly parlour-maid in a black dress and a white apron and a cap with streamers, and she looked at me, and I said, 'Please, I've come.'

I was taken to a big schoolroom with the other new girls. We were given a book, *The Water Babies* in the 'Read to the Children' series, and we were told to read it to ourselves, or if we couldn't read it, we were to start to copy it out. It took me half the morning to write 'Once upon a time Tom . . .'. So never have I forgotten that *The Water Babies* starts 'Once upon a time . . .'.

My friend and I were only seven, and the next youngest pupil was ten, so for the first year we had a class to ourselves. We had a charming Scottish teacher whom we called Andy Pandy, and Andy Pandy taught us our letters and our tables. That year was wonderful, because we really got a little bit of foundation and then I think afterwards we were always able to catch up. We were always in forms with girls older than ourselves.

I liked needlework, and I loved figures – mathematics – and literature. But I had no arithmetic talents, and I had no musical ability at all. My mother was very musical, my father fairly.

I was never very brilliant at sports, hockey and tennis. We never played cricket. There were a lot of girls who were extremely good. You see, the college nearby was all run on the house system and a lot of the housemasters' families went to the school.

My school was originally started by the refugees of the French Revolution. It lapsed and was restarted again by the sister of Lord Leighton, the painter, as a school for girls. It was very much a private school. I kept up my connection with it all my life. I went there when I was seven, as a day-girl. I wouldn't leave my father at all, d'you see. After I left the then headmistress said, 'Oh you must come along and start the Guides!' and I did.

I learned mostly plain needlework. We weren't encouraged to do embroidery at all. Fine stitchery was really the object. Embroidery was considered very easy and common and you know, it was the good stitchery that mattered. One of the heads when I was at school was French, and she was convent-trained, and we had to do eighteen stitches to the inch with no. 11 needles and 200 cotton – tiny little tucks you see, and then stroking all the gathers, and yards and yards of broderie anglaise which we put on all our undies – petticoats, nightgowns, and knickers, they were all done with little tucks and all this embroidery.

The school brochure said, 'Pupils' interest in poetry, music, dancing and drama is greatly stimulated.' The school was for gentlewomen, so to speak. The aim was not to pass exams and to train you to be professional, but it was that whatever you did you would do to a very high standard. The aim of the school was – as you see in the motto – 'Knowledge is no longer now a fountain sealed'; education was opening your mind in as wide a way as possible. You had all sorts of opportunities, especially as we got older. You had to do things very well at every stage, but when we got older the girls used to be taken up to London for good music or good drama or anything like that. Our lectures were from really top people in their own field and the staff were all very much more qualified than the average staff were in those days. In the third year we studied heraldry and I found that fascinating.

The headmistress was very musical. She was a great friend of Sir Edward Elgar, and he used to come and give recitals and so on. The dancing mistress, who was also the games mistress, was absolutely brilliant at choreographing dance. She also became my sister-in-law. She produced a ballet based on Elgar's 'The Wind of Youth' – after I had left school – it was something quite unique really.

I never thought of having a career, because we didn't in those days. I just wanted to have a home. Actually, my job in any case was to look after my father and the house and my younger brother. Then, one's idea was simply that one would get married and run a home to the best of one's ability. Any leisure time you'd get you'd do things for your neighbourhood. That was the whole object. There was never any question of having a career. You accepted it. Acceptance was all part of it.

I was the mother in the family. There was no question – you just did it, and you did your best. My father always said, 'I trust you to do what you can but if you've any hesitation about anything, always come and ask me and discuss it with me and we'll decide what's the best thing to do.' I used to take all the messages from him to the gardener and, of course, in the First War we were growing all the vegetables we could ... but our old Welsh cook would no more go and stand in a queue and buy anything than – there was no proper rationing you see, and food got frightfully short. You had to stand in a queue to get things. So instead of playing dainty games I used to escape from school and go and queue in the shop to get a little bit of fish or a pot of jam or some sugar or butter, so that my family wouldn't be starving. A group of friends and I used to breed rabbits.

I did all the mending in the house, and I used to really look after the house from the time I was twelve. We had two Belgian refugees who had been tailoresses, so I had learned tailoring too, when I was fourteen. I was sixteen when the war ended. By that time I felt I could cope with anything that came along. One didn't think it was strange, one just accepted it.

We went to the Grand Hotel in Minehead for a week in 1917. There was a dear old gentleman who took a great fancy to me, and he greeted me every day with 'Hello Mona Lisa!' because I had an enigmatical smile. Afterwards he sent me a great big picture of the *Mona Lisa*.

After the war I joined the St John ... the fact that I knew nothing about these things, and at the end of the First World War everybody was coming as VADs and that sort of thing, and I was terrified of meeting an accident or having to deal with an emergency and I thought, well the only thing was to know what to do and then perhaps I wouldn't be so frightened.

At the end of the war there was an artificial feeling that we should be happy now, but it was very artificial. ...

Your great thing was that you mustn't ever expect anything. When I left school my allowance was five pounds a quarter, and I had nothing but my school uniform. I saved up two quarters and bought a coat and skirt. I don't think it was at all suitable but it was the only thing I could buy. I had learned to make a lot of things. I had my own ideas.

Very often I felt I had too much responsibility. One was terribly conscious of that, and hoping one would do the right thing. But my father had an older sister who lived very close. She was a spinster, one of the people who fell into the trap when her parents wouldn't allow her to marry unless she married someone who could keep her in the same environment she'd been brought up in. The right background, you see. Her parents were very caring, but to their own family they were frightfully strict.

She used to think it was frightfully wrong for me to have any authority and say in things. She thought it was quite ridiculous, but my father said 'No, I trust [her] and I want her to do it herself.' But I know it was very unusual.

AS   : Have you ever been in love?
Miss X: Well, one's had one's ups and downs in that way, but that's one's private life.

I've never been engaged. One's always had great friends, shall we say ... for one thing, I've never felt I was free, because I always had my father or I had somebody. I suppose if I had been completely and utterly over the moon I would have pushed everything on one side. I've never got to that stage. I think partly I've never let myself. I think I was – not exactly shy, but not very confident in myself, you know, and I felt well, I'm sure nobody would feel that I'm the only one they'd ever want. I could have fun and friends, but I never really – I've realized that it was never going to work. I had too many responsibilities to think of marriage. My father was very fragile and I couldn't have left him. Your home was the thing that mattered then.

It was a funny time you see, and I was in a position where I felt I had great responsibilities in other ways. It was such a strange time at the end of the war. I left school in 1920, two years after the war, when everybody had settled in. In those days when you were eighteen you were just going to come out.

My father said, 'You must be presented', and I said, 'No, nothing doing, I'm not going to', because for one thing I had enough practical common sense to realize that it was quite useless. It would be a complete waste of money because we weren't going to live in London and have a season and I hadn't got anybody to launch me, as it were. I hadn't got a mother or anybody and my spinster aunts were much too old and uninterested anyway. They'd already got so many other nieces. ... But the war put a stop to everything like that.

I was to have gone to Paris but Paris was so unsettled then that my father was advised it wouldn't have been at all wise, so I didn't having anything like that. I just emerged, I brought myself out.

I always imagined that when the time came I would get married and have my own home and my own children and that would be that.

Really you just took life as it came each day. I used to see quite a lot of friends and I used to stay with my relations. I was always the niece who was free to go and look after auntie if she was ill or anything like that.

... I thought the Suffragette Movement was the wrong way to tackle things. I had no wish to be political in any way. I thought things would evolve, and they were evolving – evolve to fairness and equality all round. But I was quite content with my own position as a woman. I suppose in a way one hadn't much contact with the slum conditions, and some of the deprivation there was. I didn't come across it that very much. In that way one lived a fairly sheltered life, I suppose, in a residential town. But we cared for everybody locally. I never wanted to get into Parliament or do anything for women's rights. I thought what I wanted was to improve the general lot of people, and to do everything one could, like everybody did in a village in the old days – looked after all their neighbours. It was much more the community spirit.

I was doing quite a lot of Guiding, and I felt one was helping all the Guides to learn how they could contribute something to help other people. Teaching them how they could think of all the little things, and the caring things which would make them able to help, so that everybody was doing what they could in their own locality to make everything a little bit better.

The whole village was part of your life. For instance, my grandparents had six sons and four daughters. Everything in the parish really depended on them. There was no village school, so as soon as my oldest aunt was about thirteen or fourteen she and her governess started a village school. Under the guidance of the governess she was teaching the children to know their letters. My grandparents had a very strong idea that people didn't want charity; they wanted to contribute themselves, so although there were very small wages and large families, every child brought a ha'penny every Monday morning, and that was their payment for their school.

My aunt had to keep a little book, and all the names of the children were written down, with a little tick for every ha'penny. Every month they had a little meeting with the eldest children and my aunt and the governess, to count out the ha'pence, see how much they had, and say, 'Now what do we want most? Shall we buy a new book or do we want some more slate pencils?' – and they spent their own money, you see.

In the same way my grandfather collected from his friends quite a number of books that they were able to spare, and they had a village library. Anybody in the village could borrow these books. They paid a ha'penny a month. These ha'pence went to buy books they wanted.

That was the way a village was run. Everybody could take part in that village. They had an annual flower-show: everybody could take part.

... That was just a little bit of the background to my parents' attitude to life, you see. They were caring for their immediate surroundings. ...

After I left school my father would never let me go anywhere by myself, but provided I had a young man to go anywhere with me, he was quite happy. He never thought of people behaving badly, and they didn't, because they weren't expected to. I mean, one didn't go just two of us. Probably I'd go with another two friends and there might be three girls and three young men. My father always trusted me.

I adored the little car my father gave me soon after I left school, a ten-year-old Singer made in 1912. I called it 'Araminta'. It had brass fittings and oil lamps. You took a raw potato and cut it and rubbed it over the windscreen to stop the rain settling on it. In intervals you had to screw up the batteries. I had six lessons from the local garage – one in driving and the others in how to look after the car.

My first mishap was with a herd of pigs. When they saw the car they were all startled and instead of running away from me they ran to me, with such force that they broke the steering arm of the car. Great big sows. There were no garages and practically no telephones. I was stranded seven miles from home. My father wouldn't have a telephone in the house. He didn't believe in any new-fangled gadget. I had to walk into the village and take the train home.

I got familiar with my car and learned to drive it into Cambridge in May Week. That was when I was twenty-one. It was one of my great things. When my brother left Cambridge he had a car, and my father said, 'You must give up yours.' I had to part with my precious Araminta. He said, 'Oh no, you mustn't feel possessive about these things.'

By great good fortune a godmother died and left me one hundred pounds, so I bought an Austin Seven – my precious little box one that we had at Brooklands. I had an allowance of fifty pounds a year to do everything. I wasn't brought up to be extravagant.

I used to follow hounds on foot because I used to take my aunt. I had no time for what I call *artificial* riding – from commercial stables and so on, and during the war the horses had gone to the Yeomanry, so there really were none.

I haven't travelled a lot. I used to go over to Ireland, because I had great friends there, nearly every year. One had quite a variety – Guide camps, conferences – you met people of your own background and interests. And I used to visit all these uncles and aunts ...

One's life was a very ordinary one in a way. Because the war made a great difference. There was much more the trend towards equality after the war, because the men from all different backgrounds had been fighting together in the trenches. I think there was gradually evolving a much more even society. But there were too many impatient people who wanted to turn it all upside down.

The General Strike was a tragic time because we couldn't see it was going to do any good to anybody. It was a protest really, and there was a lot of deprivation and I suppose people just couldn't wait any more. One's first idea was, 'How are we going to cope?' Everybody who could, who wasn't on strike, just turned to, and their great thing was to do what was needed – they weren't thinking of having a fight.

There was a wonderful feeling of help and service in the Depression, but on the other hand there was a terrible feeling of helplessness, because it was such a big problem and there seemed to be nothing that anybody could do.

In 1925 I was very much tied at home, keeping house and looking after my father, so I said to him one day, 'Oh, I've got a job!' and he said, 'What? What have you done? What have you done now?' I said, 'Well I've been offered a job teaching needlework.' He said, 'Oh, I think you'd rather enjoy it.' I thought he would say, 'Oh no, my dear, you mustn't do that – plenty to do in looking after your home.'

I was so surprised. I told the headmistress that he was quite willing. For seven years I taught needlework, and then they started a Domestic House, so I taught dressmaking too.

My uncles were always very kind. I did receive a lot of support after my father died. My father had very little capital. He had to earn enough to support his family. After my father died I had a little house of my own and I had a maid who'd been our kitchen-maid and who came to me as everything. She *loved* looking after me, that was her great joy. Somebody came to see me one day and said, 'Oh, has she got a baby staying here?' 'Oh', said Doris, 'We've always got a pram at the gate.' Wasn't that marvellous! My friends used to leave their babies, and we used to look after them. I could send any baby to sleep, because I held them firmly. I never woggled them about or anything. I got very expert at weaning babies, because when my friends were trying to wean babies, if they hadn't got a nanny and tried to do it themselves – well you see, poor baby was used to its food coming from *there*, and the mother had the greatest difficulty in persuading baby to take anything else. But if the mother wasn't there, you got a few tears at first and then the baby was hungry and it accepted something else. I found very soon I could cope with that. It was a little side-line, you know.

But I was only twenty-six and I didn't want to live alone. I went to join my old cousin who had this great big house in Gloucestershire, with twenty bedrooms and one bathroom. We had to pump the water with a windmill. We had lamps and candles and a kitchen range. There were no mod. cons. at all. Huge log fires. It was a beautiful house, full of wonderful treasures, family things; hundreds of years of real beauty, shall we say. In some extraordinary way all my family seem to have had right back for generations very good taste, and they've only picked out the things that were good. There were lovely Cosway miniatures, there were paintings from Turner, Constable – all these people. Beautiful Chinese Chippendale furniture, and some much older. You see, it all blended together – it had all been lived with, even the curtains and the wallpaper. It was a wonderful background in a way, and a very sad one, because obviously finances were getting so strained. They got worse all the time, because capital had to be spent to keep things going. Yet she simply loved it and couldn't bear the thought of giving it up and she'd got a young cousin whom she wanted to inherit it, and she really wouldn't sell any of the silver and china and things, so it made it a little bit difficult. But it was living a life of graciousness, but on a very modest scale and rather a sad one as it was all declining rather.

My cousin had great personality and loved young people and she was always asking young people to stay. They used to come and think, 'Oh, here's the most lovely house, and we can bring all our friends', and she would put on a good show, and there would be cream and eggs and chickens and everything else when they were there, you know. They didn't realize that afterwards she was going about in wellington boots with holes in them, and one candle, and that sort of thing. She was generous to a degree. She was known to the whole neighbourhood as 'Cousin Floss'.

She had refused to get married because her only sister had died of a heart attack when she was in her early twenties, and Florence was engaged to a man who owned an adjoining property, a very beautiful place, and he came from an old family, and it would have been very suitable, although he was killed in the First War. She wouldn't marry him because she wouldn't leave her parents once her sister died.

That was the Victorian way, you see. She had to be the

daughter at home. If there was only one then they mustn't go. If the other one had been married and had produced a family then she could have gone off and done the same because there would have been continuity, but she couldn't leave them, you see. In those days I think the family could be very demanding, sometimes, and that was a case where it was.

I went for three months and actually I was there for eight years, until the war started.

I think there's a niche for everybody in the world. ı always wanted my home to be a welcoming place where people would like to come. I was never a pioneer or anything. I never had any wish to be a leader.

I've always loved children. The Guides who interested me most were the ones after school age. Then it used to be fourteen. Between fourteen and eighteen I felt that they were just starting life, and they were very often a little bit out on a limb, and by our group activities we could always talk about things.

I ran a little Ranger company among the villages round about where I lived in Gloucestershire in the early 1930s. In the house where I was living the stables were empty and I used the harness-room for my Guide HQ.

I've had a lot of great sorrows and I don't think I can talk about them. I wouldn't ever talk about them. I suppose the greatest sorrow in a way was my father's death, because my world had just gone – disappeared. My only brother had been married a few weeks to a sister-in-law who was older than him and a very dominating woman and I had no rapport with her at all, and she was never going to let me have any contact with my brother if she could help it.

I had quite a lot of illness in my early thirties. I thought it was grumbling appendix but it turned out to be other problems and I had several quite serious operations. Luckily it was nothing malignant. And I've always had back trouble all my life. I was born with a double curvature of my spine.

I went to Switzerland for International Guide Training and I had an accident then. I fell down some concrete stairs and caught my back and it concussed my spine.

I was X-rayed. The machine was in the doctor's dining-room. It was like an enormous metal four-poster bed. My spine was fractured. I'd been walking about like that for two months. I had to lie flat on my back for three months.

Afterwards, I went to India, to stay with my cousin and his wife. I got ill on the boat going over, and had to return home before the hot weather began. I had a holiday on a house-boat in Kashmir, and once I inspected the Camel Corps. It was most interesting to see the camels all line up, sitting and standing to command.

India was terribly sad and terribly dusty. There was so much indescribable poverty and such different values among the native people. There were such inequalities. The boxwallahs treated the Indians as though they were dirt. There was a tradition of Anglo-Indian service in our family. I hadn't expected all the deprivation and the dirt and the smells and the dust.

I think the thing I wanted more than anything else, because I have had a great many worries and problems to cope with in my life, is peace of mind. That's the hardest thing to find, isn't it? Yes. I know I worry terrifically about things that I shouldn't, and it's stupid, but if you're tired little things do get on top of you. Peace of mind is such a rare thing now with people because everybody, even the young, have all their problems. In fact, they have so many.

How wonderful it would be if all the worries ... of course, as the world is now it gets more and more complicated, doesn't it? In many ways things were simpler than they are now.

I've had wonderful friends, that has been the great thing, but there were always the anxieties and the tension. I suppose if I had been a person who had got married that would probably – if I'd had my own baby, that would have been my thing, because I always wanted to have children, that was my idea – creating a home, you see. I think I've always managed to, even if I've only been running a camp. I could always make it welcoming and comfortable. That was my great thing.

I did full-time St John all through the Second World War. After a time I became commandant of a hospital for eye cases. I was there for a year, then they asked me to go and open a new hospital for the women's services. The Queen Mother visited once. She gave the place an atmosphere of serenity and peace.

In the last year I had to leave because I was 'a bit wore out' – my tummy gave out. You wouldn't believe this, but we were working fourteen hours a day and fire-watching all night, and the food was ... well I was in University College Hospital for three months, then I did what was considered a part-time job. I went to the St John training centre to be deputy organizer. We had fortnightly courses. It was run by Mrs Beckwith-Smith. It was her home. Her husband was commanding the Guards Brigade at Singapore and was taken prisoner and he died in a prison camp. She was perfectly charming. It was her own staff – her cook and her housemaid and her gardener and her butler and everybody, you see. I had to clear up afterwards and do all the correspondence, even to type, which I'd never done. I had to teach myself.

Before the courses there was an interval of about ten days which I used to spend working at Belgrave Square St John headquarters, and I was Mrs Beckwith-Smith's staff officer.

After the war I started doing things with youth. I was a county cadet officer in the St John's.

All my shortcomings and my insecurity feelings – I don't want to talk about that, but I don't want to sound as though I had all the answers and could put the world to rights or anything; but I do think we had certain values in those days. That didn't mean we were any less human and ordinary.

Nothing was ever talked about sex in our day, and one didn't sort of think about it somehow at all. It didn't come into one's thoughts really in a way. I mean, you could have friends and be perfectly natural but you didn't think of it from the sex point of view. I don't think 'sex' was a word we ever thought about. The facts of life had to emerge as time went on, and I was very innocent – extremely! – even when I was commandant of a hospital. I've laughed since sometimes to think how *frightfully* innocent I was. I must have sounded quite ridiculous, but still – I managed to keep discipline anyhow.

I always had a terrific instinct. I couldn't bear unfairness. I used to be so hurt myself as a child if I was blamed for something I hadn't done. I couldn't bear that; I couldn't accept that, and I always thought that one of the things that matters most is fairness. But it was awfully difficult, because one of the things I found in the war was, if you did something on compassionate grounds – and there were often very good reasons why you should – immediately everybody was up in arms, because they said why should so-and-so have a privilege that we have not. They were so much on the look-out for that. That's what happens in Parliament all the time, doesn't it? The way they twist things in the most extraordinary way, and put words into people's mouths which aren't there.

I did full-time St John all through the war, then after the war I took on the youth side – this is a woman who never had a job! One of the things I got very much roped in for was camping, because I'd done the camping with the Guides.

I belonged to Guides for twenty years, from 1920 to 1940. Then I was doing full-time St John's and I had to give it up. In 1927 I joined the Women's Institute. In 1932 I was secretary of one of the branches. I was twice over president of another branch after the war, then I did committee work, and I retired from them in 1981.

After the war I hadn't got a home, for my old cousin in Gloucester was more or less a nursing-home case. I wanted to stay in Surrey. I couldn't find a small house, so I rented a house on my aunt's property and divided it into three. It wasn't very easy because, you see, the army had been there during the war and when they left it there was no means of cooking. Until I could get an Esse cooker, which was several years after the war, we had to cook on oil. And we had no electricity except a petrol engine, which would just give us some light, which wasn't very much fun. There was no gas, there was no main water, we just had a private supply – same with drains and everything else. There was nothing. We were completely rural. The garden had had six years of neglect. Anyway I struggled somehow.

I gave up my lease of this in 1956 and I managed to buy a little cottage. I made a garden. Then when my eyes began to give me trouble, although I could still drive a car, I moved to Haslemere. I loved gardens, and my thing was, the plants must be happy. Don't put in something just because you like it, put it in because it likes growing there.

Do you remember Lady Reading's scheme for one in five? For

teaching all the women in the country how to defend their family in case of nuclear war? This great scheme was started ... Lady Reading realized that if there was actually a nuclear bomb dropped – and this was the days when all this trouble with the Berlin Wall – the great thing was, if you could protect your family from fall-out. So they had a meeting in London of Lady Reading and her WVS committee and the various voluntary services. I was asked to go as the representative of the St John's. At this meeting they were talking such utter balderdash as to what you would do, how you would manage to cook food, and what will you do with the sanitation – oh, the most elementary things from a Guide's point of view, you see – not a clue as to how anything would happen. The people from the Red Cross had some very strange ideas. I said, 'But wouldn't it be a good idea', you know, very diffident voice, 'to do so-and-so on the principle of this and that', you see, and what about trench fires with a few bricks, which would be more effective than trying to have these primus stoves and things, for they probably wouldn't have fuel for them and they wouldn't know where to go to collect them. The idea was that if you could keep people safe for forty-eight hours it would give the authorities a chance to make any plans and to know where there was a danger of fall-out.

They were so interested in what I had to say, that I got a letter from Lady Lucas-Tooth, who was dealing with that department for Lady Reading, saying would I come up to London and have lunch with them and discuss the plans for sending it all out. I produced my little handbook. They asked me to come on to the WVS committee as a speaker on the national level. I said, 'My first loyalty is to St John. I don't know that I've got time.' They said I could do it just when I had time. Anyway, I wrote to St John headquarters. There was a very sort of snooty reply from the deputy superintendent-in-chief, saying that my first responsibility must be to St John, but that provided I didn't neglect my duties ... and you see this was all voluntary work and I was already doing about forty hours a week for them. It was very funny.

Later I took on Meals on Wheels, and I did that for twenty-five years.

I always kept in touch with the school. In 1960 the

headmistress, who had been head for thirty-five years, retired and sold the school, and it was bought by parents and old pupils, and I became secretary of the Old Girls' Association, and this [*she brings out a large scrap-book*] is the record of the twenty years I did that. Then I was made the president. I gave that up in 1980. So that's something I've done all my life, you see; ever since I was seven years old I've had a connection with the school. I think that's something a little bit unusual perhaps. I can count at least a dozen friends to this day whom I met at school.

I would always put in for every Gardening Society show, and I always won awards.

One of my other interests was the English Speaking Union. I was on the committee of that. My special interests ... we used to give a scholarship every year from this branch to a boy or girl from the neighbourhood for a month's friendship visit to America. I was one of the selection committee who chose them.

We organized a verse-speaking contest between the schools, and for quite some years I was one of the judges on that. These were my two special things in the English Speaking Union.

... I've always been very keen on fine arts. I joined the Decorative and Fine Arts Society, and joined in various things in that. I've been to various weekends. I went to a week in Vienna, and I went for a week to the Châteaux of the Loire and other things. One year four of us organized a display of period costumes which we owned, in aid of the local educational museum, of which I've been a member for many years. We had it open for a fortnight, in 1981.

I think I am very interested in anything creative. I am very patient. I have got a capacity for patience and even for stillness if necessary. When faced with a crisis I keep completely still; that's my first instinct, I hold myself in and hope that I can see a way of coping. My natural instinct is to create a home. Wherever I am I want it to be like a home.

All our health advances have meant that all the weak and the disabled and the elderly survive, and in a way I don't know whether it's really kind. I remember in the war one of my cousins was head of the physiotherapy department at a children's hospital, and there were 1300 children in that hospital; she had a staff of eighteen. I used to go over there when I was working at Barnstead when I was off duty. There was one ward there where all the children were blind and deaf and mental, and they'd been born like that, and they were going to be looked after for the whole of their lives by trained people. Well, what life could they have? They would have died in the old days. And the elderly people used to say that bronchial pneumonia was the old people's friend, because it was a very quiet way of passing on, but now people can live when they're not capable of enjoying life any more – when they've gone senile: they don't know what's happening, they can't contribute anything, and they are occupying people who could be doing valuable jobs. I don't think it was meant, really.

I think we've rather gone beyond the development we were meant to have. I mean, science has gone beyond – I always sort of feel that it comes back to this business of eating of the tree of knowledge, and if we hadn't discovered how to split the atom we wouldn't have some of the present problems, because we'd be much more localized and things would be smaller. Also, television is giving people the wrong ideas. Knowledge has outstripped what was meant. When we learned how to split the atom that was the beginning of it all.

... Regretfully, in the world as it is, the only way you can keep peace is through strength. But if this rivalry can be kept in moderation, not this building up and building up of weapons. The great problem to me is that on one side we're dealing with the oriental mind, where so long as you can make people believe a thing, that's truth; that's very much the oriental way of looking at things.

If you go back and look at history there have always been frightful abuses. I think human beings altogether have not learnt to behave awfully well. When you think, the animal kingdom doesn't behave like that. On the other hand there's been a tremendous lot of good.

A great deal of our problems at the present come from all the publicity and the media and wanting to be more important than your neighbour and to catch the attention of everybody. If one could only go quietly back to the past. All one can do is what one can in one's own corner.

My life has been very humdrum in many ways, but on the other hand I've been fortunate enough to meet quite a lot of interesting people and to see various sides of things, because not having a career but doing voluntary work as far back as I could I was fortunate enough nearly always to do it on a county or national basis and not just completely local. So in a way ... I think perhaps I've always been interested in people.

The most important thing in life really is to be given the strength to deal with a crisis and to be wise over it. I think that matters so much, and when people come to you with troubles be able to say the wise thing – not the immediate thing that comes into your mind but something that is really going to prove to be good advice. I think that's the hardest thing ... I sort of pray that the instinct to say the right thing will come. Because it is so terribly difficult when you're suddenly faced ... in an emergency. I think that's one of the things one dreads and one only prays that you'll be able, when someone really needs your help and advice, that you will be able to give them wise counsel.

That wisdom comes from a power that's greater than human, that puts the right words into your brain, and gives you the guidance – it's something you can't explain. To me the whole fundamental is that there is something beyond human comprehension and that in what happens here, we are making part of a pattern. What we do makes a certain pattern and in a way that will always have certain repercussions, that go on and on like sound-waves. But I don't feel it's all about an individual thing. You see, I feel it's all part of an enormous whole and we're just a tiny speck in the pattern of life. Because if you think of evolution and how a thing has developed and another and another, it's – now that they've got all this scientific knowledge and can realize the intricacies of life and the development of life, it has all worked out to some creation. There are many blotches on the way, aren't there, and many cracks and breaks and so on, but through it all I think it must all be working some way to something that is far beyond our comprehension.

I was brought up as a Christian. I mean, I believe. But to me the great laws are to believe in the Infinite Power and to give service to mankind. I think there are many ways of doing it. All the actual details of the different religious groups are man-made. I once heard things described in a way which to me means something, and that is that the whole universe is based on a wheel and that the hub of the wheel is beliefs. There are many spokes leading to that wheel. They are all rather straight and narrow and provided you stick to what you feel is your own belief it is all going to lead up to the hub. The whole thing is joined together by the rim of the wheel, so that everybody can contribute to that. That is something that gives me a bit of strength when I am ... you know, Doubting Thomas, that there is a purpose in everything.

Mary (right), and her sisters

Mary Coull

⇥ 5 ⇤

Mary Coull

'No regrets, all my life.'

Mary Coull was born in Peterhead, Aberdeenshire, in 1903. Her father was a fisherman; her mother had been a domestic servant. Mary was the eldest of five children, three girls and two boys. She left school at fourteen and helped her mother in the house until she was seventeen, when she began work as a herring-gutter in Peterhead. The herring-gutters used to follow the fishing fleet down the east coast from Lerwick to Great Yarmouth during the herring season. Mary worked at this until she was thirty-seven, in 1940, when she married John Coull, a fisherman. She had a son and a daughter. Her son, Billy, is a builder in Stirlingshire, with two daughters. Mary lives in Peterhead with her husband, her daughter and son-in-law, and her ten-year-old granddaughter.

I met Mary when I was writing an article about women in the fishing industry in the old days. A friend whose mother had been a herring-gutter in Peterhead told me that she would be the best person to speak to because she had done the work for longer than most, and had a vivid memory. Interviewing Mary turned out to be an unforgettable experience: the richness of her dialect in itself evoked a whole vanishing world, and she is a born story-teller, reliving every incident as she recalls it. As I left that time she handed me some reminiscences that she had written down for her own pleasure.

The 'ben' was the living-room, dining-room, bedroom, baking-room and wash-house all in one. It had a big open fireplace with whitewashed sides and a 'swey' – a swinging rod with a crossbar and a strong chain with a large hook: the girdle for baking the oatcakes and scones, the pots for the potatoes and herring, fish, soups and broths were hung on this and swung back over the fire. A long fender stool lay in front of the smaller fender, with 'Home Sweet Home' on it, or 'Peace and Plenty'.

The bairns coming in from their play made for the fender stool and got a lovely warm, also they got the potatoes left from dinnertime, lined up and toasted on the sides of the limed grate. There were no ovens, stoves or cookers then: everything was done on the peat fire. The country folk came in with carts laden with peats, the townsfolk got out the herring baskets and every household got an equal share. A pound for a cartload of peats would have been a good price.

There were no prams then; babies were carried in arms, with tartan plaids round mother and bairn, sharing the weight. Every cottage had its wooden rocking cradle with a knitted cradle-string two or three yards long, which was fastened on the four knobs to keep the baby in.

Toys... Father gave the girls a bit of side-rape off the nets: he bound the two ends with thin twine to keep it from opening out then twenty girls could play for hours. A cocoa-tin lid with a hole knocked through with a nail and a piece of string knotted and passed through it would run at your side all day if you liked; you could have a hoop off a herring-barrel and a bit of stick to drive it. We played at shops with buckies [shells] for money and a piece of flat iron and a bit of stone for weights. Dandelions and dock-leaves were rhubarb and vegetables. We played at seeing who could stay longest on the rocks when the tide was coming in. Sometimes we would light a fire and roast the wifies' fishies off the rocks.

Everyone was more on an equal footing then – cosmetics, perms and beauty parlours were never heard of: good soap and water and a good scrub and everyone was as right as rain.

The big washtub would be taken to the fireside and the bairns bathed one after another; then on with the flannelette sarks [vests] and worsted combinations. A petticoat and a thick tweed frock and you were dressed. Often you wore a pinafore too.

The floors of the but an' ben [room and kitchen] were usually hard clay sanded over. At the weekends the hard sand was swept up and clean sand put down. The tables and chairs were taken outside and scrubbed till they were white. There would be two stools as well, and a sensible dresser with its two white china dogs or figures of Rabbie Burns and Highland Mary.

There were box beds in all the houses. Some had doors on them which were closed all day. These had wooden bedboards and straw mattresses, then tyke-beds, full of chaff, which were always emptied and refilled at cleaning times. The women went to the farms with their creels and carried down the new chaff; the same was done with the boats' beds.

The blankets were washed in the big washtubs and trodden by foot and then laid on the beaches to dry in the sun.

The second time I visited Mary was a Saturday, and all her family were around her. They were intrigued to know what was going on, and came and went as we spoke. Mary meanwhile referred to countless photographs in envelopes and albums – 'There's just everything in here but the Children of Israel!' – which she would dig out to illustrate what she was saying. Behind my armchair were two huge heavy-framed photographs of her mother and father, and she managed to lift even these out for my inspection.

Her daughter, Mary-Alice, brought in a tray with tea and the traditional teabreads of Scotland. Mary-Alice's husband George came in at different times to show me some popular religious books by the Rev. William Barclay, which he had read and reread, and insisted on lending to me.

George is the son of a cooper who worked in the herring industry. He himself is a stonemason by trade, but he works in a factory now. He had undergone a religious conversion the previous Easter, and was so impressed by a series of coincidences that had befallen him in connection with Dali's *Christ of St John of the Cross* that he had written to the press and the Queen Mother about it. He showed me the kind reply he had received from Kensington Palace, and gave me one of the copies of the New Testament, in a black wooden case, that used to be placed in the fishing-boats by the National Mission to Seamen. He also brought me a bookmark with the Dali painting on it, and a postcard view of Buckie, the nearby fishing-village with which Mary and John had strong connections.

Johnny Coull came in at one point during this. He had been to the harbour to get fish for dinner. He sat down and Alwyn, trained by Mary, immediately began to lecture him about sitting on the good settee in trousers he had worn round the fish-sheds. It was quite comically clear, as Alwyn kept calling Mary's attention to Johnny's misdemeanour, that Mary was bringing up her granddaughter in the matriarchal traditions of the fisher-folk, and there is a special bond between the two of them. Mary resolved the situation finally by having Alwyn fetch a tea-towel to put between Johnny and the settee. She commented proudly to me, 'I got this suite from my son. He had it for umpteen years, and never a mark on it. I don't intend there will be a mark on it now!' Seeing I was going to take her mother's photo, Mary-Alice suggested that Mary change into more formal clothes. Mary asked me if I wanted her to do this; I said I preferred her as she was, and she was happy to stay in her apron.

She invited me to have lunch with Johnny and herself (the others were going on a picnic): 'We always have porridge on a Saturday.' I went to her tiny kitchen with her to watch her make it. She discovered she had run out of oatmeal, and roused Johnny from his seat in front of the television in the dining-area where he was watching a crucial cup-final match, to go out and get it. When the porridge was made we ate it in the old way, with bowls of cold milk beside our plates to dip our spoonfuls of porridge into. Afterwards Mary walked with me to the bus, although the weather was heavy and her chest is bad. She would have carried one of my bags if I had let her. She waited to wave to me on the corner as my bus passed.

Soon afterwards I had a postcard from her, then a letter about a holiday she had had with her family in Buckie – 'We have seen two beautiful sunsets and hope to see more.' They returned to news of the disaster on the Piper Alpha oil-rig: 'We were all reeling with the horror of it. There are awful things happening, Anne, if we hadn't our own personal hope fixed on God for our Salvation we would have nothing, with Him we are prepared for everything.'

Meanwhile I had been interviewing two sisters, Kathleen and Rosetta Pinder from Pinder's Circus, which toured all over Scotland before the war. When I wrote to Mary about it, she replied with her memories: 'Oh, the thrill of going up to the show park, hearing the music, seeing the goldfish.... We never afforded to go to the circus but we loved to go and watch the artists coming out between their acts.' She wrote about her son's daughter at university, 'It's funny, I never worried about learning. What I knew I knew and that was all about it.'

While researching my article on the circus I had come across a story about women boxers ... big hefty lasses, who took on all male comers – in fairground booths at the turn of the century. I asked Mary what she remembered. She replied:

> In my young days there were a lot of daredevil women who were afraid of nothing. A menagerie came to Broad Street, all barricaded up to keep the wild animals in. They put a placard on their caravan platform saying anyone who went into the lions' den would get five pounds. One young woman went in, and they wouldn't give her the money, but one of the businessmen in Peterhead went to see them and they paid up. I suppose they never expected anyone to go in, but there was that type of woman then. They could easily have boxing matches when they could face a den of lions!

Later that summer I phoned Mary to check some facts in my interviews. 'She's away up to Fraserburgh in the bus with Johnny to look at a caravan for sale there', Mary-Alice told me, and added, amazed and amused, ' – isn't that something at her age? I said to her there's hardly any summer left, but she said, "There'll be plenty other summers to enjoy it!".' Shortly afterwards Mary caught two of her fingers in the door of a friend's car, splitting them open. She did not consult her doctor: 'I wasnae seekin' tae cause nae carry-on ...', she said, and added, 'I've come to that in life now that I don't worry. We give it every day to the Good Man, and it's up to Him what we do with it. I don't put myself about; I don't hurry – I'm not able to hurry. I just take things as I can get them. I worry my head about nothing, and everything seems to fall into place. That's the thing I wonder at. Things come to me without any effort now.'

THE INTERVIEW

We were all fisher-folk. My father had a little boatie, and they all went to the small-line fishing. We gathered the mussels and shelled them, and baited the lines for the inshore fishing: cod, haddock, whiting.

My mother never liked the fishing. She came from Inverallachie and worked as a servant, for two and sixpence a week and she met my father. So you see I'm a half-breed: Inverallachie and Peterhead.

I adored my father. He was a good man, and I was the first-born; the first *survival* – I was the third birth. Being the third baby I was thought the world of.

After I was born I had fits. I had to lie with my head packed in ice. When my mother watched by my bed night after night, she blew up. She was over twenty stone and she never lost any of her fat. She blew up with want of rest and always being on her feet. She was afraid that anything would come over me; I was the third birth, and the first one to live. When I look at my mother I remember what she had to do for me when I was little. She was stern, but she went through a lot.

There was me, then Bill a year and a half younger, then Sally two years later, then there was two years between Beattie and Sally, but Beattie was twins when she came; then two years between the twins and John. John was her last birth. She prayed to the Lord that she wouldn't have any more after John, and my father was angry with her for that. But she didn't care, for she was the one who had to do the suffering.

My mother was always for doing good. But many a time I said she'd be better off doing more in her own house. She wasn't house-proud, but she should have been. I was expected to do everything in the house. But my mother was a grand cook. She made neeps and tatties; broth; and stovies; chappit tatties and milk, which I hated. When the tatties were beginning to grow black I'd say, 'Pick some whole ones out for me.' But I can take anything now.

Fishermen used to get settled up at the end of the fishing. We had to live on tick, and pay when we got my father's money. He was a smoker. It was a good job he didn't drink. The money wouldn't have been there – it wasn't there for the tobacco. I grudged ticking tobacco and cigarettes: Wild Woodbine, twopence for five, twopence ha'penny the ounce for Bogey Roll tobacco. The woman we got our errands from told me to tell my mother – for my mother never went for any errands, Muggins went for them all – 'Tell your mother to get a pound of tobacco from Fyfe and Duncan, and just take off his ration every day.' So when we got a settle-up of two or three pounds at the end of the fishing, the things that mostly needed to be paid were settled up immediately, and the shops all got their share. My mother bought the pound of tobacco, and she used to go to the kitchen in the morning and take my father's ration off the roll, and break it up. He used to say, 'Is that all you're giving me?' And she'd say, 'That's plenty. If you smoke that you're doing fine.'

My mother definitely wore the breeks in our house. But I wear them now, where are you? You don't know women from men – unless they take their breeks off of course!

When margarine first came in, Lipton's had a special offer – 'Lipton's Overweight' – if you bought a pound you got a quarter free, or two ounces with half a pound. That's what we lived on. But my mother said to me one day, 'Will you go to the mannie Chowie' – a grocer, he sold mending twine and hooks for the lines and fishing gear, but he was a grocer too. (He would have been a fisherman like all the rest of his folk but when he was learning to work, his mother had no patience with him, and she gave him a haul one day and she hauled him out at shoulder. That arm just hung helpless all his life. But he made his fortune out of that shop: folk have to eat to live . . .) So my mother said to me, 'Go over to Chowie's and get a quarter of butter to spread on my bread, because I'm scunnered with that margarine.' Now, the quarter of butter had to be ticked, but I went for it.

You got four biscuits for a penny; two rolls for a penny; two cookies for a penny, and two big rolls for a penny. For threepence your bag was full – that was the kind of living.

Coal was three and sixpence a bag. Often we could just get one bag. In the very poor times, when my father worked in a small boat, my brother would go down with a herring-basket (there were four baskets to the cran) and he got it filled up to the lugs of the basket for a shilling. When they were coming home from Yarmouth they'd stop in at the coaling ports and buy two tons of coal each at thirty shillings a ton. That did us a long time.

Then when she got her fishing-money my mother would buy a bag of potatoes – a hundredweight; half a boll of oatmeal – two or three stone; and the same of plain flour. She did bakings of scones and pancakes, but we always bought our bread. Oatcakes and butter – she made the oatcakes – was a lot of our diet.

To make a dinner she had to buy the beef – one and sixpence – or even a shillings worth of beef made a lovely pot of soup or broth. There were seven of us, and we got two platefuls each: fourteen platefuls out the pot for one meal. It was a great big soup-pot; we hung it on the open fire. We didn't have any oven baking. Potatoes and a dozen and a half of cured herring was our Saturday dinner: three-quarter stone of potatoes; we put them in the wash-house and stirred them round and round with the handle of the broom to take all the muck off them then I took the eyes out the potatoes with the sharp knife and put them in the pot. There was never a thing left on our table after a meal.

My father never had a big boat, and we never had big money. He always made sure his nets were in good condition. His new nets always had to be paid for off the fishing-money. And his clothes for his work. That was his money broken.

The herring-fishing started in May and finished in September. I don't believe my father ever had sixty pounds for fishing in his life. Johnny and me get more for an old-age pension now between us than my father ever earned.

I was the oldest and I knew my mother's poverty; I was brought up with it. I was always aware of the money that was owing.

When my father used to come home from the fishing, there was a lot of washing. Men can't wash. My father could wash his face but that was all. So there was weeks of washing after the fishing. A poor woman used to come and wash for my mother then, on a Saturday, for half a crown – for the whole day. That was a lot to take out of your purse at that time, but the labour she did was worth its weight in gold.

She came to my mother at the beginning of the week and said, 'Sarah, that half-crown you gave me did my whole week in errands, and I had threepence for my pail of coal out of it.' She had gone to Allan the butcher's and said, 'I'm seeking something to make a potful of dinner for tomorrow' – she had five or six of a family, her man was a cooper and coopers were often idle. He was often in his bed. He had a great thirst. So the butcher goes away and rolls something in a bit of paper. 'Threepence', he said. She had her peas for her broth and all the rest already. But when she opened the butcher's parcel she had three flat bones, with everything scraped off them.

Back she went to him: 'Now Allan, if I'd been seeking the broads [covers] of a book I would have *sought* the broads of a book, but I was seeking something to make a potful of soup for my man and my bairns!' He said, 'Well, Belle, that's all I have for threepence', and he gave her her threepence back. She took it and went to Kenny Smith the butcher, and told him the story. He away and got the great big knife and yakit [cut] off a big round of steak, off the cow. He didn't need to weigh it: he wasn't charging her. He rolled it up and said, 'Now, take your threepence along with you.' He was a Christian man – 'inasmuch as you've done it to the least of them'. Belle said, 'I made a potful of meat that done us two days.'

That was the kind of thing; that half a crown did a lot. My friend Peter was remembering that when the coal boats were in half the children didn't turn up at school – they'd be in the harbour scranning [scavenging] the coal . . . and all the lies next day: toothache, sore head, diarrhoea – just excuses.

All women at that time had a hard time, harder than the men.

There were two folk came in to visit us one night, a man and a wife when Billy and me were just bairns. I would be six and Billy would be four and a quarter. We were able to know right from wrong. When these two folk were leaving they gave us twopence each. My mother put it into a corner of a drawer in the chest and went to convoy the visitors through the close.

Whenever they had gone I said to Bill, 'Hey, that's *our* money she's put in there.' 'Oh but', he said, 'you'll be killed.' I said, 'I'm not caring, I'm going to have it.' I hauled out the chair and put it against the chest of drawers and climbed up – when I saw the height of the drawer! – and took the fourpence. Then I said to Billy, 'Come on, we're going to spend this.' 'No!' he said, 'no Mary, I'm not going. You'll be killed.' I said, 'I'm not caring, it's my money.'

Now you see if my mother had given us a ha'penny each I would have been satisfied, but she kept it all.... Well, there was a shop down the road. It had gas light and red curtains hanging at the window, so the gas light sent a red glow round all the window, and at night it was like looking into fairyland, looking at this shop-window.

She had birdcages hanging up; sweetie-cages, with bits of curtain round the four edges of the cage, and a sweetie bird perched inside – it was a sweetie-cage. With the light shining through – oh! Twopence; that was beyond us you see ...

We bought jaw-stickers [toffees] and black sugar straps – they looked a mile long to me. That was twopence. We were standing outside the shop and I was watching this cage out of the corner of my eye. I said to Billy, 'We've spent twopence. Now I'm going to buy a cage. We're not going to eat it; we're going to keep it for a long time and look at it' ... *pride of possession*, even at that age! Billy said, 'Mary I haven't any money left. We've eaten our straps and our jaw-stickers. You're taking it all!' 'No, no; you're getting half of this cage, and all the time I have this cage, you're having half of it. It's going to be combined operations.' He was thinking about his twopence. He wasn't sure about it, but he gave in to me. He had to; he would have got a smack round the ear if he hadn't. So I bought the cage. It was big; it filled my hand.

We went home; 'And where have you been?' asked my mother. I said, 'Well then, it was our own money.' She said, 'No, you stole it out of my drawer', and took the cage out of my hand and put it in the heart of the fire. That was the sort of mother I had – stern, strict. If I had it all to do over again I would. But I got a sore smacked backside that night. Mind you, that was nothing new, for it was always happening, for the least thing; it taught you respect. But I took my own way that night. I had then the spirit that I have yet, for my own rights: it was there. I have the sense to know that now.

Well, I'll tell you, poverty put you on your mettle. I proved the hard times, and that's why I think so much now of the good times. There's not a day but I shed a tear for my mother. Oh, the difference, when I go into my purse and I've five-pound notes and ten-pound notes when the coalman comes. You've five pounds and forty pence for a bag of coal; you've three pounds for a small bag of coal: you never have silver in your purse because it's all pounds you have to pay out, and you get pounds back in change ...

We went to church on Sunday morning, Sunday school, and church at night. In the summertime the Sunday school was held in the open air, and we liked that, sitting in the grass.

I have a full understanding of the coarseness and vileness that's going on in the world.... I was only eleven years old when my father was the skipper of a boat at Scapa Flow. His pay was nine pounds a month, and he used to send it to my mother in a telegram envelope, and I went and drew it at the post office. Nine pounds a month to keep her and five bairns, and pay the rent and everything. For the four years of the war my father did that.

He was at Thornbush Pier for a refit, for they had a high ship there. My father and my mother – oh, they had an awful love for each other! Oh *what*? My mother idolized my father! My father, he liked his sex you see, and she grew that she just wasn't able. But they liked it when they were young. So when he was in Inverness he took a room for us: my mother and the five of us in one room. We were three months in Inverness for a holiday and we went to school there. That widened my knowledge too. I was always learning, all the time.

Inverness is a great place for brambles, and my mother was a good jam-maker. So one bonny Saturday we went to the brambles; me, mother and father and Sally and Beattie and John. John was just two years old. We all had a tin mug each, to fill and empty into my mother's basket. It was a bonnie green park. Sally and Beattie and John were just children; they didn't have to worry about pulling the berries, so they were playing down in the park. Bill and my mother and father were pulling the big juicy blackberries. It took no time to fill a mug. I was plucking berries off on my own in a dip, and listening to the children fighting and playing. There was a man came into my view, among the thick trees. I wondered what he was doing, but he wasn't my business, and I went on plucking the berries and filling my tin. Every time I looked he was nearer to me.

He said, 'Are you just here yourself?' I said, 'Oh no, my father

and my mother and my big brother are with me.' I just had a
feeling. I said, 'Look, that's my brother and sisters playing in the
park.' I don't think he believed me. He said, 'I'll pluck two or
three berries for you' ... but I was watching him, and all the
bonny berries went down his throat. He was eating as he was
plucking. Of course, I didn't want him beside me at all, but I
couldn't say, 'Go away', for I'd no business to.

It was quiet. I was surrounded by brambles and I couldn't get
out without passing where the man was. I wasn't looking at him;
I was praying to the Lord, 'Keep me today.' Then the man said,
'Look round! *Look round*, you b——— of h———! Look
round or I'll kill you!' When I looked round he was down on his
knees urinating, and a great big long pink thing that size in his
hand, and I lifted my eyes to heaven and I screamed. That's
what I say now, they ought to be taught to scream. I screamed
from the depth of my being, 'Father!' He knew when I said that
that my father couldn't be far away. I don't know what
happened after that, for I must have passed out for a minute.
But he never touched me. The scream I let out was what did
it.

Two minutes elapsed and there was my father with a great
lump of wood, running. He said, 'What is't?' I said, 'A man.'
'Did he touch you?' 'No.' My mother was lumbering at the back
of him, with Bill.

There was no more bramble-hunting that day. My father
went to the police and reported it. I had a feeling that that man
knew every inch of those woods, and watched them; I had a
feeling that his gimlet eyes were watching from the trees. If there
had been nobody with me I'd have been killed. I would have
died.

That put me off lads. I didn't bother. There was a bonny fine
chap that sought me when I was twenty-two, but I said, 'Oh no.'
Thirty-seven years old when I was married. I wasn't interested in
them. I didn't care what anybody else did: it wasn't for me.

I've been in Inverness an awful lot of times on bus runs since.
It's a beautiful place, but to me it's bad. At eleven I was just
coming to be a woman.

He was a tall slender man, when I went out I used to wonder
if I was passing him. He was a beast – the type that's doing all
the damage now. When I hear about it my own experience

comes back. I can understand it. They should emphasize children to scream.

If you're in company with a good person, you feel better for it, but if you're in company with evil it also spreads, more so because the Lord's able to keep you. It made me wise in a way I hadn't wanted to be wise, because we knew what it was they were after. That experience changed my life to a certain extent, because I wasn't interested in boys after.

I knew when it came time for Johnny Coull that married life meant that, and then it was different. No romance like you read about: I wanted the companionship. But sex was necessary with a man and a wife you see.

I started the herring-gutting when I was seventeen years old. I left school at fourteen because my mother had her family to bring up and she couldn't afford help. When I was fourteen I had the qualifications for the Academy, but they had twenty-one shillings to pay for books and they couldn't afford it, and I never got to the Academy: I left. But I got a merit certificate and a 'very good' in every subject – that would have taken me into a good job.

When I left school I worked in the house. I was a servant. I helped to bring up the family. I was nine years old when my youngest brother was born, and I entered him into school when I left. I was a second mother to the younger ones, for if there was anybody in the town not well – cases of need – my mother went. She sat at a lot of death-beds and attended to a lot of folk, so somebody had to be mother in the house, and it was me. I believe many's the day my mother thanked the Lord for me, for she could depend on me.

Once when I was single and my mother was ill I thought, God, what would I do if my mother was taken away? To me at that time, that would be the end of everything, for all the punchings I got from her, I was like that with her. She didn't hit me when I grew up. I would have held her back, when I was angry. I have an awful temper – in justice. If I deserved it I took it.

When I was fourteen it was twenty-one shillings for books to go to the Academy. I was disappointed. I would have liked to go to school for more, just general learning. What I got was, 'Hing in noo Mary, grow up a big quinie and be a servant to your mother', so that was my ambition. I was quite happy to leave school. That was my life, working in the house. That's how I knew all my mother's affairs; I knew every penny in her purse. It was meagre.

When I was young I never saw far before me, I just took every day as it came.

I used to make rag rugs. My mother cut them and I rolled them up and I thought out all the patterns and made beautiful rugs. Beattie got two, Sally got two, and John got two when they were married.

There was always plenty to do at home, because we were learning to be housewives. My two sisters, I made them work in the house, and I've only proved it in latter years how much they resented that. Because you see I said, 'If I'm left with it you can help. You're not going away to play and me doing the work.' They hated my guts for it. And yet we never fought. People used to ask why, and I said, 'I never gave them any cause to fight.'

My mother never knitted on four wires. Twice when my father's boat was in for a refit, after I'd left school, she went away beside him and I was housewife. I learned to knit on four wires when she was away from home, from a chum. My mother never knitted. She had a sore back. But she was a grand sewer, and a patcher and darner. I learned all that from her. There's nobody will patch behind me, or sew or darn.

I knitted ganseys [fishermen's jerseys]. I didn't get it out of a book; I had it all in my head, all the patterns – anchors, diamonds, and hearts and waves. We used to go down the Mission socials, and the choir would all be in ganseys, and I wore mine.

I knitted my father's socks. He wore thick stockings up to his knees, and serge drawers that came down over his knees and tied with tapes. The fishermen were well-clad, because they'd a lot of weather to stand. I weft his stockings and ganseys to fit him.

A hundred loops on all your wires – three hundred loops for the ganseys. I never had great sight, I knitted by lamplight, sitting by the sink. I did a new gansey for the men every year. When Sally grew up she weft the same, but nothing like me: I was the wefter.

I baited the lines for my father, and shelled the mussels for it, and mended the nets and weft the ganseys and gutted the herring.

I was converted when I was sixteen. We were brought up in the church, always went to Sunday morning service, Sunday school. My father took us to church on Sunday morning while my mother cooked the dinner; she didn't get much to the church, her church was at home, at the fireside.

I always knew when the mannie was preaching that I'm among the goats: I was no sheep, and I knew it. I needed something I didn't have. I knew, because you see when you're brought up with it, it's in you, you can't avoid it. Well, I was always listening and when people went up converted I thought someday I would be like that, but not yet.... When I was sixteen there was a Faith Mission woman came to the Baptist church. She wore a little bonnet and navy-blue coat – there was no dressing up with them, poor things, hardly a shoe on their foot. After I was converted and went into church I entertained an awful lot of that kind of folk, poor creatures: I just gave them a share of what there was, after I was married and had my own house. They didn't get much in my mother's, because there were too many of us coming and going there already, and anyway her house wasn't grand enough to entertain folk.

Faith Mission ... they'd faith for their pay, and the Lord provided for them.

This woman was preaching. There was a Bessie Buchan, two years older than me, who came to the meeting with me every night. Now this craiter, Stir-Alice was her name, and she held the meeting in the Baptist church hall. Every night I was enthralled with her speaking: there was just something about her different from the minister and she got through to me. So on Friday, the last night, Bessie's mother came over and said Bessie was too busy to go. When she told me, she looked into my face and said, 'Are you awful sore seeking to go to this?' I said, 'I'm seeking to go to it.' She said she would go with me herself, and she did.

The Faith Mission woman was talking about Revelations, and all the things that's going to come. 'Oh me', I thought, 'I'm bad enough now, but what will I be when it comes to that?

There will be no room for me at all. I'll have to do something about it.' And I was convicted inside. I just felt like a bunch of filthy rags. Comes to the last hymn and I wasn't able to stand on my feet to sing, I was so put about. My sister stood up. I took a hold of her skirt and said, 'Tell my mother I'm staying on at the meeting tonight.'

My father had an uncle, his father's brother, a good mannie – his prayers and everything were real – he came down to where I was sitting: 'Well Mary?' I said, 'I'm going to be saved, for I'm awful feart for that that's going to come, because there's nobody but them that has the Lord is going to stand that time.' He took me to the front and went down on his knees with me. He poured out his soul to the Lord on my behalf. When he finished his prayer, I was laughing and speaking to everybody, but I felt no different.

I went home. My father was home from the war ill. He took insomnia and neurasthenia and he was a year and a half in the hospital. He was lying in the back room with a muffler tied round his head. He had to be kept kind of quiet. I went through beside him for the quietness, because I wasn't clear in my mind about *anything*. I didn't feel a bit better for being converted.

Some friends who had heard about it came in to see me. One of them shouted through, 'Mary, haven't you anything to tell us tonight?' I went through to the living-room and said, 'Oh, aye', and they all shook hands with me: 'That's fine, you're a real sister now.' The tears ran down my father's face. I went to bed.

You see, my mother put a lot on to me. When my father was discharged from the navy he got some extra money and he bought a brooch apiece to us. She was raging all over the house, but she couldn't find the brooches; somebody had taken them. Of course, I got the blame. This day, the day I was converted, she volleyed and she called me for everything. It was *she* ought to have had places to put these things, so she'd know where they were, but she knew nothing about it, going through all these drawers.

It was the time for the errands. She would put a big shawl round me and give me a basket to put them in. When I was coming back it was a beautiful moonlight night, away from the lights of the town. I walked along a lonely road myself. . . . Since that night I've believed every word about him that was walking on the road to Damascus – Paul – and got a bright light. There was a clear moon right enough, but there was a bigger light than the moon. I couldn't understand what happened, but it happened. And you know this, my burden was away and it never came back. I was as light as a feather. The Lord did that for me. After that, my mother's roarings and fightings of me – I always tried to do my best, you see – hadn't the same effect, for I had more strength than my own, to combat that kind of thing. That's never left me. That's reality to me now.

I've doubted, and I've asked questions since, but I've always submitted to the Lord's will. When I see all these things happen ... why is the Lord taking away folk that are so sore needed? And leaving others that are not?

My mother just hated the gutting. She only went once. I liked it. I did it twenty year. I loved going about, to Lerwick and Yarmouth and meeting all the folk.

The herring-gutting was the only thing that was going – I was glad to get out to earn a shilling. I had to hand my pay to my mother. I started with a learner crew, and any soft herring, over-day's herring, the learner crew worked on. My boss taught me how to gut. He said, 'Now put in your knife like that, and pull.' When I did what he did the whole thing ... the heart and the gut – there's three different things that came out, and then the herring was ready to preserve. We didn't take off the head.

What I liked best about the gutting was the pay. We were happy in our work. No growling and girning and vying with other folk; what other folk did never bothered us. We were engaged for seven or eight weeks, for a fishing. Then when the fishing finished you were up the garret mending your father's nets, ready for the next fishing. We were four weeks at home. We gave all our money to our mother, and she kept us. She would buy our riggings-out for the Yarmouth fishing – three coats (one each), two vests each, and two pairs of knickers each. She was responsible for all that. She was the keeper. We never got money to deal with. We never did a thing without asking her.

I went to Yarmouth every year for seven or eight weeks, and we dwelt with the poor. They were glad of six shillings a week from each of us – they made our very beds, and I never had a bad landlady.

We wore an oilskin overall with a bib. At first we had leather boots – we were killed with them, all the long days standing. But rubber boots came on the go, right up to the balls of our legs, and it was heaven.

Our fathers kept their old oilies from the fishing, and we cut them up into aprons to protect the coats. Then, in our day, women wore mufflers. We were always tidy.

We started at six in the morning. We got an hour to our breakfast, from eight to nine; we went back and worked till one. From one to two was our dinner break, and from five till half-past was our suppertime. Then back again, and we gutted as long as there was daylight in the summertime. We went home and went to our beds, and up again at five.

We got tenpence between three of us for packing a barrel. It took four big heaped tubs to fill a barrel. Two would pack and one would gut. Twenty-four barrels would have been a good day's work. When we were topping up the barrels we got fourpence an hour. The herrings pickled in the barrels and the salt that they were in mixed with their own juice and made pickle. When they had been lying for nine days the coopers came and put in bungs. Two women would pour the pickle off, and the fillers-up came with the tubs of herring and topped the barrels up. When you were doing this you picked out the bonny herring, the best, and you pressed the bellies of them and made a top tier. The coopers put in the ends again, and they pickled them again.

I have the marks from the gutting on my hands still; they never went away. Sometimes the bad salt ate holes between your fingers, and my knuckles were often skinned. When we went gutting at Lerwick we had to carry our chests from the end of the road up to the huts, and that was a long carry. Well, I fell once carrying my chest and I bruised every knuckle – and we were in among salt and brine, and pickle and everything. I took a whole fishing before I healed.

Once I worked with awful bad salt; it was heavy like soda when you lifted up a handful, coarse salt. It played havoc. My mother used to chew oatcake, and filled the holes in-between my fingers with it, and I tied the cloths on, and they stayed on my fingers till they healed. Oh, we had sore hands ... but of course, we got accustomed to it. It was our work.

There was a mannie Diamondstein, who worked for the Scottish Russians, a little buyer, and when he came into the yard to look at the cured herring, to make an order, he would take a bite out of the back of the neck of the herring, and put his finger into the pickle to taste it.

... There was a Russian woman who used to buy the trawled herring – she had her own markets and her own trademark – at the end of the fishing the Aberdeen trawlers would start trailing the bottom of the sea for herring. My father said, 'You've gotten them but you'll rue it!' Well they drained it [overfished it], same as they're doing now. There were no scales on the trawled herring. When the drifters came in, they wouldn't buy herring with no scales on it.

A lot of it was changing the dates when it was bad quality – rubbing out – I knew Christian folk that went in for curing and quitted it, because of the carry-on.

The war ruined the fishing. In 1939, the markets were all closed, because our best buyers were our enemies – Germany, Poland: we were the first to suffer.

Some tried it on a small scale after the war. There were some English firms, but the English never had the knack of curing herring like we had. The wifies used to come down to cure herring with white aprons on – they just skited along [skimmed the surface of the work].

I was seven fishings at Lerwick. There was a gey lot of babies conceived at the fishing in Lerwick, I'm telling you; there were no landladies you see, and there were some impudent men came to the hut door – especially with drink. But they never darkened our threshold, me and my sisters'. A lot went on, because there was no control, and all those fine hills and valleys. We three sisters went together; we would never go in with anybody else. If we didn't get a hut to ourselves, we wouldn't have gone.

It was lovely – wonderful! – because it was the only time in my life I'd had a shilling in my pocket, because my mother was pursekeeper. We got fifteen shillings a week wages, beside our gutting money, for our daily keep. We had no lodgings to pay; we just had to buy our food. A bus came certain days, to run into Lerwick. We had to pay our fares, and we had to put in our church collections, and when we got to Lerwick we used to buy fish and chips, and our sweeties for the week. We had always something left over in Lerwick. Our cookies and our milk were left on the doorstep every morning; we had porridge every morning: porridge and tea and two morning rolls, every day for our breakfast. Every day we had a dinner. We would stay up till one o'clock in the morning to prepare our dinner for next day. We'd put the pot at the side of the fire, and during the day the packer would go up to the hut and turn it – broth with a bit of beef; I never believed in bones for soup. A bonny bit of beef, one and sixpence: one and sixpence made a good dinner.

We got fifteen shillings a week for our keep at Yarmouth. We had six shillings to pay our landlady. Oh, I liked our landlady! Six shillings a week each, and she fetched and carried for us for that. We bought our own food but our landladies cooked it. We did well. We never went to the pictures or anything; we couldn't afford it, but anyway we weren't brought up to do that – we were Christians you see. Me and my sisters were called 'the holy quines'. Oh no, you see, we tried to do it in our living too. It's no use just going to church if you aren't going to live the life. We wouldn't buy their twopenny sweepstakes and raffles – no, we'd never do that! It wasn't the pictures, it was what was going on after that was the trouble. And it wasn't the dancing – there's no damage in dancing – but it's what comes with it! So no.

At the beginning of the Yarmouth fishing our fathers took down for us on the boats a big stock of errands, that our mothers bought for us – biscuits at four a penny; a box of oatcakes – there was half a stone of oatmeal eaten every week in our house; jam and sugar and tea, and our neighbours would come in with cakes for us to take with us. We would have enough cakes for three weeks. Our fathers and friends would come up to see us on a Sunday night, and we had always a spread table at suppertime.

I remember I was with my sisters, Sarah and Beattie, in a big shop in Yarmouth, a gorgeous shop. They had towels, 'His' and 'Hers', and pillow-cases the same. My mother needed table-cloths. I saw some bonny white ones with mauve borders. I took two, and 'His' and 'Hers' towels and pillow-cases, and a pair of cushion-covers. My sisters were furious: 'Why are you doing that?' I said, 'Well, with what we have left over every week, we can come up and pay some of this.' Sally called me for everything. But we had to buy my father his tobacco too. He was seven years on the same boat, and every blessed year he'd be further back, deeper in debt. It was awful days of poverty.

In Yarmouth that time, the first day when we were sharing what was left over, it was a Saturday, I put my hand across the table to take Beattie's money. She said, 'Oh no, Mary, I'm taking my own money.' I said, 'You are?' – it was like a knife in my heart, because she knew what Sally got: Sally got everything there was to get. It opened my eyes to the drift I was on [what was being done to me], because you see my mother was the boss. So Beattie kept her own money. But her pouchette was stolen when we were coming home from Lerwick the next year! I said, 'It would never have been stolen if it had been mine, because I would have looked after it.' I used to sew a hankie on to my petticoat, put in my money, and sew it up again. For this was the money coming home to my mother. It was always my mother I was thinking of; I never once thought about myself, that never entered my mind.

I said to my mother when we came back from the fishing, 'I'm putting ten pounds into the post office.' Beattie said the same, and my mother wasn't pleased.

When we needed clothes, it was three coats; when it was bloomers it was six pair of bloomers, vests – for all three. My mother did it all. You never got a choice. I never got to choose my own wedding-coat even. I did what she said.

Beattie married a man that went to the line-fishing out of Aberdeen. He was well-off. She had an organ when she was married, and she had a house, and something like seventy pounds. She was all right.

Everybody that was in Yarmouth took a revival home with them – there were an awful lot of conversions. But I was saved already.

When my father gaed to sea, if they had a quern of fish ... they'd have got twenty-five shillings for a box, but only one and six for a quern, and that was what the fishwives bought. ... I said to my father, 'If we take these home we'll dress them ourselves and I'll take them and sell them.' I was in my twenties. I went and knocked on the doors, with my creel with my fish codlings, my basket with the yellow fish, and another basket with half-blown haddock – split and sweet-salted and out in the draught for a day. Lovely for roasting, just put them on the brander – they went like hot cakes!

When I hear them speaking now of getting one hundred pounds for a box of codlings – my father couldn't get fifteen shillings. It's made them millionaires. And they look down their nose at you. That doesn't affect me, because I can't see them looking down their noses or up to the sky, because I'm blind, but our quine sees it. I say to her, 'Never mind them, because the Lord sees you.' They fancy themselves because they've got two or three pounds. It makes you laugh. The Lord's a great recorder. He knows all about it. And we're quite willing to leave it in his hands. We can't begin to judge because we're inadequate; we're ignorant, we only know our own ken.

If I had my life to begin again it would just be the very same because you see I didn't know, I hadn't the knowledge to know better. When I left school I could have just said – well nowadays they say, 'I'm not biding in the house. I'm going to get a job' – and I would have been independent, but no, no, 'Bide in the house, be a servant to your mother.' Well, I knew I'd never get anything from my mother, and I never did. Not even when she was getting a wage from my father.

The war came on. There was a fishing. My brother John was married and he got a berth on the *Trustful*. That's the first time our John went to the fishing and I wasn't gutting – always during the fishing, in Peterhead or Lerwick or Yarmouth, I was down to the boat with his present, for I brought him up. He came down with carpets for my father and mother, and a teddy-bear for Beattie, because she was expecting, and slippers – and he hadn't a sixpence-worth for me, and I was thirty-five years old.

I didn't get married till I was thirty-seven because I never got the chance of a right man. I saw the rest of my family all married. When my turn came my mother hadn't a sixpence to give me.

Sarah was married first; she married a stone-cutter. So ... it came to my turn now. There was Johnny Coull. I met him in Lerwick. I just say thank the Lord for Johnny Coull, because you see I never went out with men. When I was younger there was nobody took me on. I used to look in the mirror and I thought, well there's nothing here that anybody would run after ... and I got the chance of two widowers, and one of them I would have taken – the boat was there and everything, but my mother wouldn't allow it, because he was a widower with three of a family. But I could have coped with it, because I had coped with hers! . . . And there's nobody could be worse than them.

She said, 'These two hands will never get you out.' Her two hands would never get me out anyway. I had to get myself out. But her word was law . . . and you see, she had a lot of poverty: if it hadn't been for the tick we'd never have been brought up. That's the honest truth.

She always made sure of the dinner. You couldn't tick from the butcher, but we always had our dinner – but, come time for the supper? – we couldn't have many suppers if it hadn't been for the ticker . . .

I'll tell you a story: There was a man who used to come round, we called him 'Silk-for-Blouse'. He wore ay the long robe. He was a foreigner, a Persian or something. He had a great big leather bundle on his back. He stayed in the Palace Hotel, and kept a lot of stock there and carried samples of it.

One day I came into the house and Silk-for-Blouse is sitting (they can sit cross-legged for hours, you see) with his wares spread out in front of him. My mother said, 'Now Mary – he's told me that he'll give me five shillings off three sets of dishes.' They were two pounds fifteen shillings the set. I said, 'I'm not seeking any dishes from him. If ever I need dishes I'll buy dishes I can use. If you buy these there'll never be tea in them' – they were yon see-through stuff – 'You take my two pounds ten shillings and go and give it to Isa Bruce' (that's the woman we owed for our groceries). The mannie got wild. He said, 'You dare speak to your mother like that!' I said, 'I'm not speaking to you.' He said, 'When I'm at home I say like it says in the Bible, when I say come, my servants come; when I say go, they go.' 'Well', I said, 'go away to your servants. I'm talking to my mother.' I was in my twenties you see, and I was beginning to assert myself. Oh, the mannie roared, but he gave her the two sets. I said, 'I'm not for it.' She gave one to Beattie and one to Sally, and they were thrilled, but not me. My mother went down to Isa Bruce's shop then, to give her her share of the fishing. I said, 'Mind and not give her any of my money for the dishes.' When she came back she said, 'Mary, there's only a little left to pay off the whole account.' I told her to go back and pay it off and be clear. So she did it, and Isa Bruce gave her a beautiful shirt for my father for discount for paying out the account.

We never took any more tick with her afterwards, but she died a year or two later. Half of the town of Boddam had to pay her, but she had no organization of her book-keeping; she'd just put it down as 'Mary, ninepence; Mary, one shilling' – and so the lawyers never got a penny of debt in. I said to my mother, 'Are you glad now that you paid her? You've a clear conscience and so have I.'

My two sisters got their dishes, and they never had tea out of them. When I was married my mother would have bought me bed-linen.

It was the thing for me to be married, because I hadn't sixpence to – well, I had sixpence but I never got more. I'd get married younger if I'd to do it again. If I had taken the first lad who came and sought me when I was twenty-two, I'd have had it different. Yes, I've had a happy marriage, in spite of everything I had to do. It helped me in life to carry on and make the best of everything I had to do. I never had time to sit down and mope.

I was my sister's bridesmaid, and I kept the frock. I didn't wear it. So when I was married to Johnny Coull he didn't have to buy a dress for me. The man always bought the woman her dress and hat and coat. Johnny's sister came from Buckie and she bought my coat and my hat – that was the style. The woman bought the bedroom suite; the man bought the sideboard and the table and chairs. The easy-chair was bought off the present-money.

But even when I bought my wedding-coat my mother was with me, and Johnny's sister. I was determined on a bonny coat, with a fur collar and such. My mother said, 'No – no!' – she was always looking forward you see; she was thinking about the time when I would be pregnant. I wanted a close-fitting coat, but she made me get a wide one that I would get the good of then. She was wise enough … I was a year and five months married when I had Billy. I hated the coat I got; it was five pounds, cheap fur on the collar, and it was wafting about my feet – I was never happy about it, but I took it, through her persuasion. After that she got no business with what I got.

When we were about to be married my sister Beattie's baby

was born. It was taking fits. It only lived for twenty-four hours, and she was at death's door, poor soul. Johnny came ashore to get married. We went to the hospital and sat with her, and she recovered. She said, 'When are you getting married?' We said we were waiting for her to recover. We were all ready: the bedroom suite was in the garret. 'Well', she said, 'as quick's you can now!' And we just went ahead. We were married in the Baptist Kirk, and our reception was upstairs in the Rescue Hall. We had quite a good turn-out.

I paid for every article myself. I never got sixpence from my mother, and my father had a job, building the air-force place, getting a wage. So, I had to seek a loan of five pounds from my mother, because I didn't intend to leave Peterhead with any debt. I had paid so much on my photos and everything, you see, so it wouldn't come so hard at the time. Of course, Johnny got the sack for going ashore to be married, and he was five weeks without any pay. I had twenty-four shillings in my purse after we bought our tickets to Buckie.

I sought the loan of five pounds from my mother. She got the feathers for my feather beds from the country, and filled it – the feathers were going out of her all ways! I had to pay that, and two tubs and my washing-steels; scrubbing-boards and brushes – I use my scrubbing-board still; it makes things cleaner. I needed five pounds, for I was *determined* I wouldn't tick. I said, 'I've had a life of it, but there will be no tick with me!' So she gave me the five pounds and I paid everything and went away to Buckie.

Eleven shillings was what you got from the means test if you weren't getting any unemployment pay. We had that for two weeks, then there was a woman flitting, and Johnny helped them with the wardrobe. She gave him a shilling. He came upstairs and gave it to me. I said, 'Oh Johnny, you should have bought a couple of packets of Woodbine, man!' He said, 'I'll never smoke a fag till I get a job Mary.' Did I think anything of him? He was a dear man.

Two or three times we went up to his sister Janet's and got our meat. He had been good to her before he was married. A man came in, seeking her man to go to the Boom Defence at Scapa Flow, to join a trawler. Janet's man couldn't go, and Johnny got his chance. He was three weeks over his trip, which meant that I was three weeks waiting for my first pay.

His mother said, 'Go down to Paterson's and get your errands, the same as I've done all my life, and pay when he comes back.' I said, 'Never – *never*!' And I managed. Seventeen pounds he put into my hand when he came back – seventeen: I thought I was like a queen; nothing to come off it except five pounds to my mother.

I never expected my mother to take the five pounds but she did. That's all I got for being the oldest daughter – all the extra work I put in. There's a bit in the Bible that tells you about folk that started to work in the morning, and folk that started to work at dinner-time, and folk that started to work at suppertime, and they all got the same. I thought, 'That applies to me.' There's nothing can beat your own experience.

My man was a fireman, a second engineer, and a fisherman at the trawling. I got his unbroken pay-packet every trip, and I never knew what it was to want a pound. I got a good man, and I thank the Lord for him every day.

We lived upstairs in his mother's house – [*ironically*] I was *tarred wi' luck*. I had my mother-in-law for seventeen years. There was two years she couldn't work, and I took her about. Her sister was ill for three months, and I nursed both of them.

There were three old folk in his house when I got married. There was a brother over eighty; Elsie – she was wearing on, and Johnny's mother: she wanted two months of eighty-nine when she died. Billy was seven weeks old when the brother died. A while later Elsie took ill, and my mother-in-law took ill. I had their two beds in one room. Johnny's mother was fly. When her sister started to fail, she started to buck up, and she was on her feet when Elsie died. She lived another two years. I did all the cooking; I gave the two sisters all their food for ten shillings a week. My brother-in-law was a widower, he lived across the road, and I cooked for him too. Johnny and his mother had brought up his daughter, for his wife died when she was six months old.

I had all the ground-rent and taxes on my mother-in-law's house to pay after we were married: she never paid a penny. I said to Johnny, 'Well, we'll pay that but I'm not giving her a penny for paint' – you know what the Buckie folk are for paint – 'I'll do our room but that's all.' So she bought the fine paint for the strokes, all round the bricks. Johnny painted the strokes round the bricks and put the spots on. I had a house for my bairns. They were awful folk for swearing. I had to tell my mother-in-law that I'd keep my bairns back from her if she didn't stop swearing. I hated it.

Sometimes Johnny will let out a bad word, and I said to him, 'Hey . . . I courted you a year and a half, and I thought you were a Christian man – but you aren't. You say bad words.' He said he wouldn't, and he doesn't often, because I don't give him cause.

Johnny . . . he's like the sea on a bonny day, but rouse him and his temper's vile. He doesn't enter into conversation with you. He could speak right enough about his work. He's not a singer. We were always singers – full of music.

I didn't worry when my man was at sea. My mother was a worrier. She had her man and two boys, and if they'd been to the trawling we wouldn't have had a dog's life in the house with her. But you see, I realized the common sense of it. If they were at the trawling, my mother would get a wage, and we wouldn't have had the poverty: seven shillings and sixpence a day they got at the trawling, and that was a living wage then. We had nothing, but she had a carry-on.

I didn't worry when Johnny went to sea, because he was in the Lord's care. I knew he'd be taken care of.

My son Billy was only six and a quarter pounds. I was thirty-eight when I had Billy, in the house at Boddam. Oh I wanted bairns!

When I was going to have Billy I just thought it was a sore belly. I ran to the lavvy, and I was a dozen times to the lavvy in no time, and my mother said to my brother's wife, 'Go over and tell our Mary to come in.' When I came into the house I had to take a bucket, because it didn't take away the feeling; something came every time I went, and I was always getting relief.

He was only six and a quarter pounds, and I thought my body was racked. The doctor didn't come till my last pain. My brother John got him. It was the time of the air-raids, and he was always around when the wardens came out. The second war had begun. We were married on January the twelfth 1940, and I was a year and five months married when I had Billy.

I remembered the Saviour, because it says, 'And he suffered as a woman in travail.' Our Sally had a fireguard. I couldn't lie in my bed. I was up and toddling, and I gripped the fireguard. I often remember that, the pain and the agony He suffered for us, and I understood it.

It's my faith that's kept me going. When I went into labour with Billy, with my first pains I said, 'Lord, you and me and this.' And He definitely brought me through. I just got over the bucket and started to push. My mother came through: 'Quine, rise off that pail!' I said, 'It's the only way I'm getting any relief.' She said, 'Rise, or your bairn will go into the pail!' I said, 'I'm not caring where it goes.' I was in the kneeling position and I could push. I couldn't push standing on my feet. I said, 'Go and be quiet – go away to your bed.' I gave a groan when my brother John came in. He lived upstairs you see. He was a bit bothered with his nerves: he was in the navy and went off the deep end at the mines. He said, 'How long has our Mary been like that?' He went and demanded the doctor to come.

The doctor wore a beret. He came in and took it off. 'God', he said, 'those nights – those nights!' He was wild at having to come out to me.

Billy was born with a stricture between his stomach and his bowel. He weighed less when he was three months old than when he was born. He spewed everything. They had to operate on him at three weeks old. He had eight stitches across his belly. During the air-raids – there were thirty-three people killed in one house down the street. But never mind that, it was the war and we try to put that away. Billy's a big bonny man now. He went back into hospital for more at six weeks. He had about forty wrinkles – his skin all grew but he had nothing to fill it. 'Oh no', I thought, 'he'll never come to anything.' But he did. When I got him home I could see every bone in his head. His father was away at the war. If he'd come home I would have asked him what we'd call the baby. I hadn't asked him because we didn't know if everything would be right or not, if it would come or not, and we never bothered our heads with that carry-on. I'd have loved it if he'd come back to see the baby, but that wasn't in Johnny's make-up; there was none of that fancy stuff about him ... very little romance. [*Laughs.*] What had to be, was now, and I was a good wife to him, but I wasn't sorry when we got over that bit of a hurdle, sex.

I called Billy after my father, William Buchan Coull. When Billy was born my father was the best man in the world to me, not counting Johnny Coull. Billy's in the building in a big firm in Stirling now. He's done well. His wife's got a grand head on her shoulders. He has a car and she has a car, but they're too far away to be any use to us. If we're not able to walk we can bide in the house.

When Billy was born my father was at the salmon fishing at Cruden Bay. He said to my mother, 'I think we'll give Mary her pram', but she said, 'I have four married besides her and there's none of them gotten a pram, and she's not getting one either.' I said, 'Thank you for nothing, for that's what you've given me – nothing!' She was a hard woman, but she got her eyes opened before she left this scene of time.

Six pounds, nineteen and sixpence I paid for his pram, and who was like me when I hurled [pushed] it out with him? Nobody! And I had the quinie in it till she was nearly four years old. She comes in now and says this one and that one's all dressed up, and I say, 'Hold your tongue, I'm scunnered at you, speaking about dress!' When I went out I never saw nobody like me. I was as good as any of them, washing my costume and going into the choir on Sunday, in all their grand hand-sewn silk costumes, I never saw them – I never looked. I just look at their faces. What they had on didn't affect me, and doesn't worry me yet. It's trivial – when the breath's out, where are they? With all their thousands, they've only spoiled Peterhead; they've ruined Peterhead. There's not a factory standing now where young creatures can serve their time. It's a tragedy. The fishing in Peterhead used to be something that did the whole town good. There wasn't a garret that couldn't be let, and three pounds from the curer for taking in three quines. All the women who could get out, when their bairns were running about, were at the gutting, and the shops all got their turn, and the town was full of strangers spending their earnings. A great time of fishing. It's not like that now. It's making two or three millionaires, putting their bawbees in the bank. It's all money, money, money. I never go into company because their conversation's all about it. Everything's put into money. And of course, in a lot of cases you're judged by your bank-book, and I'm gey far down the ladder with that ...

With Mary-Alice, three years later, I never knew it; I never knew she was coming, I was only three hours in labour, but with

Billy I was from six o'clock at night until half-past three the next morning. When you think of it, you wonder how you manage.

Mary-Alice was born with the cord round her neck, on our bed, with nobody in our house. I just got into bed and out she came. The midwife came and cut the cord. Mary-Alice was a treat. I could have had a dozen like her.

My mother was years and years ill, with bronchitis. My father spent a fortune on her, for the doctor charged three shillings and sixpence a call. The doctor came in to my mother that morning. I said, 'Are you going far away from home today?' He was laughing. He said, 'Are you started?' My mother said, 'You lummer, you don't tell me till you're started.'

When I had felt a pain coming I just went upstairs to the bedroom you see, and she never knew. I was supping cabbage soup when the doctor came in, and my mother had a plateful too. We were enjoying our dinner. The baby was born at half-past three.

I only went to the gutting once after I was married. I went one year to help a crew, just for seven weeks at Buckie, and left my two bairns at home, and my father gave me the rough edge of his tongue for doing that. He said, 'You'll never go and leave that quinie again.' He went upstairs and saw my daughter every night when I was away, and she was always crying. I was sorry that I did it. That finished the gutting and the curing.

I was a strict mother. They grew up to respect me. I think I was right; they had to be corrected. If I had my time over again I'd do the same thing.

I think a lot of the crime that's committed with children now is mothers going out to work, and the children are brought up any way they like. I feel a mother's place is in the home; I say her bairns have the first claim on her. But that's not the feeling now; it's the nursery as soon as they're out of their nappies, and other folk looking after them. In our day the man was the breadwinner: he went out and worked and the mother had the house and the bairns to look after, that was the old-fashioned way. And the oldest bairns brought up the youngest. You were always strung with bairns.

I looked on my mother as being a bad kind of manager, you see, because I knew what I did with my own. When I got my children I said, 'There's nobody will take advantage of them.' Their pay grew as they were working; I took two pounds a week from them for board, and never a penny more. Mary-Alice had nearly twenty pounds a week, but I never took more. They had their own bank-books, and our Billy when he was married paid a thousand pounds for a flat. We gave him sixty pounds of a wedding present; we gave Mary-Alice her wedding. I made them independent. Mary-Alice is doing the same with her quine.

When Billy was born, I had so many friends that came in with presents I had little to buy him. He had three of those romper suits that buttoned between the legs, that he never had on: they did for frocks for Mary-Alice when she came. I just did away with the buttons and took up a hem. I got so much for him I didn't need much for her.

I had the two of them at school, and a house with five rooms in Buckie, my man coming home every fortnight from the trawling with huge washings, and two old folk to look after. I sat at three death-beds.

There was a woman across the road from me who used to watch my children when I went to the meeting on a Thursday. I hadn't seen her for a few days, and when I went down she was ill. I watched her for a fortnight till she died. There was nobody else lifted the latch of her door except me. I gave the doctor the works; I said she should have been to the hospital. 'You couldn't take Kate to the hospital,' he said. 'You couldn't take her?' I said, ' – *I* took her and washed her and put her own clean clothes on and bedded her. She thought she was in heaven.' She had a daughter in London; she didn't come to her mother's funeral. She told me she couldn't afford the fare.

I had two beds: Johnny's mother was in one and her sister was in the other one. But she was fly his mother, when she saw the auntie was failing she began to get better.

Johnny's mother was a bit more learnèd than his auntie, but there were none of them bright; I was always thankful to see my boy and girl. The auntie couldn't read or write. She was a member of the Auld Kirk; she was a great curser.

Both Johnny's mother and her sister became incontinent. It could be embarrassing, especially when I had missionaries staying with me. But there was always something happened that made you see the funny side. When I would be washing things and hanging them out and there would be a spot of rain, I'd say, 'Please Lord, give me just an hour.' I always got it. Everything I sought like that I got. My Lord and my God stood with me in everything I ever attempted. I've proved Him and I call for Him when I'm in trouble.

When I was attending to Johnny's mother, she used to say, 'The Lord will bless you, Mary, for what you've done for me.' I'd answer, 'Well I couldn't do less for you: it's absolutely necessary what I'm doing. Somebody has to do it, and there's nobody here to do it but me.' Johnny was on the ocean billows. So I did it.

On the night she was dying, he came home a half-trip. I said, 'I'm all right through the day, but I can't sit up on her the night.' I had her two and a half years that she never walked. I didn't want to put her into hospital. In fact, I took her out of hospital. I got her with ten bedsores. They didn't want me to take her home. I said, 'I didn't put her here to die, I was just going to see my dying father.' He had cancer; I looked after him. I had to get a woman in to look after my mother-in-law while I went to see my father. Neither her daughter nor the quine she brought up would do anything for her.

That was Johnny's cousin. Her parents stayed across the road. Her mother died, and Johnny and his mother brought her up.

I was always healthy, never in hospital except to visit, except to get out my teeth. My mother was the same and she lived till she was two months from ninety. If I get anybody to be so good to me, when I come to be like that, as I was to her, I'll be happy. I've nothing on my conscience. I'll meet Him with a clear head. No regrets, all my life. I can't remember any big mistake I made at all; I just always think my life was planned, and what's before you won't go by you.

The thing that my mother and father were most acquainted with in all their life was poverty. They were never fortunate; they never had money. The hardship we had makes me appreciate what we have now. The old folk – they don't need anyone to weep for them; they're attended to hand and foot in these houses, and they've nothing to do. My sister, she's three and a half years younger than me, is in a home. She makes her own food, but she has a room with a carpet. We never had carpets; we had canvas and rag rugs. I made a hundred rag rugs.

I was president of the Women's Auxiliary for a year, in the

Baptist church. I go to Boddam Evangelical church now, just a wee kernel of folk. The Baptist church now, it's got a new minister, and you've got to be there by five o'clock to get a seat. The dormobile comes to the door to take us to Boddam. I'll speak all day so long as I don't have to walk.

I was twice in Canada, holidays with cousins. My cousin said, 'If you manage the fare we'll manage the holiday.' We had two trips. I've been through the Rocky Mountains, and in Victoria, and I have slides of them all.

(... My cousin had four husbands. She was awful wise. I don't know but I would have done the same thing myself so I never say nothing when I hear them saying, 'What is she doing taking all that men?' She knew what she was doing, and so would I too – of course, not now; I would never start on it all again.)

I never got a penny from anyone all my life. After I was married I saved my ha'pennies and we had a holiday every year. I never spent money foolishly. I dearly love a holiday in a caravan.

I've tried to give you the good side of me, not to decry me in your vision. I believe that the Good Man has brought us together. That's the secret, if you can trust – you've nothing if you don't trust: it makes companionship.

Josephine (left) with her sister Lydia, and her mother

Josephine Pasternak

⤞6⤝

Josephine Pasternak

'I thought that the three of them – my father, my mother, and Boris – were three geniuses. They were like three suns, you know: major sort of things in the sky.'

Josephine Pasternak was born in Moscow in 1900, the third of four children, the eldest of whom was Boris Pasternak, author of Dr Zhivago. *Her father, Leonid Pasternak, was a distinguished artist, a friend of Tolstoy, and illustrator of* Resurrection. *Her mother, Rosa Kaufman, was a concert pianist and, at the time of her marriage, Professor of Piano at the Imperial Odessa Music School.*

Josephine went to school in Moscow, then to Moscow University, where she studied natural science. For a while after the Revolution she worked as a copyist in a government office in Moscow and rose to become private secretary to the council responsible for the leather trade. She left Moscow to study philosophy in Berlin University, where she took her degree. While she was in Berlin she married her third cousin, Frederik, and moved with him to Munich. They had a son and a daughter.

In 1938 Josephine and Frederik moved to England with Josephine's parents to join her sister Lydia, who had married an English psychiatrist. Josephine studied philosophy at London University. After her mother's death she and her family moved to Oxford. Her husband died in the late 1960s, when he was ninety-five.

Josephine has published two volumes of poetry and numerous articles on Russian literature. She edited the Russian and English editions of her father's Memoirs, *and has been working on a philosophical treatise on the relationship between zero and one.*

In 1982, when I was editing the *Literary Review* and working for Quartet Books, a friend who was doing some reviewing for the magazine asked me if Quartet might be interested in his wife's translation of Josephine Pasternak's edition of her father's memoirs. He showed me the catalogue of an exhibition of Leonid Pasternak's paintings, and I liked them enormously.

Pasternak had been a friend of Tolstoy, Rilke, Scriabin; he had painted Rachmaninov, Chaliapin, Einstein – the list was exciting. I put the idea to Quartet Books and the publisher, Naim Attallah, was interested, so I went to Oxford to discuss the project with Josephine and the translator.

From the outside, Josephine's is quite an ordinary semi-detached Oxford brick villa. Inside, the walls glow with her father's paintings; every room has the magic of their life and warmth and colour, and the house is dreamlike.

Josephine herself had a warm natural courtesy that went beyond mere sociability. Little and fragile, with her slippers set to heat above the gas fire, she discussed her father's work in a strong Russian accent. She was concerned about how many of the paintings we could afford to reproduce in the book, and about the quality of printing of the colour plates. In between times she waxed passionate about the incompetence and cliquishness of Russian art critics in her father's day. When I asked her anything about herself, she turned the question aside with a mixture of diffidence and impatience.

As the *Memoirs* were being translated and going through the press Josephine and I kept in touch. I visited her a second time, and warmed to her even more. She liked my Scottishness; her son-in-law, of whom she is very fond, is also a Scot, and I reminded her of him. I liked her passionate intensity, her uncompromising intellect, and her readiness to laugh.

After the book was published we wrote back and forth. I loved it when she told me in her letters about the latest sayings of her cousin Matilda, who was in a nursing home and whom Josephine regularly visited – Matilda was about a hundred years old then, and pronounced upon people and events with a dignified, comic bluntness that reminded me of my own grandmother. But the correspondence gradually fell away because we were both too busy with our several projects. When I decided to write this book, I took it as the ideal opportunity to meet Josephine again.

She had become more frail; she ate very little and had to rest in bed a great deal of the time. She had all her favourite books in her bedroom – Tolstoy, Chekhov, poetry, and dictionaries – and she read and thought and spoke to Russian friends on the phone: 'The telephone is my indulgence', she said.

A young student and his wife were living with her (on my previous visits her nephew had been there but remained invisible). There was something wildly incongruous about sitting by Josephine's bed discussing the weakness of Aristotle's thought or the origins of Boris's *Zhivago* then going downstairs for coffee and being enthusiastically guided through the students' wedding album, or invited out to the cinema to see *Crocodile Dundee*.

Josephine sent me over to the Ashmolean to see some of her father's drawings which she and Lydia had donated to the Print Room there. Most of the time she was fretting about the suitability of a gallery in New York which wanted to hold an exhibition of his work. While she feels it to be her mission to make Leonid's paintings better known, she dreads succeeding at the cost of having him cheapened by being relegated to one of the many categories of minor artist. Her son, a distinguished biochemist, visited on the last night of my stay and tried to calm these fears, but to little effect. Next morning she was fretting again. Her devotion is absolute, and probably intensified by her sense of her own frailty.

Everything came back to her father. Usually when we notice the children of genius we sympathize with them for the burden of trying to measure up to their parents' achievements. We rarely consider that they might feel a heavier duty to keep those achievements before us until they are accorded the recognition they deserve.

Her parents were artists, and they had taught Josephine that art is sacred. She recalled in the Introduction to Leonid's *Memoirs*:

> When I was already a grown-up, I remember that in an angry mood I said to a friend: 'My parents ... you know ... even they are not absolutely faultless...' She looked at me in surprise: 'What do you mean? Did you think that your parents were the incarnation of perfection?' That, I suppose, was just what I thought and cannot help thinking to this day. Of course, they had their weaknesses or else they would not have been human, but even these weaknesses made them lovable to us as marks of their character.

She did not feel herself overshadowed by her father's and

mother's genius as one may be by parents of lesser talents and greater ambitions, yet she kept insisting to me that she herself was not interesting, and reverting to the subject of her father's work. The only way I could draw her away from this was to get her to talk about her mother. Josephine has written a memoir of her mother in Russian and poems about her. She concluded her introduction to the *Memoirs* feelingly, 'When Mother died it was as if harmony had abandoned the world. When Father died it seemed that truth had left it.' But these qualities live on in their daughter, together with the quality Josephine described when she wrote of her father's painting that he 'knew how to instil into domestic scenes, into humble manifestations of life a tenderness, a poetical note of his own'. Hers is a very gentle honesty. She is sensitive, and generous to a fault; although she was far from well, she never made me feel as if my presence was an intrusion. Her doctor had told her that she must not talk for any great length of time, to avoid tiring her heart, but she ignored the advice to help me with my project.

Because of the success of *Dr Zhivago* much has been written about the Pasternaks, in many places. Most of it, Josephine says, is rubbish. After I had interviewed her, Mr Gorbachev lifted the ban on Boris's novel. She told me that the family had been pestered by phone-calls from the press. She had made no comment, because what could she add to what had already been said? What could she say that would mean anything to the readers of tabloid journalism? She only lamented the fact that her *father's* work is not on exhibition in Russia now.

THE INTERVIEW

My life is not really interesting, at least not as outward things go. As to the so-called 'inner' life, it was a very perturbed and strange life. One teaches us that crystals break up the light in its constituent colours. Certainly the light which penetrated my so-called 'inner self' was broken up in so many colours, or anyway constituent parts, that I am at a loss to collect, to integrate them again in what might be called 'this person'.

My cousin Matilda just is 105 because she didn't write about her inner life. You see unfortunately my – how should I say? – my stupid life all consists of this little box of grey matter.

[*Points to her head.*] It works all the time, and what is worse, it works in so many different directions. What I call 'the different avenues', and the older I get, the more different and more alleys and avenues there are in my brain. Because, well, when I was young it was poetry and perhaps history, religion . . . but now it is everything – geography, history, whatever I read – then all of a sudden I have some idea about . . . let's say some writer, Pushkin our greatest poet, and I want to write about his *Eugene Onegin* that he wasn't right what he wrote – you know, things like that, all of a sudden. Then, of course, I have no time to write it down, and now being so old I am also not physically able to do all that I want to do. No, the interesting part are my parents . . .

[Josephine wrote in the Introduction to her father's *Memoirs*: 'We spent the summer of 1931 as paying guests in a country house . . . on a mountain slope over Schliersee, a Bavarian lake. As usual, my father worked enthusiastically. . . . In the evenings one had music. And then my mother was asked to play . . . when later in the evening we were back in our rooms upstairs, in a voice of pure admiration Father said to her: "I now realize that I ought not to have married you. It was my fault. You have sacrificed your genius to me and the family. Of us two you are the greater artist." ']

They were both artists of genius, but very different from other remarkable artists. Unlike with other famous people, their mark was humility, modesty, and, shall I dare to say, a kind of sanctity. Because, you see, they were interested mainly in art of course, but life had its priority. Whenever they were with art, art was everything, but they were 100 per cent *with* the art, through and through. But when life called, life had priority. And you see, as my father said to my mother there in the summer, she had sacrificed her art – she was a great artist, a pianist – to him and to her children. And we feel it all the time, of course – can't forget it. And my father also, of course, sometimes sacrificed his time to my mother, because she had a nervous heart.

They met at a soirée in Odessa. My mother was a *Wunderkind*, a child prodigy. My father might have been in the army at the time. Anyway, they met and for my father it was love at the first . . .

His parents were poor people. His mother, she came almost

from a village, but she was a marvellous woman who loved flowers and with her pennies she would buy roses. They were very much against my father becoming a painter, because they thought a painter is someone who paints houses and walls – always dirty, always having no penny to himself, and they wanted him to become either a lawyer or a doctor. To please them, he went to university. He studied first medicine – he did anatomy. It's all in the book.

My father didn't want to marry, because he thought a painter must be free. But not free like the painters who want to have so many women, and so on – on the contrary, more like a monk. He must be *absolutely* free from mundane things, and only for his painting, and he knew that a family and a wife will be something that will interfere with his painting.

I think that in the end he was so much in love with my mother, and she tried to do whatever he wanted because she loved him also like that. In the end my father had a breakdown for a whole year, and then he decided to marry.

He met my mother, and fell in love with her, but he thought if you are devoted to a spiritual thing you mustn't marry, because the family would interfere with the purity of his art. And they were the years of his, I would say, suffering, because my mother at the time was in Vienna. Sometimes they met abroad. She was with Leschetitzky, a pianist composer, a very famous man.

My mother was a girl in Odessa and Anton Rubinstein came there, because his mother lived there. He heard about my mother, because she was a *Wunderkind*, and he heard her playing, and he was *so* taken by her – she was fourteen at the time – that he became friendly with my mother and her mother. He invited them and he played specially for them, which was a great sort of thing. Then when Rosa's – my mother's – parents said, did he think she should go to finish her musical education in Petersburg, in the Conservatoire, which Anton Rubinstein and his brother founded, he said, 'No, she's much too good. There's nobody in the Petersburg Conservatoire who can play like her.' He said, 'There's only one man in the whole of Europe, that's Leschetitzky, who lives in Vienna, and she should go there.'

But my mother's life was also very tragic, because ... Then

Rubinstein said that he will help them. She had different concerts in Kiev, and other big towns in southern Russia. When they set out to Petersburg, she and her mother, Rubinstein met them in Moscow. Even in these times in Russia there were all these things with passports and papers, and by the time – she should have given a concert in Moscow, but all these official documents and so on took a long time and Rubinstein introduced them to his very great friend, a very rich woman who took over and helped them. They came to Petersburg because it took too long a time to do anything in Moscow.

In Petersburg she was introduced to the very highest aristocracy, and this, of course, made a very great impression on the girl. She came from a provincial town to somewhere where there was *brilliance* – and well, I probably could have said I even wrote a poem, a sort of sketchy thing about my mother in Petersburg. There was this very modest provincial girl with an enormous talent in her, and she met these ladies of the world, and altogether in Petersburg there was *the world*, and instead of feeling alienated from it, she loved it.

But it was a very tragic thing, because an orchestral concert was arranged, to be conducted by someone very famous. My mother, of course, was taken to different soirées and things, but she was a frail girl. These ladies were absolutely taken by her. When she played, some of them even cried, because it went to their heart. A few days before her big concert – she had played Mozart with the orchestra in Odessa when she was nine – before that, she went to some kind of party or soirée, and when she came out she was shivering. And then she was ill, very ill, and it was typhus. All the doctors who came to her, they already knew who she was. That was a terrible time.

When she came to she probably even had forgotten about the music. For her mother, it was bliss that she could talk. All my mother wanted was to look at *things*, to feel that she was alive. She was a girl of fourteen. Her mother kneeling next to her bed gave her tea and bread and butter; she looked at everything, and all of a sudden she remembered: 'Music', and she thought, 'Music ... No ... Can I ever return to music?'

She became better. The doctors said she must go to the Crimea to recuperate. She and her mother went to the Crimea for I don't know how many weeks and in this time she became her own self, and probably this process of Petersburg and illness and so on made her very grown up. She returned to Odessa; her sense of responsibility was awakened. Her humanity. That was the first thing, 'Oh, does God want me to be a pianist?' She had a very nice teacher, Tedesco.

She had started when she was a child of five or six – I've written it somewhere, but it's in Russian, I think. My mother's family was quite different from my father's family. There was always music and people – just the opposite from my father's entourage. (My father's family were poor and puritan. The mother was a very kind person; the father was a bit strict with his children and with his own life.) Her father had a soda-water factory, but actually he was a mathematician.

In her family there was a very old piano. They had a cousin living with them, a young girl, who had music lessons. My mother as a child used to creep about the piano and hide and listen to this music, and one day the teacher said, 'Why are you always here and listening?' My mother said, 'I like piano music.' And he said, 'Would you like – can you play?' She sat at the piano and played all the things her cousin had learned, by heart but properly, so that was like a miracle. Then this teacher said he will teach her. When she was eight it was her first appearance. This Tedesco, also a famous teacher, he was even known abroad, heard her. He was a Pole. Tedesco and his wife were so fond of Rosa.

Tedesco said to her, 'Would you give up your public appearances because you must take it very seriously. I will teach you and only when I find you are ready to appear in public ...', and very seriously she said 'Yes'. They had no children, so he treated her as his child, and she simply fell in love with this teacher, because he was so serious. There were a few years that she went there, and when he said, 'Now you're ready to give a concert', then she started.

When she came from the Crimea she was a different child. She went back to Tedesco. He was surprised, and everybody – her father – they were all surprised. Her appearance, everything was different: more beautiful.

I don't know how many years passed, and this Tedesco says he thinks that she would be ready. What she did, she did with all her heart, and her devotion to her teacher was so great, she would love to give him pleasure.

He said now she was ready to go abroad, and she should go to Leschetitzky in Vienna, a Polish composer and a very well-known teacher. At that time he was world-famous. He said she could give a few concerts, he would arrange it for her. She went out with her mother, and two days after she arrived in Vienna she heard that her teacher Tedesco had died, and she had brain-fever. It is my feeling that she thought that was punishment, because she only thought of her music, and she must think of those she loved: in her heart she thought she deserved it – I mean, she didn't *really* deserve it. This typhus in Petersburg and now this, her brain-fever, were sort of 'sent'. She must not think of music. It was touch and go again, this illness. Doctors thought it was the end but God granted her and she recovered. Of course, for some time she wouldn't touch the piano, perhaps for a year. Gradually she became better. But there were the seeds of all her future life, that music – she was music herself you know – she must forget about it. But then gradually, she went on tour in Poland I think, Warsaw, and they were also great music-lovers. And one time she played. She played Chopin. From this time on Chopin was her main thing. I'm speaking now actually from my own things that I tried to do in a poem about my mother – sort of sketches. So Warsaw was for her – she had the feeling she is Chopin, and she and this Tedesco were all amalgamated in one.

Then she came back home. Tedesco before he died was saying that she should have a European tour, but of course there was nobody to arrange it now. In the end she came to this Leschetitzky and she had lessons with him. She gave very soon a concert in Vienna. Her press reviews were incredible. Some wrote that her playing is better than Liszt or Rubinstein ...

I thought that the three of them – my father, my mother, and Boris – were three geniuses. They were like three suns, you know: major sort of things in the sky. And we three, my brother who is an architect and Lydia and I, were satellites. We were attracted one time to one and one time to the other. In my youth I was attracted to Boris. Later on, when we were in Berlin, I was attracted to my mother. In later times I was attracted to my father. Lydia remained attracted to the three of them. I changed a little bit more to my father's side. Shura was always more attracted to my mother.

When she and my father married – she was a complete artist, of course, she became at the age of twenty Professor for Advanced Studies at the Petersburg Conservatoire in Odessa – gradually she gave up for my father and for the family. Because you see, everything that was in her heart was with such a vehemence that the two couldn't live next to each other. She sacrificed her music. But sacrificing her music was like sacrificing herself.

They came to Moscow, because my father loved Moscow. He made up his mind that he was a thoroughly Russian painter, and Moscow was the most thoroughly modern town, because Petersburg was a little bit foreign and Moscow was the heart of Russia. They were very poor in the beginning. My father had decided not to marry and became a recluse for the painting. He sold his wonderful painting, *Letter from Home*, a painting of soldiers from life, and was able to be married with that money. My husband's father – he was my father's cousin, and he also lived in Moscow – when my father went to him and said, 'Do you know what? Tretyakov bought my picture!' He said, 'Now do you have any sort of qualms. Go and marry Rosa. You will never find anyone better for you as a wife.' And then he married her. It was a very happy marriage.

My mother thought it's not the material, sort of outward existence, but inwardly she must think only of love and so on of the family, so gradually she developed this heart neurosis. It was not a real heart illness, but a neurotic heart. As I put it in my things which I wrote about my parents, it was the revenge of her inner self for the fact that she left music and her heart illness was revenge.... But as I say, even in my own life, instead of becoming something, I became also a nervous wreck. Nowadays I believe so much in all those genes in the biochemistry. With my father it was art and with me it was religion.

My mother was a much too good mother. For instance, when we were invited to a party or something, and one of the children was sneezing, she would give it up. We had a nanny and servants.

I had very bad memories about my early childhood. I remember my nanny; she was almost a saint. She was still from the time of serfdom. Serfdom was abolished from the time she was nineteen or twenty. She never spoke about this time, I don't know. Her manners and everything were those of an aristocrat ... it's funny. My father made many paintings of her.

I probably had a very bad illness when I was six, and it must have somehow affected me without me knowing what it was, and when I was seven I remember how I used to ask my father or Boris: 'Will I die tonight?' and they would say, 'No, you'll be all right', and then I went to sleep. I didn't know, probably, what death is, I mean, but still I asked every evening. A few weeks ago when I had my doctor here, I told him that with me it's all anxiety, anxiety, anxiety, and told him about this seven-year-old girl asking 'Will I die?' He laughed and said, 'Well, if in the last eighty years you haven't learned to know that you will not die, what can I do now?' So altogether I think I'm a coward, a great coward. And if you are a coward you can't change it.

I was ten and my sister was eight when we entered school. My mother was very much against it. She was always afraid of bad influences or ... for instance, I had very long hair. If I had my hair washed the evening before, I mustn't go to school because I can get a cold. I suppose that this went along with the fact that she had made this sacrifice and didn't like our going to school. But my father said, 'No, they should go. One can't exclude them so much from everything.'

At school I was outwardly so much more liberated than I was at home. It was a much more easy atmosphere. So much so that when we had a party at our leaving school, with some theatricals ... I was small, and since I was very good at imitation, I was chosen to represent the merchant instead of a nice girl. It was like an insult, you know? So I didn't even learn my lines, and when I was on the stage I was mute. But after that, one of the French mistresses knew that I was very good at impersonations, and she said this, and I was asked to get on stage and imitate all the teachers and the headmistress in their presence. People were in stitches. After that everybody thought I am going to the stage.

There's another facet in my life. I was afraid of mice, and I thought I'd never go behind the stage. It's a deadly fear – and in Russia ... no, I don't want to speak of that.

When we went to school it was marvellous. Right from the beginning the girls in my form took to me; I had this ability to imitate. At the beginning of my father's career, they also thought that my father would be an actor, but the funny thing is, we didn't like the theatre! We thought it wasn't good enough, perhaps.

Before the teacher came in, I would get in her place and I would say, 'Vanova!' or someone, and I would imitate how she comes up to the teacher and how she speaks in a trembling voice, then how he speaks, and they were all on the floor with laughing.

I fell in love with the German mistress. She was very strict. She was not handsome – on the contrary. She liked me because I could speak good German. It was, I should say, absolutely a destructive love. I must have been twelve at the height of this. And when she spoke, the voice and everything.... Perhaps it was the same thing that always attracted me, this feeling that this person, neither beautiful – intelligent but not terribly intelligent – but also his or her own, that I'm outside and I just – I don't know how to explain it: the inner strength of these people. Frederik was twenty years older, and he was supposed to look after me a little bit when I came to Berlin because my parents were troubled when I was on my own, and he was very strict. He said when I have to go to bed and I mustn't do this and I mustn't do that, and then all of a sudden – probably he liked me from the beginning but he didn't show that – we had a long walk and he said, 'I can marry you – if you want.' [*Laughs*.] Something like that. Then, of course, he became really enamoured, then he became in love, and I became in love.

At school, I didn't have any make-up or anything – they thought I was beautiful, but a sort of plain beauty ... I don't know how to express it. I remember then there were dances, and who would ask me to dance: the teacher of orthodox religion! He was the only one.

I asked myself.... My father was absolutely in love with Tolstoy. Tolstoy was to him like an idol. But why did Tolstoy like my father so much, that he even asked him to come and make illustrations to *Resurrection*? ... I thought and thought and – Tolstoy wrote when he was very young, 'Sebastopol'. He wrote three chapters about Sebastopol because he was there when he was a young man, and in one of them he says, 'But so-and-so was not the hero of my story, nor was it the officer so-and-so, nor was it the simple soldier so-and-so. The hero of my story is truth.' Would you believe that someone would say the hero is not a man, nor a woman – this, this, this – *nobody*: the truth. And probably my father's art appealed to Tolstoy because the hero of my father's art was the truth. You can't speak of Realism, Naturalism, Impressionism, nothing of the sort – Futurism – nothing, because these are post-Movement things, but not the thing that is *in* you and can't be defined, and that is truth. And that is probably what appealed to Tolstoy in my father. I'm glad that I found this ... comparison, because otherwise you couldn't understand why he sought him out. He worked so much on the illustrations that he had a slight nervous breakdown, simply out of tiredness.

My mother played to the Tolstoys and the Countess wrote one day afterwards to my mother, 'Somehow the spirit of your playing is still in the house.' I have a book downstairs which Tolstoy's wife inscribed to me. The one I remember is Tolstoy's daughter. She came when I was eight or nine. The funny thing is that I remember people who went to see my parents when I was a schoolgirl, and I remember what they said, and you see altogether, when I was a very small child – I have a very bad memory actually, but what famous people said I somehow remember. I remember the Tolstoys' daughter – we were sitting in the drawing-room, and they were talking and she said, 'Of course, you know how my father is, he is such an *anti*-feminist, he thinks women should sit and knit or mend socks.' [*Laughs.*] But with Tolstoy it is not as simple as it sounds.

Religion came in. Prayer and so on. And the trouble – you see, I always try to show people that I am not so stupid and so on – you know, I mean more or less normal. Some don't believe, some laugh about it. The trouble is that probably I am 50–50: 50 per cent rational and 50 per cent irrational, and they fight all the time. You see, if you are irrational, just religious, it's OK. Or if you are rational it's OK. But if they're balanced 50–50, you're

neither one nor the other. And, of course, the minute when I'm
rational, I feel guilt: I feel that I am sinful. And sometimes I
know that – I think it's called the original sin? – I feel the
original sin, and people say, 'How can you, a clever person? I
mean, believe in original sin?' And I do.

I kept getting in love with people when I was a girl. Perhaps so
they didn't know that I was in love with them – that sort of
thing. And when I was thirteen we spent the summer in a very
nice place. The Russian owners of big estates, they used to go
abroad in the summer, and then they let the house. Perhaps a
very big house of the eighteenth century to two, perhaps three
or four, families. My father liked this sort of thing, because
there were very few people. He didn't like what is known as
Russian *dacha*, they were little places where there were lots of
houses and people – you know, theatricals and music and so on
– he couldn't stand it – and so we always went to a place where
there were very few people. Anyway, I fell in love.

First of all when we came there I was only thirteen and it
probably was the awakening of myself more or less, and I
remember the main thing was the birds at three o'clock in the
morning, and the fresh air. It was like paradise, the whole
business. So it was a very, sort of, wonderful summer and I fell
in love with someone.

He was the cousin of the composer Scriabin, but he was quite
different. He was an officer in the army, but also he wanted to
become *what* he was. He was double my age: he was twenty-
eight. I didn't say much, but everybody knew that I was in love
with him. He had a sense of humour and so on.

The next year, we came there, and he and his mother were not
there, so that was terrible – but anyway, we were there.

And then, the war started, and *that* ... I can only say one
thing, you know, there were big alleys – the linden alley, the
birch alley, and so on – beautiful places. One day I went and I
had a kind of Kleenex with me, which I had in my hand, and it
was nowhere. There was no wind, there was no rain – there was
nothing – and it was gone. I was absolutely shattered. I didn't
know what that was.

Every day when I went for my walk I went to the clearing and
started looking around. It wasn't there. Then all of a sudden the

war started. When it was declared, I thought it was the greatest sin, and I being part of humanity, it's my sin too – you know, a girl of fourteen, instead of going to dances and so on, these things must have done quite a lot of harm to me. I went into this clearing and said, 'God, if you are there, and if you forgive me, let me find this bit of paper.' And I bent and it was there. And I called it a miracle. All through my life. He gave me a sign.

But also from this day onwards I thought I must do things – penances. From my fourteenth year I started to do it, and that was not easy. On the other hand, at school, I was regarded as someone very jolly and I loved my friends, they loved me. My main thing was imitation and people always thought I'll go to the theatre or something. That was an absolute split of the personality really – but I never showed it. I thought I must react to life as if I was absolutely normal. I could do it.

But meanwhile I also did *frightful* things for these self-imposed penances. One thing I tried all through my years, and sometimes I succeeded, was not to sleep till the morning. In summer nights, which are very short in Russia, I did it. It went on year after year, which was perhaps why I suffered so much from insomnia later on.

I said to myself, when I will be sixteen I will have done with the penances, and then life will begin. But this non-sleeping business. I couldn't have done with it. So when I was sixteen I still had to do it, and whereas I was jolly at school, in my nights I was in a terrible situation.

I didn't like to speak about sexual things so I will not speak about it, but, however, there were probably some difficulties with that, at nights.

I believe in God. And miracles. But I had too much rational feeling, and that rational feeling leads me to this guilt of 'Oh God, you *are* there, but ...'.

When I think that I believe in God, I believe in Jesus, but I don't believe in the spirit. In Russia there were quite a few sects, but the main thing is the Trinity. But I somehow have the feeling that this Trinity is a Greek influence – the *logos* and the Spirit were confused, and I think that the *logos* is pagan, and it has influenced Christianity in a very bad way, because, well – I think the Greek *logos* has contaminated two things: science and religion. It was a very pagan thing; it was the human mind, which we don't know anything about, and it was *added* to Father and Son. Aristotle thought that *logos* can be the creator and the created. Now, you can't mix up the created and the creator. After all, we never know what the creation *will* be, and Aristotle thought that he can make a sort of diagram – a syllogism. Very simply: if Socrates is a man, and if all men are mortal, then Socrates is mortal. But in order to know that Socrates is a man, already implies his mortality, so it's a circle. So nobody ever discussed it.

Of course, the English empiricists felt it somehow, that the whole basis of logic is nonsense, and everybody was a bit afraid. For instance, Bertrand Russell, who was very revolutionary – even he didn't want to shake the whole business. Then they started speaking in mathematical logic, where everything is in symbols instead of words, but they forgot that the core of the thing is deduction, and if this deduction is called logical it's nonsense, because we never know what the mind, what kind of deduction it will make. So I'm writing now that instead of speaking of mathematical logic, which is nonsense, one should speak of mathematics. Because mathematics is a conventional thing. It's not a natural truth. It's just for our convenience. Therefore everything that speaks of the Spirit is very uncertain. And if I say I believe in God, it's just that I believe in God who is not knowledgeable, but I believe in miracles. Now I find that modern science says more or less the same as I'm saying. They can't define things. For instance, the wave and particle theory: is light waves, or is it particles? One of the physicists invented the word 'wave-icle'. Physicists don't like it, but it's just it.

We had a Russian philosopher, Feodorov. He had a philosophy which was a crazy one. There will be resurrection of the body – with atoms and so on.

More and more I know that everything is biochemistry, but not the *logos*. But what can we do? I can't stop thinking it's some computer, but who works it? God. Who can understand it except God?

The only thing that I should have done and haven't done is that probably I hoped that there is time ... there is time. And I had the same thing as my parents, this feeling of life's priority. So you see, first it was my parents, the priority of their – I did incredible things because I thought, well, I have to do it:

penance but also this feeling. . . . For instance, this place we went in the summer, when I started having all this religious guilt, I wanted – I thought, 'Oh God, make my mother live!' I was fourteen, I suppose and I thought, twenty-eight years. . . . 'Make my mother live till she is . . .' – I don't know how old, but you have to do something.

I had to go to a forest, a very typical Russian birch forest . . . something in nature which you can't describe, the time when the sun goes down but it is not down yet, when there is not day – then it is the Greek Pan's . . . he rules it. When I went to this birch wood, it was just such a time, and I became *panicky* and I was afraid. There was nobody there and it was a few miles from the house, and I thought, 'Oh, I must return I must return! I can't do it!' But then I still did it. I went through this thing, trembling like anything, for my mother to live so many years. I can't remember what I had to do – kiss the ground, I suppose – it was the usual thing. I went back. I don't remember what I did for my father, and then one night for my grandmother. This went on into the years I was already in Oxford, things like that.

When I was twelve I remember how Boris used to come to the nursery and he would read to me or talk to me. I remember how my mother from the other room would say in the evening, 'Leave the children alone, they have to sleep! Go away!' He would read to me perhaps, poems by the Futurists. He would read to me one or two of his poems. There's a letter that he wrote to me while he was in Marburg studying philosophy.

The things that have been written – the amount of books about Boris – stupidity and so on. I didn't write anything, but then a few years later I was slightly annoyed because people thought this *Dr Zhivago* business was a continuation of one of his earlier pieces, which was unfinished, *The Childhood of Luber*. I thought, I *will* write something and I did. In the *London Magazine*. It is from what I call the horse's mouth. I know, and Boris talked to me and so on, different things, different situations, before he wrote this book. About female beauty. When I was a child he used to talk to me. And I thought, good God, now I will write what I think, because I didn't like the *Zhivago* very much. Some places, yes.

The biggest change I have seen in the world was the change

made by the Russian Revolution. None of us were politically minded, so that although it was a big change in the world, it was not such a big change in our everyday life. My father continued painting. He, of course, painted Lenin. He got a permit to go into the Kremlin so that he could paint different things – meetings and so on.

I remember Scriabin. He was a terribly sensitive man in his music. He spoke of the arts, that they should get together in a conference, between music and colour and so on. I remember a few months before his death he was in our place in Moscow. He had lunch with us; there was only he and my parents and I. My father and Scriabin started talking. Scriabin said that the arts must come together, and he spoke of a piano that every key you touched, certain colours should come up. And my father said no, that's a very bad idea – altogether arts should never interfere with each other.

I was so much with my father, because each art has its own language, and the minute you – and you know what, one time I was reading Tolstoy and he was speaking of – I must find it – he says, 'Of nothing has been said so many stupid things as of art, painting, because art and language have nothing to do with each other, and that's why so much stupidity is going to be said by art historians.' I made a note ... Tolstoy and Chekhov, these two I know them by heart, so to speak. No – that's something from Seneca ... I can't find it because I'm trying too hard. ... But also in *Anna Karenina*, in the scene where Anna Karenina and Vronsky look at the pictures of the painter in Italy, Tolstoy says, 'They spoke softly, as people at exhibitions. You will find people speak softly because it's too easy to say something stupid!'

Things were simpler when I was young. For instance bribery, which one finds now in art. You see, one always thought that the commercial world is bribery, and the business world, but I find that in the arts, perhaps because it's even more shocking – I don't know what kind of bribery, but I find in the arts there's something not very pure.

I had my degree in philosophy. It was something called 'experimental psychology', and the whole thing – I started thinking of it while I was still in Moscow. I went along the Moscow river; it was in winter and there was this fantastic red disc of the sun, and very cold. All of a sudden, while I was walking, an idea struck me, something about – it was more a kind of mathematical–philosophical thing. The zero and the one and the relation between one and zero. Then, of course, I forgot about it, and then when I finished school I spoke with my brother Boris, who was in the Philosophical Faculty in Moscow and found it a bit boring. He found the Marburg philosophy much above the Moscow business. When I finished school both my father and Boris said, 'Don't go to the Philosophical Faculty, because they won't teach you anything. Go somewhere which has to do with science.' The funny thing is, probably I was interested in science, but I wasn't mature enough, or I didn't have the capacity to concentrate, so I went to the different lectures in natural science, and I couldn't get on with it, so I made fun of it.

In 1920 I was bored with always being at home. Everything was difficult. We did everything ourselves. I was never exactly starving, but on the way to starving. Sometimes, especially in Moscow or Petersburg, you couldn't get rations. I was never strong, so I did the lighter work in the house. It was a very boring life. I was also at university but I didn't like the lectures either. I thought I would like to have some office work, some work away from here. Someone said they knew where I could go, not far away from our home. But the mother of Olga Freidenberg, who had this correspondence with Boris, and the whole family too, were terribly proud and also a little puritanical, at least the father ... when she heard that I was going into an office, she said to my father, 'How *could* you let your daughter go into an *office*, where she doesn't know what sort of people she will meet! It's terrible that you could *think* of a thing like that!' And she was right.

First of all a man interviewed me: 'Do you know what incoming and outgoing correspondence is?' I said no, I had never heard of that. And he said, 'What! And you want to come and do something?' But the man who had introduced me said, 'Oh quiet, quiet, she will learn very quickly.' So he said all right.

But the first day I went there, it was just what my aunt was horrified about [*Laughs*], because it was a huge hall with different tables and people sitting at the different tables doing some clerical work. One girl shouted across to the other, 'Well, how was the outing?' And the other answered, 'Oh, it was fine! I had on – oh, say rather I *didn't* have anything on.' I was absolutely delighted to hear such talk after the puritanical upbringing where you mustn't even mention the word 'love' or anything. Then, since I had this gift for imitation, I very quickly got the different people who said this and that, and I gave sessions of imitations when the man wasn't in, and they simply roared. I remember, I was always late. In the morning I would never get there properly. The supervisor was a real communist. He was always in black; he carried a revolver, and wore boots ... but a small man, he was a Jew. I felt sorry for him, because he wanted to make himself very majestic and I don't think he could do it. But he was a member of the *Cheka*.

One morning I was late again, and he said to me, 'Comrade Pasternak, if you are late one more time I'll send you to the *Cheka*' – that was like a prison, you know – and he looked at me. I knew that he liked me, and so I said, 'Oh, heavens! Not to the *Cheka*,' I said, 'because there might be rats there!' and he couldn't keep from smiling. He turned away to smile.

Very quickly I came from copyist through second grade to first grade to the central something for some industry. I didn't care, I just wanted to be away from home, you see. And also I got a little bit more of butter or sugar. I was there for a year then I decided to go abroad to read philosophy in order to be able to say that philosophy is nonsense and there is only Christianity. [*Laughs*.]

Before I went, there was the main bureau – I became the private secretary to the council or something, the highest for the leather business. I could have reached something there, and become more or less prominent.

All of a sudden I had the feeling that I must go abroad and study or read philosophy, in order to show that philosophy doesn't give the answers and only Christianity does. I thought, I will become a preacher of Christianity – absolute rubbish! I went to Berlin. What I did to my poor mother, you know, because there was no postal exchange yet. When I went there, the first thing I started trying to get was visas for my parents. I succeeded. They came in a few months' time.

A revival of pure Christianity ... I tried – I started reading philosophy. Nothing came of this. (Theology is the worst thing that can exist in the world, because theology is somehow connected with Aristotle. He was a genius in other things, but in logic a fool.) But this thing about one and nought and about something actually connected with maths ... I started writing something worthwhile while I was in Munich, and gradually I developed my idea; it is epistemology. But also I had a nervous illness. I had a very good professor in Berlin. He was the one who went away when Hitler came, and he was teaching in America. Kohler, Wolfgang Kohler. He taught the *Gestalt* philosophy. That was quite interesting, because he did not stick to all these Aristotelian things, and he was a very handsome man.

I know that he didn't like me. I don't know why. I had a friend there. She was of German origin, she was an emigrée probably. I think he loved her and she loved him. She committed suicide – must have been '23, '24 – she tried three times to commit suicide. The third time she went into a forest and drank poison and died there. When she tried it the first time – she was still sort of high-spirited – I once went to see her. Her family was very rich. She and I sometimes had these sessions of psychology. We laughed at it and made jokes together, and didn't think much of it. She was a very jolly one. Psychology ... I knew that it was a bit mechanized. There is no real psychology now, I mean.

I was in this *passion*, then and I continued with my non-sleeping. But there I had the light on and read, and again I couldn't do it. I was fed up, and I thought, 'Now, it's enough.' I was, of course, a coward. I would never have committed suicide; I don't think so. I said to myself, 'I'll go out, and the first people I meet, if I'll hear the word "life", then it's finished: I don't continue with this kind of penance. God has forgiven me. But if I hear "death" – or something like that – then I must finish my life.' Ten minutes or so I was walking, then two women came and I heard the words they said: ' ... Yes, of course, life is like that!' So I went home and I said, 'That's OK – finished.'

I was extraordinary, let's say. I tried to live up to the figure of a very normal person, and my husband was a very sane person –

what I call abnormally normal – and perhaps that's why I felt so protected by him, just because he was so normal. He was much older than I – twenty years older. Someone brought me a little sketch-book that I had been given when I was six years old, to make my paintings in. I found on one page, where I was just learning to write, a sentence, 'I would like to see Frederik' – and I was six. So it was probably fate.

My husband was my third cousin. He was very fond of my parents; my parents were very fond of him. He used to come to Moscow to visit us. I fell in love with him in Berlin. It went on a few years then – oh yes, then the religious things came in and I thought, I must not marry, I must become a nun or something, you know, and that was also up and down. Then he went to Munich and I thought, oh well I can't stand it without him, so I married him – but that's a thing on its own, another chapter.

When I came to Munich, he worked in a bank. He was not a banker, but he worked in banks. And so we had a sort of typical bourgeois flat – you know, all that sort of thing. But I was not interested in this. I was interested in university and so on. Then, of course, the usual split of my personality was very outspoken, because when I went to do my psychological tests at university I was one person and everybody thought ... whether they knew or not that I was married – and when I was with Frederik and his friends it was quite a different person.

I was twenty-four. Then, of course, I thought, 'Now life's finished. I am twenty-four and a very old person ...' I found out that before I was married men had a life before they married, and women were not supposed to have such a life, and that made such a ... it was a personal experience, I mean, I needn't talk about it with my husband, and all of a sudden someone from his former life ... a whole year I couldn't look at films, I couldn't read, I couldn't speak, because of knowing there are women whom people desire because they've been mistresses, and that made me sick, and very gradually I sort of recovered from it because I spoke to different people. My younger brother in Moscow – they came to visit – to our doctor there, he was our friend. His son, Schmurel, was the one who Hitler shot – the White Rose Movement later on, you know.

This Dr Schmurel, the father of Schmurel, I asked him, 'Tell me, is it true that men can't exist without having these mistresses?' He said, 'It's not true. I never had one. My first wife was the first woman.' So that made me feel a little bit better, that the world is not constructed like that. My younger brother also said he never had anyone except his wife.

It was the feeling that some women are treated like a lavatory. It was this feeling that, how can men after that think that they are noble or so on.

Oh goodness, my whole life was a repression, more or less! And feelings of guilt and so on. And when I married my poor husband – he proposed every week and I said yes one week and I said no the next. Because I was in love with him, but I thought it was a crime to marry. In the end I married because he got a very good post in Munich, and he would be going away from Berlin, and I couldn't stand it, so in the end I said yes. One doesn't speak of these things ... you wouldn't believe it, but I put a golden cross on me the night of my marriage and I prayed so that I should remain pure. Only many years later I knew that something was wrong with me. I mean, I was very sexy but there was no – it was only by imagining things but not in real life. I became like stone. I gave satisfaction but I didn't have any. But on the other hand I didn't mind. It was not revulsion. These things are very complicated.

Although I was not brought up in the orthodox church, my first night with my husband was spent in prayer to the Mother of God that I should remain pure. [*Laughs.*] My husband didn't notice anything. He was not very sentimental. He wouldn't ask me what I felt. He was very kind, but ... probably organically there was something wrong with me. I was very emotional. I thought that perhaps it was his fault, although he was very potent.

If the woman has an orgasm, then the woman should not be monogamous. But, of course, the main thing to me is that the partner should know. One should not do it secretly. If the partner knows, they either part, or he accepts it, she accepts it, and why not? Even in *Anna Karenina* she has different dreams when her husband and her lover are together and she thinks, 'Why not?' I am absolutely also thinking, 'Why not?' Of course, men, probably, their constitution is somehow more sexual than women. Not all of them.

There is platonic love; there is sexual love; and there is simply love, which is in-between somehow, and I don't know how to combine this love with sexual desire. Somehow I feel that they don't coincide. When all of a sudden someone appeared with whom my husband had an affair before he married me, and he wouldn't let her into the house, and I saw that, I was so indignant that I tried to find this woman in Munich but couldn't. She wrote him a letter. She wanted to blackmail him. But I was on her side. And when I remember a man who had sort of courted me a little bit – he was an Austrian aristocrat, we were friends – we went somewhere and spoke, and he said, 'I wouldn't like to be your husband, because you would like me to be faithful to all the women I had before I met you!'

The Berlin period was very fortunate for my father. The government gave him a permit to go temporarily to Berlin, because of his heart trouble. My parents became friendly with the Soviet Ambassador, and my mother played sometimes at his soirées. My father painted his wife. My father got commissions to paint the diplomatic people, and that kept him going.

My mother had to be present always when my father had models, so that they had a more lively expression, so she talked to them, or she played the piano, and for instance, she played the piano to the anarchist Kropotkin.

When my father painted Einstein we lived in a rented flat in Berlin in the twenties. My mother was busy with something, so she could not come and amuse Einstein, so my father said, 'Could you come and amuse Einstein?' I started talking about philosophy, and then all of a sudden Einstein started laughing, or anyway, a beautiful smile, and my father said, 'Ah, that's good, good! Remain like that!' Of course, he wasn't listening to what I was saying, and Einstein said, 'Oh!' he said, 'Your daughter talking of philosophy reminds me of these experimental dogs by Pavlov! They are showing meat, and salivation starts. Your daughter speaks of philosophy, and for a few years I haven't thought of philosophy, and now she makes me think of it again!'

There were so many things like that.

AS: Did you want to have children?
JP: That's a question I can't answer. That's one of the questions that I don't want to . . .

I was afraid ... I think the whole business with maternity feeling and so on – I didn't feel it. Though, mind you, Boris's wife came and I gave all I could to my nephew when he was three or four. And when he went away and I saw a child there were floods of tears, because I had this feeling, 'Oh – !' But then I had the feeling of fantastic responsibility, and how can people – my first illness was a little bit connected with this. ... Will they find life acceptable, and this sort of thing.

I enjoyed being with my children. I was very much with them, although they had a nanny. I was sometimes two hours, three hours, playing with them. That was not because of duty but because I felt somehow that playing funny games with them was good.

But my parents: you wouldn't think that artists would lead such a very modest life. Of course, it has something to do with the Russian intelligentsia – the sphere where they moved was very unobtrusive, you see. I had already my children in Munich, so I was a grown-up woman, but when my parents came to visit and when they saw that I had a cigarette – *'What*? *You*? *Smoke*?' I was over thirty. Or they'd say, 'Oh, Josephine – don't use *lipstick*!' So when I was a bit flirtatious or something, well ...

One thing I remember when we came to Britain first is that one day we were asked to tea by someone in the British Museum, the director of the print room. He knew my father's work before he met him, and he bought a few things for the British Museum. ...

That was a terrible time, the first winter in London – we weren't used to that sort of thing. On the continent we had proper central heating. We had to find to live somewhere; we had not much money. We found a few rooms, it cost thirty pounds a year. We had part of the house, and someone lived above us, but she had to go through our flat. We were ill, especially the females ...

The summer came, 1939. The man invited us, he was a music-lover. His daughters played the violin and so on. He himself was also a painter and played some instrument. We were expected to have tea with them and to play. He said he wanted the Quintet of Schumann – and so my mother started preparing, doing exercises. And honestly, when she did her exercises ... she remembered that she had played this piece as a girl so many years before in Moscow – my father writes it was her swan-song. It was already pure delight to listen to her. It was a very long way, so we had to go by bus. We had tea. Everything was very English. There was no table-cloth. There were three girls and their father. After tea we all went to the drawing-room and they started playing together. They were all very astonished, because my mother looked a very modest, middle-class woman, and then all of a sudden ... she played Bach and Chopin, because they asked her to play solo. When she finished she *never* made any fuss. She would get up and smile a little smile, as if to say, 'Did you like it?' – absolutely as if she was not an absolute genius.

When she played I felt a real pain in my heart, because I had the feeling Mother, who had this nervous thing, and now she is playing like someone absolutely strong, and playing like a genius. And when she plays she goes on to somewhere else, not here with us, on a height where she is alone where nobody can follow her, and this feeling that nobody can assist her on this height, on this absolute solitude – so when she is finished, I was really suffering.

While they were playing my father made a sketch of this man's wife, and gave it to him. So we had to go back by bus. And then when the bus came the man helped my father to get in, not my mother. And this I *can't* forget! I simply can't forget it. Because he knew my father's name, and my mother, who was a greater genius than he, he didn't know about her. Then in two months' time we went through that part of London with my mother's coffin. ... I didn't like the word 'happy'. I'll tell you why. We were in Bournemouth. I was with the children. It was our first year in London. We were ill. The children were ill; my mother was ill. It was a time when one was afraid of Hitler's war coming. Many people went to America, and Frederik also said, 'You must go to America.' My parents lived in a little flat in London, and my mother, of course, thought it would be the end if we went away, so I didn't want to go. Anyway, the doctor said that I and the children must go somewhere because we'd been ill with the English cold. One day I went with my children to a park in Bournemouth and we sat on a seat. All of a sudden I felt like fainting – a *terrible* feeling, so much so that the children looked at me and said, 'What is it mother?' Then I got a little better and we could go with the bus back home. In the afternoon I sat with them at the beach. I met a friend, and I said, 'I am happy now, because we are not going to America.' In the evening Frederick rang and said that my mother had had a stroke. And since I had said the word 'happy' on this day, after that I avoided the word. For almost half a century I can't say the word 'happy'. It is excluded from my vocabulary.

A week after my mother died the war started. The worst time in my life was my mother's and father's deaths. The best time was when I wrote poems; when I became a poet. I was thirty-four or thirty-five. I wrote before that but I knew that my poems are not real poems. (This year is the first year I haven't written poems. Up until I was sixty-five or so I could write poems.) But I wouldn't like very much to talk about it, because again, as everything in my life, it is something not quite normal. Perhaps if I fell in love, but nothing came of it, it was not real. Chekhov, when I read him it is as if he wrote things connected with me, or about me. One short story, a young man falls in love with a young woman who is married, she has children. She says to her husband at one point, 'Look, let's travel', and he says, 'But oh, my dear, I must go to my business. If you have this feeling, go abroad, but I can't go with you.' She says, 'No, you must go with me', and he says, 'You know I can't. Why do you want it?' and then she says, 'You must do it because I think I have fallen in love with someone else, and you must save me from it.' He says, 'Oh Olga, what a fantasy! Who is he?' She says, 'I needn't tell you the name, but it's enough to tell you that.' He says, 'Oh, you're imagining things.' It was as if Chekhov had heard me talking to Frederik. Mainly you are in love with people who are not in love with you.

When we came to England, and I was thirty-eight, I thought, 'Well then, my life's finished.' Because then I had so much to do and there was nobody to help. It was difficult to live, and then the war started. I never thought that I could have another husband. It was then that I started being so close to Frederik, and he was already fifty-eight. But I never had sexual satisfaction. We lived together till he was ninety-five and when he died I knew that life was over – even before that – but then it became a kind of fantastic ... like they used to be in Victorian times, you know? At one time I even thought that *he* might be bored, although he was always telling me things. When he was young he didn't show his love so much as when he was older. He was in love, but he wasn't at all demonstrative. We were very, very close. The funny thing is, that I always thought that my husband was more superficial, you know, being, sort of, in the bank. People asked him once, why don't you write your memoirs, because he'd been in Russia and he was old, and he'd been in different banks in Sweden and Germany and with different people, and he answered, 'I'm a simple man. I'm not Montgomery – let *him* write his memoirs.' The most revealing thing was, when he was already ill, in bed, and I praying and kneeling, and he looked at me, he smiled, and he said, 'It's difficult for you to establish connections with Gabriel.' And I thought, 'God!' Because, you know, I was always thinking that my prayer ... I have to repeat it or do it differently. That's what made me sometimes ill. In fact, I think my last nervous breakdown was because, you see, my nanny – I had learned this kneeling of the orthodox church.

Kneeling, kneeling – and at the time of kneeling I mustn't think of this and I mustn't think of that, because I'm afraid something might happen to, not only my own family, *anybody* – a neighbour, you know. And the last few nights I was kneeling many times, and I was tired but I kept doing it because I thought I was doing it wrong, and I thought '*Again, again, again*!' – that will bring me a heart attack, and it came a few days later. Of course, I didn't tell it to anybody. It is connected with my nervous illness, all this anxiety.

I am a coward because I don't like to die, I suppose that's my cowardice.... When my husband died I was next to him the whole night, kissing him all the time – that's also strange.

I wrote recently. All of a sudden I noticed that in physics nowadays there were ideas which were very much like mine, but I approached from an epistemological point of view, and they from the scientific, but at a point we said the same thing. I showed it to Mikey, who is a mathematician. I said, 'Tell me one thing: is it nonsense or not?' He said, 'No, it makes sense.' And I said, 'If you say it makes sense I shall work on.' He said, 'Yes, you should.' My friend who is in university in Denmark, a pupil of Karl Popper, is very interested in it.

All this going to the moon and so on, how could human nature think of such things? I say in the end, that the miracle also is, that nature, or the human mind ... that mathematics is already *given* somehow, and the human mind simply imitates: it is somehow an imitation of mathematics. I call my work 'Indefinability'.

I had the feeling that my husband and my cousin Matilda thought I was a fool when I was typing it. I had the feeling that they think I'm a fool because, what does she want to do this typing for, instead of making a nice cake?

The Russian language I associate with art; we had a German governess so I started speaking German very early. The English language I associate with philosophy and politics and all this, sort of, very objective knowledge. Lydia's translations of Boris are the recreation of poetry. She also writes poetry. If I write something I'm always not satisfied with what I have written. I have all these dictionaries. That shows I feel at home with three languages. Sometimes even something strikes me in French, and I sometimes spend the whole day finding the right word, looking through all my dictionaries. When I think, for instance, I should go and stay with my daughter, the question is, can I play around with the dictionaries – I must have them all.

My poetry is as if I was simply a tool which puts down on paper something that is beyond me. When I have arranged my father's exhibition, I will concentrate on my own things, my third volume of poems.

Kathleen Tacchi-Morris

7

Kathleen Tacchi-Morris

'Because God doesn't do it, somebody's got to do it.'

Kathleen Tacchi was born in Johannesburg in 1899. Her mother had been a nurse and her father was an engineer–inventor; they had two sons and three daughters. Shortly after Tacchi's birth her parents returned to London. Tacchi attended Acton Central School, from which she was expelled when she was ten for leading a strike against excessive caning. She then went to boarding-school near Manchester but was again expelled, this time after only a month. The rest of her education was conducted at home.

When she was fourteen Tacchi began to work in a draper's shop in Leytonstone. She soon moved to a haberdasher's in London's East End and became a buyer there, but when the First World War broke out she worked for the RAF in London. At the end of the war she was working for Aquascutum in Regent Street. After the war she became a typist for a film-booking agency in Wardour Street. While she worked there she played small roles in a variety of silent films.

Tacchi had begun to study dance when she was seven, and when she began work she continued to attend evening classes, by then to study the Dalcroze method of Eurhythmics. In 1922 she went to Paris to study with Dalcroze, and opened a tiny studio of her own there. Later she danced in America to earn enough money to open her own studio in London. Eventually she had studios in Hammersmith and Notting Hill Gate. She continued to dance in France every year, and managed a troupe of dancers.

In 1936 she married an RAF officer and moved with him to Malta. The marriage was a failure and Tacchi returned to England to open a school in Somerset teaching Kallirhythm (a new system of dance she devised) and managing the teaching of drama, sculpture, and painting. During the Second World War Tacchi took in the illegitimate children of black American servicemen and English girls. She was married again in 1944, to an estate agent. By 1949 she had wound up her school and was lecturing on dance all over the country.

In 1950 while lecturing in Sheffield she accidentally met Picasso, an old friend from her dancing days in Paris and Nice, at a peace conference. Picasso persuaded her to involve more women in the peace movement, and she started Women for World Disarmament, which she ran until 1987.

In 1986 I wrote a series of articles for the press about abuses in residential homes for the elderly. A researcher from Central Television's programme for retired people, 'Getting On', contacted me. I told her in passing about this book, and she urged me to interview Tacchi, who appeared on one of her programmes about elderly peace campaigners.

When I phoned Tacchi it was like speaking to an old friend. We arranged that I should go down to interview her after she had returned from a trip to London in connection with her organization, Women for World Disarmament.

Tacchi lives in a rambling fifteenth-century manor house outside Taunton. She could only walk with a crutch because of a long-standing hip problem. We sat in the kitchen with my photographer and a German translator friend of Tacchi's from the BBC's World Service, round a huge refectory table. Tacchi's husband Rod, a gentle, frail little man of eighty-nine, could not seem to do enough in the way of hospitality. It was more like a party than an interview in the end, with Tacchi's iconoclastic asides causing great hilarity. In the face of the AIDS scare, we invented a new organization, Women for World Condoms. Her humour is always to the fore, and her habit of hospitality was evident from the comprehensiveness of the range of cooking materials on the shelves that surrounded us in that huge kitchen.

Next morning I spotted John, an alcoholic ex-army officer whom Tacchi and Rod had taken into the fold. He was in charge of the garden, Tacchi told me. On subsequent visits I would catch only the odd glimpse of him. There was also a middle-aged rough-and-ready Birmingham woman who had run away with her lover and children. At first she had lived in a caravan on Rod's land, but now he had loaned her a cottage. This woman came in in the mornings, washed a few dishes and, probably, made the beds. To maintain a house the size of Tacchi's properly would have required a full-time staff of two or three.

The great difficulty in interviewing Tacchi was to get her to talk about anything other than Women for World Disarmament. Everyone she met was roped into her campaign somehow – when she went to the hospital for a check-up, she was recruiting the nurses. In the end I had to bargain with her to speak about her past life, and ended up almost before I knew it as press officer for her organization. Tacchi has great charm of persuasion, and she is relentless in her efforts for disarmament. In one letter with a list of addresses and instructions about people and organizations I should write to she added: 'Here's £10 to help with the stamps – I sold a cockatoo today!'

When I next visited her she had injured the ankle of her good leg and was bedridden. Rod had severe circulation problems and was attending hospital as an out-patient, and to crown it all, some of the water-pipes in the house had burst in the freezing weather. Tacchi had a camp-bed in what had been a maid's room above the kitchen. She occupied a corner in a sort of literary hibernation, surrounded by heaps of papers and journals.

Her little dog, an old chihuahua which had survived the days when she used to breed them and donate the proceeds to the peace movement, nestled in her lap under a hand-towel. Tacchi was as optimistic as ever; she did not seem to mind in the least that she could not use her bedroom, which was too far away for Rod to toddle up and down and attend on her. She soared above her circumstances, buoyed by a sense of mission.

I had seen Tacchi's own bedroom on my first visit. It was perfectly, in every detail, what I imagined a filmstar's bedroom of the 1930s must have looked like – all glass and lace and fine things, with a four-poster bed: it was stunning. There were little pots and jars of lotions and potions that have not been manufactured in decades.

Add to this the large aviary of tropical birds beside the back door and a beautiful rose garden, the old barn that had been a theatre when Tacchi had her school, and the picture of glamorous country living in a bygone era is complete. Inside the house, among its splendid furniture, the dining-room had some of the Kaiser's silver, a plate painted by Picasso, and the fridge where Tacchi kept the tonic water for her evening G and T. But then all over the house on odd tables here and there, where you might have expected to find faded copies of *Punch* and the *Tatler*, were piled solemn, dull English-language magazines from Eastern-bloc countries. I tried to imagine what Tacchi's Russian visitors must have made of all this, and failed.

Rod, of course, as an estate agent and landowner, was a dyed-in-the-wool conservative, but he did not hamper Tacchi in whatever she wanted to do. He simply financed it all and adored her, treating all her guests with the quaint, extravagant courtesy of another world, while effacing himself from the whole proceedings. Tacchi said he was very like the Duke of Windsor, whom she had known in France. Rod was small and neat in the same way.

Her own background could not have been more different from Rod's. He was the son of a long line of estate agents and auctioneers, established in the same village time out of mind. Her father was the son of an immigrant Italian gilder, based in London; her grandmother was a French opera-singer.

Tacchi gave me a copy of a cutting from the *Somerset Gazette*, which, to mark her parents' diamond wedding anniversary in 1958, had carried an article about her father, 'The genius of Mr Tacchi (aged 83)'. It describes Tacchi's father as 'traveller' – he had spent five years in China, in charge of a Hong Kong shipyard – 'engineer and inventor'. At the time the article was written Tacchi's parents lived with her, and her father used her attics as his workshop. He was engaged in improving a thermostat that was about to be produced for use in industry, simultaneously with 'a revolutionary development of a motor cycle engine' and models for a sailing-boat that would travel directly into the wind.

Mr Tacchi had designed the TAC motor-cycle for the Wilkinson Sword company early in this century (he thought he was the first person to be fined for exceeding the ten miles per hour speed limit in Hyde Park in 1900). He gave the reporter a demonstration of his new wind-assisted bicycle. At one time, Tacchi mentions in her autobiography, her father worked with George Bernard Shaw on a plan to harness wave power to produce electricity.

Tacchi's father met Shaw when they both belonged to the Secular Society and then the Fabians; Mr Tacchi was a passionate socialist of the Shaw and Wells type. Tacchi went to their meetings with him when she was a child, and I think it must have been there that she imbibed her enthusiasm for making the world a better place, enthusiasm so strong as to be committee-proof, but so individualistic that she had to start her own peace movement.

The second time I visited her she was engrossed in her plans for the trust she was setting up to turn the house and grounds, after her and Rod's death, into an international centre for youth, to promote peace. She was also making the arrangements for a joint meeting in the House of Commons with Women for World Disarmament and the Campaign for World Disarmament, prompting her supporters by letter and phone. WWD was to be merged with CWD at that meeting, and Tacchi would retire. Preoccupied with this, she grudged the time spent on reminiscing to me. She told me I could read it all in the autobiography she had dictated, 'I Promised Picasso', which, like Alice's memoirs, is much too short as it stands to be published as a book, but which she will not take the time to expand. When I suggested that she ought to fill it out in more detail, she said I could stay with her and ghost-write it – 'I could tell you so many stories if you lived here' – while, of course, working for Women for World Disarmament.

In London for the meeting she stayed at the flat of an old friend, a communist journalist in his eighties, who had organized a wheel-chair for her. In previous years (for decades,) in fact, on her visits to London) she had always stayed at the Strand Palace Hotel, but this time she could not have coped. Only cast-iron determination and charm had got her to London in the first place, and the same qualities got her back to Taunton, for the vicar who had promised to call for her did not materialize. I told her this was an effect of her atheism.

She had taken pity on me and brought some brochures about her various schools to put me more in the picture. There were leaflets advertising the Tacchomo School of Dancing, Drama and Music's ballet classes in Bayswater; the Tacchomo School of Theatre Training in Notting Hill Gate – 'Summer courses in Expressive Dance' and the ordinary courses, which ranged from Kallirhythm through ballet to tap and acrobatic dancing. The Hammersmith school had a drama and arts club, aimed at 'bringing together a group of people who are interested in the Drama and Allied Arts'. The club's premises boasted a writing room and the Tacchomo sandwich bar. It was non-profit-making, and its programme for winter 1931 included a performance of original Grand Guignol plays by Anthony Armstrong ('A.A.' of *Punch*) and others; a tea dance and cabaret; a talk by Percy Allen on 'A Case for Edward Vere, 17th Earl of Oxford as Shakespeare', a piano and cello recital, and a fancy-dress ball.

Pamphlets describing the aims and syllabus of the International School (Tacchomo) show how Tacchi's ideas developed. She describes the school as providing

> A complete progressive, co-educational upbringing for boys and girls from 3 to 18 years of age (day pupils or residents) providing either
> Scholastic training of high standard enriched by wide artistic and cultural attainments
> or
> Practical preparation for theatrical and artistic professions combined with thorough general education.

In a remarkably foresighted programme she set out, through 'subjects such as Mathematics, History, Geography, etc.', to establish 'a world-wide view in the children's mind ... to form a new subject, "OUR WORLD", from Geography, History, Science and Religion'. She explains that the syllabus

> is so designed as to show the development of the human race together with the animal and plant world, the history of our planet, our early struggles and subsequent inventions, the various religions, ideas and arts of mankind, leading to our life of today. This new subject ... will lead to visions and experiences far beyond those reached in the normal separate courses.
>
> Our academic instruction ... aims at ... the development of the child into a responsible adult with a grown-up mind ...
>
> Tacchomo has a world outlook in make-up and policy. Pupils and staff are drawn from many countries and deal with the world and mankind as a whole. Differences of race, class and creed are replaced by realization of all the common factors shared by humanity the world over.

Her description of the principles on which art will be taught at the school shows how advanced her thinking was:

Before it is possible to teach technicalities, it is essential for a child to achieve a degree of co-ordination of mind. Under the guidance of a qualified art teacher experienced in child psychology and welfare this can be achieved if the instruction has an individual relation to the child's psychological peculiarities, leading it from the subjective scribble to the objective picture.

Period touches only come in when the note of subjects taught to pupils leaving school include 'Rationing', or when the list of fees states 'Own wireless 1/6 per week'. The influence of Tacchi's father is seen in the inclusion of evolution as a separate subject.

F. J. Corina went to Tacchi's school to lecture the students on evolution and wrote about it in *Freethought News*:

From the moment I arrived, the importance of my lecture receded in my own mind in contrast with the importance of what I have found. I had known about Tacchomo but had not previously been there, and my experience of the school during a few days' stay made me feel I had been in the centre of one of the finest experiments in education.

Tacchomo is a private school, set in delightful surroundings, in which children are not taught to live, but learn to live – an important distinction – and do so in an atmosphere free from the disturbing effects of religious instruction, which can often contradict so much that a sensible child may learn about life, and frequently disturbs the psychological balance by emphasizing religious differences instead of human similarities.

This does not mean that Tacchomo could be described as a school 'where atheism is taught', as some unthinking people might quite wrongly describe it. Apart from the fact that a non-religious attitude is not something that can be taught in the sense that religion is taught, the position of the school is simply one of neutrality to the question. At Tacchomo one finds in actual operation the principle for which both Free-thinkers and fair-minded Christians have contended for many years. That is, recognition of the fact that questions of religious belief are personal, or alternatively sectarian matters, and that no body of teachers, selected for their secular qualifications, could possibly give representative religious teaching to suit a school of mixed children, or even undertake general religious instruction without imparting a personal bias. This applies even more strongly to Tacchomo owing to its international character.

So at Tacchomo we get the 'secular solution' at work. The policy is, no religious instruction at school, no religious duties to be assumed by the staff, who accept the status of neutrals in their relations with the children.

Parents who wish their children to have religious instruction may make their own arrangements with the authorities of their own denomination outside the school.

To ensure the harmonious working of this system the whole staff honour the neutrality policy, and the wisdom of such a course becomes evident when it is known that the staff varies in outlook from a Freethinker to a Russian Orthodox, and an Anthroposophist! It is also a tribute to the personal integrity of the staff that so fine a toleration can be displayed.

All of which reflects itself in the free, happy and tolerant spirit of the children themselves, who, instead of growing up to regard each other as 'peculiar' because of different religious ideas, grow up with an understanding of their differences, which enables them to co-operate in essentials while retaining freedom to think for themselves.

Miss Kathleen Tacchi (Mrs Tacchi-Morris) is the principal of the school and Mr Richard Stuttaford is headmaster. Miss Tacchi is an outstanding type of woman, with a high faculty for understanding and getting the best out of children, a quality developed, no doubt, from her experience as former principal of 'stage schools' in London and Paris, when she had more than 500 children under her care.

Her methods are not freakish in either one extreme or the other. She does not accept the idea of imposed discipline nor does she accept the 'complete freedom' idea of some other experimental schools.

At the meeting in the House of Commons, with Dame Judith Hart in the chair, flanked by Tacchi and a very earnest Russian woman who spoke like a robot on one side, and two equally earnest American women who spoke like earnest American women on the other, Tacchi stood out vividly. She wore bright lipstick and a matching red jacket (which Rod had bought her for Christmas), and she radiated vitality and good humour. To see her there was like coming across Dietrich on Greenham Common. She was completely incongruous, and I wondered how in her heart of hearts she stood the technicality and the worthy boredom of it all.

But of course, the• trust she is setting up is really a continuation of the school she ran, and the school she ran, although she was not conscious of it at the time, was sowing seeds of international harmony. It all comes together to further a cause that is instinctive to Tacchi. She said in a speech to the Business and Professional Women's Association in London on Remembrance Day, 1958, 'I have lived through two world wars and more and more I have become convinced that we have done too much remembering and too little learning! I speak as a citizen of my own country and of the world, but also from the viewpoint of a woman. It may be a biological advantage or an emotional one.' Her vision carries her through.

Rod died in January 1988, after spending Christmas in hospital. The next month the United Nations Association's Taunton branch, of which Tacchi is founder president, had a meeting to present her with a bouquet to mark her eighty-ninth birthday. Professor Erich Faubert, chairman of a UNA branch in the GDR, delivered a message from the Mayor of Weimar, expressing that city's esteem for her 'untiring work'.

Tacchi may have retired, but there are few signs of it as yet. She went to the World Congress of Women in Moscow in June 1988 as usual, and as usual broadcast on Radio Moscow while she was there.

THE INTERVIEW

My mother and father met in South Africa. My mother was about nineteen when she went there. She was training to be a doctor and she thought, well, there wasn't much hope for doctors in England that were women. I don't know if she had qualified before she got married.

There was a little hut where my father was living. He was looking after the machinery in the gold-mines. My mother passed the funny little house on her horse, when she went for a ride before breakfast. She smelt burning once or twice and went into the house, turned over the steak or whatever it was, got back on her horse, and rode off again. This happened two or three mornings. My father wondered what had happened – he was outside washing. He wanted to see who it was turning his food over, and that's how they met.

My father started making bicycles with a man named Wright – Tacchi and Wright. They made bicycles for the negroes because the poor people used to have to walk for miles.

He got typhoid. My mother nursed him. They fell in love. Well, there were no other white women out there anyway to fall in love with. They did pretty well together. They couldn't find anyone to marry them, because there were no churches where they were then. They got General Von Brandeis to marry them, a Dutch general. So I've got an idea that in England I'm probably illegitimate, but I'm all right over there. I'm not really sure, but I can remember my mother saying to my father at one time, 'Don't you think from the legal point of view we should get married again?' when I was quite grown up. He said, 'If you think I'm going to make an ass of myself at this age... '. I don't know whether I'm illegitimate or not, and I don't care two hoots!

My father's mother was a singer, Ellen D'ath, French, and his father was Italian. The Tacchis came from Bellagio in Italy. They were all inventors. It's the funniest thing – although they didn't know each other.... What is it that makes a whole family inventors? Now, my brother can mend anybody's watch. My father invented the first motor-bike with four cylinders – open-framed ... I used to race it for him on the sands in Wittering. His father was a gilder. He gilded the Lord Mayor's coach and the Royal Barge. After my father had served his apprenticeship my grandfather gave him a hundred pounds and sent him to South Africa to make his way.

Later on he invented independent springing for cars and all sorts of other things. If he could have kept them all, he would have been a millionaire. But to preserve the patent on any invention you had to pay an annual fee, and he couldn't keep it up. He used to have to sell one invention to finance the next one and enable us to live.

My Mum was very English, the only English one in our family. She had been working for a white negro called Pullinger. That was about the time when the Jameson Raid was being prepared. Pullinger was on the side of the British against the Boers, and she saw how they were bringing in arms from England and hiding them in the ground and planting maize on top.

Her father was on the side of the Boers. He was killed in the Boer War. My mother joined the Boers. She carried a pistol and once the train she was travelling on was stopped and searched by the British. She hid the pistol under a carpet and she told me how she waited in suspense. One of the soldiers pulled up the edge of the carpet, but did not see the pistol. Another woman had her hair done up in a tall bun, and she hid her pistol in the bun. The soldiers found it and she was taken away, almost certainly to be shot.

There were five in the family. I was the first one, and there were two sisters and two brothers. I was the odd one out really, because at that time my father was very much with the Fabians. I was taken to all the meetings, but the others weren't, so we had different ideas altogether. Isn't it extraordinary, one family, how different we can be?

One sister was too good-looking. She drank herself to death. She was the youngest one. My mother and father were very clever, having girl/boy alternately.... The others didn't do any of the things I've done. They led quite different lives. Next to me was a brother who's still alive. He's an inventor up to a point; then comes a sister who was a pain in my life. Poor thing, it was an illness, a jealousy, because she wasn't very good-looking and she was always so upset with me. I had a hell of a life with her, because she was fighting against me all the time. I tried so much to make her interested, and get a job and work at something. The next one was a brother, who is still alive. His love is yachts and the sea. The youngest sister was very beautiful. She's the one who died of drink – DTs and the lot. She hadn't got any intellect whatsoever. She went from one man to another and they were all drunkards. As a matter of fact, I got her into a pantomime, because I was producing the dancers for pantomimes. When it came to the time – she couldn't do anything; she was put on a shell like a mermaid and pulled across the stage, that's all she did. So she could say she was in pantomime. Crikey! I laughed so much!

Large families were normal in those days. One of my grandmother's sisters had thirteen children. They lived in a large house with a lovely garden and they formed their own orchestra. The mother played the piano and the children learned various instruments. The father made a lot of money selling handmade ties for gentlemen in fashionable Jermyn Street.

Acton was still mainly country when I was a girl and the new houses all had steps. Every Monday a woman used to come round to hearthstone the step. We had to step over it all the week till Sunday, when it was due to be cleaned the following day ... for the life of me I couldn't understand why this cleaning was necessary.

We had rather more excitement than most children. Father had a house built in Nemours Road after selling an invention but soon money ran short and we had to let the bottom part. We children slept in the attic and father fitted a rope so we could slide down to the road outside. It was designed as a fire escape but we preferred to go out that way.

Father was a wonderful person. And Mother was. Quite different – she was all for health and be careful. She never came to the Fabian meetings, but she made sure I was all right and got back all right. They were a wonderful team though so different.... When I think of Sunday evenings, we'd sit round the fire and he'd teach us evolution, then the bell rang and the muffin man went up the road, and my father gave us money to go and get muffins and we'd toast them in front of the fire while he taught us. It was heaven.

There was a cupboard under the stair where he used to do photography. He made his own camera. The photos are still there – the old days of motoring. He used to get us kids to see ourselves in colour upside down. Underneath his bench he had a theatre for me, with little dolls made out of clothes-pegs. He made us stilts, then higher and higher. When we had a flood in Acton, I was walking along on stilts, and my father said, 'Be careful, keep on the pavement, or you might go down a drain. We went to school on stilts, and nobody else turned up because they couldn't get there. He lived till about a hundred.

I had a lot of long golden hair. My mother used to get so

angry when people came up and said, 'Isn't she beautiful?' 'Don't keep telling her that – she's not beautiful at all!' She said to me once, 'How can you be beautiful? Look at your nose, it's too fat.' I said, 'Well, what can I do about my nose?' She said, 'You can have an operation.' I shut up after that ...

... I remember my grandmother going with me to market once. We came back with some lemons we'd never bought. They were always pushing things on to you. The man said, 'Saul Sandy, Saul Sandy!' ('It's always handy'). I said to my grandmother, 'Where did we get the lemons?' She said, 'Saul Sandy!' They had flames lighting the stalls.

My grandmother had a sense of humour. Her family came from France. They had something to do with materials – Schulbred and Ath. That old uncle used to take my grandmother to Paris once a year to buy for Schulbred. She knew Madame Patti. They sang together once at Buckingham Palace.

I was turned out of school. I organized the first strike that ever was in a girls' school. But I wasn't only turned out. So was the headmaster. He did nothing else but beat children up, if they giggled or whatever they did. He was awful. I got so fed up with it. My hands were so sore that I could not use a knife or fork. My father wrote protesting, but his letter was ignored. I remember the exact words of the report I brought home: 'Ellen Tacchi is at the bottom of the class, the lowest in the school. She is frequently late and does no homework. Her poor work is but the natural outcome.' My father put 'QED' at the bottom and sent it back. I was put in the boys' class after that, because I was 'not fit to be with the girls'.

There was a woman teacher with nasty runny sores on her face. She would pick them then take my pen to show me how to do something. I wouldn't touch the pen, you see. So she sent me out and I was caned until I couldn't hold anything. I thought, to hell with that. Mother came in to me in the night and said, 'Why aren't you going to sleep?' I was making yellow bows for the kids that were going to strike. I got the chair from the headmaster's study, put it in the playground, and got them all to strike, so that nobody went into school next morning. There was a hell of a do about that, then he was sacked and so was I. Then when Mum tried to get them to take my young sister into that school, they wouldn't take her, yet she was such a nice little soul – she wasn't a bit like me! I was about ten.

Mum sent me up to Manchester to a boarding-school. There was a little girl there – what she did I don't know, but they put her in a corner in the evening and forgot she was there. She was there all night. I'd just been turned out of the other school. You can imagine what it was like when I kicked up hell about that! So I was turned out of that school, and Mum said, 'I don't know what to do with her.' My education got a bit, sort of, limited.

I learned shorthand typing in Inverness when my father was working there and I learned Gaelic. Why my father sent me to that I don't know. But I had more education from my father than ever you get at school. On evolution and everything. I went to all the Fabian meetings with him, with Bernard Shaw and H. G. Wells and all that lot. I think he thought I ought to learn what was going on.

Wasn't I lucky as a child to meet all these old thinkers! Shaw and so on ... I knew Rebecca West very well. The last time I saw her she was the guest of honour at a Business and Professional Women's luncheon in the Connaught Rooms. She said, 'What on earth are you doing with this bunch of women?' I was president of the thing for Taunton then.

You see, when I was at school, my father wouldn't allow me to go into the religious classes in the morning, so I had to stand outside the door like all naughty children used to have to do, until it was over. On Sundays at teatime we used to sit on the floor and my father used to teach us evolution. We could ask him questions and he brought books on evolution and so on. Then he told us about the different religions and he said, 'It's for you either to choose one, or not have one, or what have you. That's all I know to tell you children.'

So of course, I've never had a religion, and I wouldn't know which to pick in any case. I used to ask, 'Well, where's the god? Where are they?' Like I asked Tereshkova. When she came down from space I was invited to Moscow and I said, 'Did you bump into any angels or gods or anything? What did you think when you were up there?' She said, 'I looked down and I thought what a wonderful world that was. Why does anyone want to blow it up?' I've never had a feeling ... I think a religion is a kind of crutch, and if you need a crutch of some sort, that might be all right. But being a dancer – and I used to paint a little as well – I suppose that was my crutch, I don't know. I suppose we all need something, and if you don't use your brains very much and you feel you want help, perhaps it's a good thing to get hold of a god. I've never understood it – I've never needed it.

My father used to take us to different churches. When we went to the Roman Catholic church I said, 'Doesn't it look beautiful?' And he said, 'Yes, and it smells beautiful. That's the way they do it. They play on all your five senses, and they've got you.' I understood all that at a very early age. Then he used to take me also to the Freethought Society's meetings, at the opera house near the BBC. It was *packed.* There used to be that funny old girl who was an atheist and then she was this and that – Anne Besant. I knew her very well as a child, and of course Bernard Shaw and H. G. Wells. So I was brought up in this atmosphere, and it seemed to be so much more commonsense there than the other ones. It was for me to choose and what choice could I have? It was obvious to me.

At school the girls did nothing in the playground. I'd climb the walls, join the boys, and start playing cricket or something. They put that down to a *sexual* thing! That went against me too, when it came to the court or whatever they did to the headmaster, they said, 'She's got some sex trouble.' As a matter of fact I hadn't any at all; at that age, it didn't occur to me. My father had told me everything, which frightened me to death – I didn't need to be told any more what I might get.

He started to tell me about plants and animals and evolution and sort of gradually ... except that I used to think, way on when I was quite grown up, that babies came out of your navel. And then the crude thing that happened ... I was working in a film company (that'll tell you how long I still thought that babies came out of your navel) and I said to the girl, 'Well, where the hell *do* they come out of?' and she said, 'Same way as they go in.' I mean, I was working in Wardour Street, in films! It was an awful shock. Now they show you the baby popping out on TV.

You know, I'm wondering about this sex education they keep talking about. I don't think you can generalize, because some children get an awful shock with the truth. If only parents could do it gradually, like my father did with me, according to what the child's like, because the whole thing could affect the child for the rest of its life.

The kids I had here I did it with rabbits. We had hutches and they would write down which one was crossing with which one. Then sometimes they would say, 'Do people do that?' and you'd say, 'Yes, they do.'

What was so interesting for me was being mixed up with the suffragettes, because my father used to take me to their meetings. I knew a lot of them. They were forbidden free speech in Hyde Park. My father took me there. I can remember them with walking sticks and umbrellas, knocking policemen's hats off in Hyde Park. They'd be dragged down by the police, then another one would come up, and I got so excited I fainted.

In those days in Marble Arch there was a big Express Dairy. My father carried me there and gave me a glass of milk. I came to and insisted on going back again. I always remember the excitement of seeing women against the police. Really being *hit* by the police, and didn't they fight back!

He used to take me to Tower Hill too, to hear Ben Tilliot speaking for the workers. The thing I remember most is, he was up there trying to get sixpence a week more for the miners. Now can you imagine that?

We lived in Essex at the time. We took a cottage in Chigwell, where one of the Pankhursts lived. As a young girl I had tea with her there, and my father, I was so lucky to have all that, because later it tied up with my work for the Peace Movement.

On Sunday evenings we used to go to the Albery Hall when G. W. Foote used to speak, and the man before him – Bradlaugh. The secretary of the Fabians in those day was Blanco White. Mrs Blanco White was the original of Wells's Ann Veronica – Amber Reeves. She had a daughter named Justine by Wells. I don't know why names are coming back, because I can never remember names.

I always knew I wanted to be a dancer. I had my first ballet lessons in a place over a baker's shop in Acton, when I was very young. In those days you'd got to pay for the lessons. Later I got a job in the East India Dock Road selling in the drapery department. An old woman named Longehey whose daughter married Ponting's daughter.

First of all I got a job at half-a-crown a week in a draper's shop in Leytonstone. My grandmother had money, but my father was against anything coming through from her to me, and he was right. There were times when my parents, because my father depended on his income from inventions, had an awful time, so I used to run and get a job. It's amazing how I got jobs without any trouble ever. I don't know whether it's because I used to go in and smile.

In my first job I used to cycle from Woodford to Leytonstone, to get there at eight in the morning, dust the boxes and things before the shop opened at nine o'clock. One day I went somewhere where there was no lavatory paper, only newspaper. I was sitting there looking at the newspaper and there was a job advertised in East India Dock Road. I got that, and I used to go round to their homes, the Chinese. Oh, I learnt such a lot from that – the business of how they struggled and how clean they were.

There used to be a restaurant not far from the police station, where I used to go with some Chinese. One night there was a terrific to-do; the police came rushing in and I saw somebody running and pushing something in a fire bucket. I kept quiet about it. The police never found it. I suppose it was drugs.

I was in the baby-linen department. Longehey called me in and said, 'Don't you think you're too good for this? You'd better work with Auntie Yeomans.' I thought, 'Who's Auntie Yeomans?' She was the person who did the buying. I went round with her learning how to buy. They had lifts like boxes all on top of the other, and you had to run in while they were going.

All the time in the evenings I used to go to the Zelka school, because there was one a night I could go to. That meant I had to cycle from work right up to Stove Street, just off Tottenham Court Road. I got special permission from the old man to come back late.

One night I got back there were police and God knows what going on. I had to go through another woman's bedroom to get to my bedroom. She had a baby that night. There was all this going on, with the police asking who the father was. Where she had kept that baby I don't know. She hadn't looked a bit bigger.

They called him 'Tommy English'.

That old man was good to his girls really. I used to go and sit in his office and talk to him. He would say, 'How is it you're doing this job? Why aren't you doing something else?' I'd say, 'I'm doing something else presently, but just leave it for the time being.'

In the First World War, I went to Hotel Cecil and worked for the Air Force. Hotel Cecil was Air House then, in the Strand. My father had invented a new engine for an aeroplane. I was with my father talking about it with a Major Thomson and he said had I got a job and I said no and he said, 'Why don't you come and work in Hotel Cecil?'

My work was getting there at nine in the morning; at ten o'clock you had coffee, then you talked to somebody or other, and then an officer asked you out to lunch. You'd go to lunch till three, then you had tea at half-past three, then an officer asked you if you would go to dinner with him, and another one would ask if you'd go to the theatre, and I'd catch the 12:05 home from Liverpool Street to Wanstead, where my grandmother lived. Every day that was my job in the air force. That was my war effort. . . .

My father was against war. They called him up. He waited in a queue for a bit and then he said, 'What am I waiting in a queue for?' and he went forward, and they said to him, 'You wait in the queue', and he said, 'What for, I'm busy!' So he jolly well didn't. Then they called him up. He walked out and said, 'If you want to have a go, have a go, but I'm having nothing to do with this at all.' He never heard another word. Isn't that extraordinary. I think he shocked them so much, because they said such silly things to him and his answers were so good, I think they thought it was better to let him go.

He went up to Inverness, where he produced engines. He was so angry, you know, how they put it into the war in the end – something he didn't agree with. It's awful when you think about it. Any good invention, the war machine is after it. It's not for the people, it goes into the war machine.

Do you know, it's the worst thing for a girl to be beautiful . . . since I'm older and all that's gone, I can look back on it now and think, 'My goodness what a drawback it is.' I could get a job anywhere, as easily as anything. How unfair it is! They don't know whether you've got any brains or not; it doesn't make any difference.

It's just as though I've been through more than one life. Because the theatre side was like one box, and my war 'effort' was like another life, then the film work I had – I think somebody sent a photograph of me, and that did it. It was awful. They were trying to get me to Hollywood, and the men that tried to get into bed over that – it's really disgusting. I don't think it's a nice thing to be good-looking at all.

I had never been to bed with a man until I was twenty-three, because I was too busy being in the ballet and theatre and things like that. Also, you see, I developed a method for children who were disabled. I used to teach in the Maudsley Hospital. It was passed by a doctor called Arbuthnot Lane, who was very well known in those days, as a cure for these children. But then, you see, I had got so much theatre to do, and they wanted to get me to go to Hollywood and make a sort of star out of me, and I thought *you'll* be lucky – and get me into bed. I hadn't been to bed with anybody so I wasn't interested. I hadn't *time* to go to bed with men in those days, and I wasn't in love with anybody.

What started it was because I got a job. You see, Armistice Day I was at Aquascutum, in the office, dealing with wages. I was looking out of the window into Regent Street. You can imagine what it was like then – it was terrific. We were given the sack to make way for the men coming back. I phoned round different firms in the West End and said I heard they wanted someone in the office, to try and get a job straight away.

One that answered was a film company in Wardour Street. They said they didn't need anyone, where had I heard it from? I said, 'I didn't, I'll tell you the truth.' Then I had to ring up afterwards and say, 'I only have your number – I don't know where you are.' It was Weston Import. They were doing Fatty Arbuckle, *The Twelve* ... something ... *Beauties*, all this rubbishy stuff. I went in and saw him and got a job straight away.

I found myself then in Wardour Street with all these film people. One of the producers who did a lot in the firm, from Kansas, was the man I fell in love with. They put me in charge of what they called 'the bibles' – that was a long book that made sure you didn't have cross-overs for the films: double bookings in cinemas.

It was before that I was in a film, with Nelly Taylor. It wasn't much of a part. That was through dancing. That often happened to me. I'd go somewhere, and somebody would suggest something, and I'd say, 'Well, I'll go and see', and you go and see and you find yourself involved in something. That's what happens if you're good-looking. I had a small part in *Coming Through the Rye* and I was in some of those cliff-hanging serials with Pearl White, and *Men are not Gods*.

I knew Douglas Fairbanks and Mary Pickford. I've got their pictures downstairs signed.

One of the bosses had a Rolls Royce and a chauffeur, and they used to send me to places in that. There would be a film just coming out and they'd say, 'Get Tacchi to go to Keith Prowse', and order I don't know how many tickets. It was an absolute swiz you see, to look as though it was popular.

There used to be a flower-shop next to the Ritz. When they knew Mary Pickford was coming they'd send me to get a lot of roses so she could throw them out of the window, in Wardour Street. They used to have to hold her up to get her over the crowds into the car. What a to-do it was! Oh, it was a scream.

The only snag was their fight to get me involved in the films. I wasn't interested. What I was doing was much more fun. At the same time I was going to the Dalcroze school to get more lessons in eurhythmics. Then my grandmother said, 'You'll have to get out of this and get to Paris.' She eventually said to me, 'Do you want me to give you money now, and go to Paris and have a proper training, or will you wait till I die?' I said, 'Please, I'll have it now.' So she arranged for me to go to Paris. I was just out of my teens. I wanted to be a dancer because I had an animal instinct for dancing. I'd been working hard at trying to learn dancing before, but Paris did the trick. I went to the Dalcroze school. Of course, through that I met all those people – Diaghilev, Picasso. . . . That was 1922.

I had a little Douglas motor-bike. My father bought me that and I took it to Paris with me and I used to get a horse to ride, near where I had a room in a hotel.

It didn't occur to me that there was anything special going on for me then in Paris. What was so extraordinary was that old Jacques Dalcroze thought I was beautiful, so when he had special tickets to go to the Opéra, in a box or something, he used to say to me, 'Put on your best clothes now, we're going to the Opéra.' So people began to think I was somebody. I was nobody at all, just one of the students. I expect a lot of it came out of that – sitting in the box with the big Dalcroze. We were great pals. He was a grand old boy. Somehow or other I got pushed into the Diaghilev lot. I think it must have been at Isadora Duncan's parties. I used to go there on a Thursday – a lot of us from the Dalcroze school used to go. She had a place in St Honoré. Her brother Raymond – he was daft – anyway he owned that place. He'd got umpteen wives that he dressed like nuns, and the nuns used to run the shop down below, with vegetable dyes – they made all sorts of things and sold them.

I think Isadora Duncan was daft too, quite frankly. I mean, all right, she'd got something, but she really wasn't mentally fit. She did things – for instance she danced with no tights, which was a terrible thing to do in those days – her bare *legs*. I think she was right – it felt right, and tights those days were pretty awful anyway. I think she might have been all right today when she could have done sensible things. I was doing a dancing exhibition at the Negresco in Nice when she was killed. That was in 1927.

I had a letter from some people who knew James Joyce and knew the daughter Lucia. I knew the daughter was a little bit something wrong with her head and I knew she was terrible – she used to cry and go on. Well, I knew James Joyce before because he used to go to Isadora Duncan's dos, and I met him there. He was a bit sort of, gruff. He told me I was a beautiful thing and that I walked like Dante's Beatrice.

In the *Observer* there was an article about Constant Lambert and his wife Mouse, whom I knew because she was a dancer. She was in a ballet called *The Green Table*. They used to come down here and stay. I wrote to the *Observer* and said, 'Can you tell me where Mouse is? I'd like to write to her.' He said he didn't think she'd want to give her address, but if I sent a letter for her he'd forward it. Then it came back that she'd had a stroke, and her son had committed suicide, but she telephoned me, though she could hardly talk. She was so thrilled. She said,

'What we'll do is have lunch together sometime.' But I haven't heard from her since. I don't know what's happened, and I haven't got the address. Poor old Mouse has been through it rather.

I got to know Picasso because as a dancer – he used to do our décor – so he knew me as a dancer. So how he thought I was going to organize a peace movement, I don't know. He had a verandah in the South of France, where we used to dance in the moonlight. It was lovely. The scent of jasmine used to come at night. He painted a picture of me in the *moonlight*, which was extraordinary. An American who was staying in Antibes bought it. I don't know where it is. Nobody knows what happened to it.

In Antibes, by the water or in the Hotel Vatel, Picasso and I used to sit and talk about peace and disarmament, with bread and big tomatoes and a carafe of wine, with all sorts of people who were around. It was fascinating to see Picasso at work. He would take a bite of sausage from time to time and I often thought he was eating more paint than sausage. He couldn't stop drawing. On anything. During the war he hid because of being a Jew. He had nothing to draw except the roofs outside (by the way he gave me that and I've sent it off to the GDR – I gave them the whole back-cloth he made for my theatre). And he had a tomato plant in a pot, and he drew it as it grew.

I knew Jean Harlow very well in Antibes. In 1922 we were dancing in the ballet at Monte Carlo, and we had Antibes nearly all to ourselves. You know about Davidson, the millionaire who made money out of Kodak? He lived in a castle in Harlech. Margaret Morris, another dancer, and I used to go down and dance sometimes. Davidson said to us, 'Why don't you go down to the South of France, find a place down there that we can open up, and let's have that as a place in the Mediterranean where you can go and live and dance and have a summer-school, or whatever we want!'

So we went down. We found an estate agent. He went all round the coast to find what we wanted. He found a partly built house. The King of Belgium had been going to build a place there but the war broke out and he didn't go on with it. Davidson bought it, and built an open-air theatre and an indoor theatre. He had a big organ put in the music-room. It was a marvellous place.

There was a very good photographer named Fred Daniels. He had to make money out of his photographs, and he sent them to America and the film stars started to come.

The son of the man Sellar, who owned the whole property, Andrew Sellar, was a marvellous ballroom dancer. Even after I married Rod he was still there. We went down there in the car. Rod was frightened to death – there was a flunkey came out to take the luggage, and we had the Duke of Windsor's apartments with all the gadgets in. Rod said, 'I don't know what the hell you think you're doing here!' They had a card up – two hundred pounds a night bed and breakfast or whatever it was. Well, I knew he wasn't going to charge anything, because I used to dance with him, but anyway Rod was frightened to death. I said, 'For God's sake shut up Rod!' We were given a special place down near the rocks next to the Queen. Rod got fed up with it all. Oh dear, it was funny!

I had a studio in Hammersmith in the 1920s. It belonged to the King's Theatre – so I could always use the theatre as well. I had a school there, then it got too big for that studio, and I took on another one as well, down the Fulham Road. There was a theatre, which was built by an Italian, who was a sculptor. He bought a bit of everybody's back gardens and made a little theatre there, and a bungalow, and he let it out to me, so I was able to use the theatre and live in the bungalow. So that was nice.

In Brook Green in Hammersmith, where my studio was, I was sitting in the park one day and I saw a little girl dancing and jumping around. I called her over – she looked as though she could move well – and asked her if she had learned dancing. She said no, and I asked her whether she would like to – she would. I went to see her mother and she hadn't got any money, but I took the girl on and trained her. Later on she performed at the Folies Bergères and got married in France.

I used to dance on skates. I was skating in a place called Wanstead Pond. I was living with my grandmother in Wanstead then. An officer came over and said, 'Oh skate with me, will you?' and I did, and we had a wonderful time. He saw me home, went in, and saw my grandmother. He was a very good-looking boy, and he started to fall in love with me. He used to go and see my grandmother. At that time I was working with Longehey.

My sister was a baby really. My father had an accident on his motor-bike, and I was looking after my sister. So when the officer asked me to go to shows, I'd wash the baby, put her to bed, and Grandmother would look after her. She was a determined youngster. She was in love with this boy, the officer. We used to laugh about it.

When I had the studio in Hammersmith she was doing nothing. I said, 'You can live in the studio if you like, but I must do my work.' I'd put her in classes if she wanted to. She made up her mind she was going to have this man. He wasn't in love with anybody. I don't think he was really in love with me. He liked taking me out. Then one day one of my men friends said, 'You know, I think your sister's going to have a baby.' I said, 'Oh don't be silly!' He said, 'Well she looks to me as if she's going to.' So I asked her about it and she said, 'Well yes I am!' She was sixteen then. I took her up to an Italian doctor who was a friend of mine. He said, 'Yes, she's six or seven months gone', and I fainted. That was that. They had to pull *me* together, not her. Eventually my man friend said, 'I think he'll have to marry her.' I said, 'But he's so much older' – he was more my age, you see.

Evidently she played up to the man to such an extent that eventually he did take her to bed. That was it. She asked for it and she got it. The man was somewhere in the north. I rang him up and said, 'What are you going to do about marrying my sister?' He said, 'I'm not going to marry her.' I said, 'I'm afraid you'll have to, even if you have a divorce afterwards it doesn't matter, but there's going to be a baby, and that's that.' Well now, you know who the baby is [*names a well-known person*]. That's the boy. He doesn't know the full story.

Anyhow, my boyfriend went out and got a wedding-ring, and I said to the man, 'Look, you either do this or I'll get you out of your job.' I just forced it on him. I bought her a cloak that would cover up, and she got married. My boyfriend paid six months' rent on a flat in Barnes, and said, 'If I were you I should let them get on with it now. It's up to them.' Which we did.

... That was the beginning. She had two children by him –

said they were by him; I suppose they were. After that she left
him and went off with another man. That man died here. She
wouldn't leave me alone for a minute. All the time she had to be
near me and have what I had or do what I did. It was a sort of
paranoid thing she'd got. She died about a year ago, and it was
only about last weekend that I learned something about her that
I didn't know. I thought it was funny because she always tried to
aim high. If I knew Lord Somebody, she'd be there to talk
about me. She just couldn't stop it, it was awful. In the end my
brother took a friend of his who was a butcher, he owned about
five butcher shops, got a lot of money – as a butcher: no intellect
or anything, he just knew how to cut up meat and make money.
He took him to my sister because he was going to see her one
day, and they got together somehow. I thought she married
him, but she hadn't. I tell you – I don't know about my own
family.

At the time of my sister's marriage, my father was working with
windmills in Wittering. Everything was done with windmills
down there. Oh, you'd have died – you'd have thought the house
would take off, with all these windmills. When there was a
terrific wind from the sea. . . . ! One day one did come off, and he
got on his bicycle and went round after it. It could have killed
somebody, it took off with such a terrific speed.
    My father made one of the first washing-machines, run by
a windmill. Yes! But it was outside the house, you see, with the
wind going like hell, washing the stuff – it was marvellous.
Everything was done with windmills. He was a marvellous man,
far too ahead that's the thing. The motor-bike he made is in Lord
Montague's place. I had a talk with Lord Montague about Pop,
and he's got quite a lot of things I didn't know about my father,
what he invented, in his library.

I had a dancing school in Paris while I was studying with
Jacques Dalcroze. What I wanted to do, I tried to get Margaret
Morris with her type of dancing together with Dalcroze,
because I thought one was lacking the other, and I thought the
combination would have made a wonderful thing for the
children – for borderline cases and so on.
    There was one child whom the doctors had given up, I cured

completely. There was a pianist called Rodney Eden, the cousin of Anthony Eden, who used to improvise at the piano for me in the Maudsley. I'd talk to these children. The difficulty was I'd have fifteen at once. Well they'd all got different things wrong with them, but I used to take them one by one and make them all do what the one had to do. It worked awfully well. For instance, there was one little boy who wouldn't look up – he looked down all the time. I said to Rodney, 'What about the music "Playing to the Birds"? Now, there's no birds on the floor; they're all up in the trees.' We got him looking up bit by bit, then we got him walking and doing hops like birds.

He was Simon Bargate. He was four years old. They'd heard about me through the Maudsley Hospital. He had never walked, he couldn't talk; it came through an illness in the father. I put him in the four-poster room here. I used to rub his back and talk to him and get him to stand, bit by bit. I said I would take him on if the mother wouldn't see him at all until I rang up and said he was fit to be seen. That was a difficult thing for her, because she didn't know what I was going to do with him. Well, in seven months I had him walking.

It just depended what was wrong, how I handled it. But it was all done through rhythm, to get the mind and the body working together. They'd go on the brain only, but it wasn't that – you don't know whether it started with the body affecting the brain or the other way round. You'd got to get them together – I think that's why I was in love with two men, to get the two together!

Wasn't I lucky to find two men like that? But after two or three years it got so that it was really impossible. One was jealous of the other, sending telegrams to each other and all this, and I thought, 'Oh God, I've got to get out of this!' That's what made me marry the other man. Oh, it was all in the papers – 'LOVE AT FIRST SIGHT' – Oh God! One of the two came to the wedding, and he was terribly upset. He made such an ass of himself afterwards, but he got over it in time.

I didn't want any children. I had enough to do to clear up other people's messes, and I took on all these black children. There was no good *adding* to it.

People argue about birth control, especially in churches. But we've got too many people in the world anyway – quite enough to get on with! I think China was very good with what they did recently. There are too many children in the world, and to make them in test-tubes and all that sort of thing, I think we've got enough without that!

These frustrated women that must have a baby – what for? Take somebody else's and bring it up. I think it's nature. We're so like animals. We are animals really. Our brain hasn't kept up with the inventions which should help us. I think religion's a lot to blame for that – it's a kind of illness in a way, to me. I don't know – people get very angry when I talk like that.

When I left Paris ... I was supposed to get married to one of these two men, and I didn't. It wouldn't have done for me anyway. He had a yacht and I get seasick.... He was a person who absolutely stuck to me – there was no funny business with anybody else, *that* I knew. So he then was going to buy a château that was built by Napoleon to give to one of his mistresses: Château de la Perrière. We were supposed to be married and he was going to give me this château. My God, it was an *enormous* place! So anyway, I didn't. I jilted him literally at the altar.

When I first came back to England, well I went into different dances and mixed with different ballets and things, so I was dancing. I trained dancers, and I had what they called Twelve Tacchi Dancers, and those girls danced at the Hammersmith Palais de Danse and the Victoria Palace and the Crystal Palace – different variety shows. They were like chorus girls, but much more rhythmic, a little more intellectual.

In 1925 I went to America. Took my typewriter with me, and my clothes, and danced in different places. I went right through Canada by train. I danced in New York. I didn't have an agent. I just went myself. I'd go into a place – for instance there was a Greek man in Chicago named Nicolas Toucalos – fancy me remembering that name! – he took me on for a couple of months, in the Greek Theatre, doing Greek dancing. From that I got other things you see. So I did quite a lot in America about that time. Then that American wanted me to marry him when I'd finished all this – which I didn't do, of course.

I didn't like America a bit. Sex mad! Oh my God, I'd only get into a lift or something and they'd say, 'Oh, I've got a drink in my –', that's when the pussyfoot business went on, and they'd offer you to go to their bedroom for a drink. I had to keep out of that lot. Then, of course, they were after me for films too.

I suppose about that time I was the best-looking, because I was having a hell of a time. It really was awful. And you see, it wasn't as though you could get anyone to talk about anything *sensible*. It was all – well I don't know what.

When I came back from America I went on teaching and dancing. I danced in variety – anywhere they paid me. I fitted in very well. They were such marvellous people. None of them were intellectual at all, but full of fun. There was Nelly Wallace, George Robey, and all these people. They nearly all lived round Brixton in those days, and they invited each other to what they called 'tea' – what we'd call supper – and they'd have a *big* table, with bread in heaps and pickles and cheese and all that sort of thing. Everybody would sit round and take what they wanted to eat and tell jokes. Gertie Gitana, she was one of them. She always thought she was above people a bit. She was rather fun.

In 1933 a well-known American photographer, Walter Bird, took pictures of me. They appeared in the *London Illustrated Magazine*, and one got first prize in a *Daily Mail* competition. Another was used by Cadbury's on a chocolate box. I didn't even get a box of chocolates out of it, but I was inundated with phone calls from men who had somehow got my address. Then Smirnov, a Russian photographer, had an exhibition of photos of me that brought more telephone calls and letters from men. It was very confusing and very wearing.

I was with the Duke of Windsor and Mrs Simpson in Antibes. I was dancing down there, and he liked my dancing and I got to know him through that. I used to go to night-clubs with them sometimes. My friend always said, 'Why didn't you make up to him? You could have done better than Mrs Simpson!' I don't think he'd be my type. He was born in the wrong place. It's so abnormal and stupid.

The Hearst newspaper men were there like a lot of flies, and all sorts of press people. Really it was awful. They were running after me as much as Mrs Simpson. You couldn't *move*. It was interesting in a way, but also stupid.

He was not serious about her then. It was very funny because when my first husband was coming in on the *Glorious* going up near Antibes David and I were standing on a rock at the side watching it come in. We went to a night-club that night. Amy Johnson and her husband were there; he got as tight as a lord and went off with some prostitutes, and the poor thing came and sat at our table. It was terrible: he was a nasty piece of work.

I thought I'd go back to London a way I'd never been before. I thought I'd take a coach back, all through France, and what do you think was on my breakfast table from David? A big bowl of cherries – he knew I liked cherries – and a great big bunch of arum lilies: they both loved arum lilies.

I got on very well with him. I met him before that, when I had a job in Aquascutum and he came in for a trench-coat. It was lunch-time and I was the only one there. It was rather different. I think I was earning two pounds a week then.

Oh yes, if I'd married him I could have made Buckingham Palace into a school for black children.... It was a very interesting time, because I was married to my first husband when this was going on.

... I couldn't cope with that life in Malta. Talk about regiments and war – the whole thing ... the priests ... it was full of factories and thin goats! There used to be a nun teaching little girls to make lace, early in the morning. And make money. *They* didn't get it. They ran about with no shoes on. I got into all sorts of trouble there, because the man who was the governor – I was called up there and told I was not supposed to help them with the ballet and the opera-house. Being the wife of an Air Force man I wasn't allowed to do that.

Then also I used to get a *carrozza* and go out to some of these women who used to serve the drinks and things at cocktail parties. They hadn't got two peanuts to rub together, so they used to put on a black dress and a white apron and ... I got to know some of them, and found out that they were living in one room with umpteen kids and *awful* conditions. So I kicked up hell, and I got into a row for that.

I gave my husband an ultimatum: either he gets another job and I'll stay with him; if he was going to stop as he was, then I was off. I gave him a year to think it over.

I wasn't really in love with him. I had been in love before that.

I think women are much freer now. It seems to me that men and women who live together stay together longer than married ones. Psychologically they feel freer, both of them. They know that either of them could walk out at any time with no bother, but the others can't – they feel tied.

I wouldn't get married if I were young now. To get married is a religious thing in any case. It's a very complicated matter. Some women like to be in the kitchen, having children, breeding like rabbits while the husband brings back the money. That wouldn't do for me ever. But it's all right if you haven't got any other interest in life. Somebody's got to have the babies I suppose – or have we? I don't know. We needn't have as many as we're having now, I don't think. There's more in life than just having babies, but that's nature's trick, isn't it, to make women want to have babies and men to make 'em and run off. I never at all felt I wanted to have children.

My father used to say to me, 'Now look here, if you go off with a man and something goes wrong, don't come back to me, because I'm going to tell you what might happen, and if you can't get that in your head then you're not worth bothering about. Don't come to me if you get in a mess, because you could so easily get in a mess, but you've got to use your brain.' I think that put me off an awful lot. It wasn't fear, it was, 'Oh God; what should I go through *that* for?'

But the pill has such side-effects, doesn't it? You see, directly you go against nature. . . . This is what makes people believe in God and everything, because you can't fight nature. This is what they call 'God'.

Isn't life interesting? It's really fascinating. I would like to live another hundred years, to see what will come out of all this, because really we're living in the middle of a revolution. If they could organize so that people used all these gadgets – technology – so you'd only have to work a few hours, and then you could develop your brain. You'd have time for arts and crafts, and could really *live*. What fun is there, working your guts out from seven in the morning until nine at night?

I remember a time when we were all living with my grandmother, because my father was inventing something and there wasn't money then. Although the Perey side of our family had got plenty of money. They were at the bottom of bringing the negroes over to Bristol. My father would never do anything – they were religious, they were money-making people: just the opposite to my father. They used to look on my father as crackers. Mother stood by him anyway. She never got asked to their parties or anything.

Those people can't understand what working people go through. This is where I think I was lucky, that part of my family are the Pereys, and they're the people with Syon Park. When I was a kid I used to go to their kids' parties and all that and you could see what riches really mean. I think I am very lucky to have had both sides. To be rich you've got to do dirty tricks. Whether you understand what you're doing or not I don't know, but money doesn't come in a straight way at all.

When I think of that side of my family, making money out of whisky and having timber coming over from Japan, and others starving as a result of it ... I have never joined any political party. I vote for who I think will do the best. I can't put myself into a box.

I really think the Russian Revolution is the most important event in this century. When you think what they've done in the time! You see, I've been to Russia every year for I don't know how many years, and I've seen it progress to such an extent that I'm nearly knocked backwards when I go there. And the GDR the same. Some of the socialist countries have got a long way to go yet, but I think the USSR and the GDR have been the biggest influence in the world, to bring the feeling of people working for people, instead of what I call 'moneybags'. I think now all these awful things you hear about going on, murders and big business doing dirty business, has all come as a result of a kind of socialism which is winning. If it wins too much, this is what I'm frightened of, because you'll get people like Reagan and Thatcher saying, 'I'd rather be dead than Red', and blow up the lot. The more we win, the more angry they will become. It is a matter of capitalism against socialism.

When I came here first, Rod had so many servants, and a cook and a chauffeur – the top floor was full of servants. I said, 'Rod, I'll give you a year to think things out. If you want to marry me you'll get rid of the lot of this.' I jolly well made him sack the lot.

His business had just been given to him on a plate. When you think of what he did, being brought up as a Conservative – it shows you what love can do. Poor Rod, he should have married a nice little girl who collected the eggs in the morning and ... he's had some awful shocks with me. How his family were livid at him marrying me. To start with, they didn't know anything about my politics. I was a dancer. That very weekend I came down with all my stuff, I was in the papers having been in a film or something. There were the pictures of me. People said, 'We don't want bloody film stars down here!' That alone was enough.

Then I had different people from the theatre coming down here, because I had a house across the road. The composer Ferrari came down. He wore a big black hat – you know how they used to – and a cloak. He liked a guitar too. He used to go round the village with his guitar playing under people's windows to see if any girls would come out. Sokolova would wander round the village followed by a lamb which I had brought up on a bottle. Sokolova was really Hilda Munnings, a niece of the painter Sir Alfred Munnings.

When the war was on there were a whole lot of pansy-boys got in a lift in the theatre then the lift went Bang! down on the floor. They all tipped out at the end quite shattered and said, 'I think we'll go down and see Tacchi! She's somewhere in Somerset – let's get out of this.' My dear, a whole lot of pansy-boys turned up here and I filled up all the rooms with them and Rod's sister came and saw them from the walled garden escaping from one bed to another. She never came again. That was the end of Rod's sister as far as I was concerned.

According to this village I'm a raving communist. When I started the new UNA in Taunton it was terrific, we were packed. About a fortnight after I had a telephone call from the committee: 'We're very worried, can we come over and see you now?' They came and said, 'You started UNA and we put you on the committee and we don't think we can any more, because we hear you're a communist.' I said, 'Well, now, you tell me what a communist is and I'll tell you if I am one.' And they couldn't.

In the village I've been a communist because I brought up

some half-black children here with white mothers. Poor little devils, where they'd have gone if they hadn't come here I don't know. That made me a communist then. They ran about the orchard in summer with just little pants on and I had people coming round and saying, 'We heard you're running a nudist camp.' I thought, 'I've been accused of most things but ...' I couldn't think where it came from. I racked my brains. It was these little kids running around in navy-blue pants from Woolworth's.

We were raided by the police at the end of the last war because people said we were communists, harbouring Germans. It must have got very hot. I didn't know it was happening. I'd gone off to Taunton shopping. When I came back I saw all the cars and thought there was a wedding going on. The place was full of police. They'd been through the drawers already. We were ushered into the kitchen and told not to come out.

We'd had some refugees, whom nobody else would have. They were Jewish refugees who had somehow escaped. One or two of the people took some people who'd had their houses bombed, but they wouldn't take the Germans. I took them and they were wonderful.

After it was all over ... Cyril Maude QC came down as well ... we all sat in the music-room and I gave them whisky. I asked him, 'What did you mean when you asked what did I understand by dusters?' It turned out the refugees all had different jobs about the house every day. One of them, an Austrian woman, used to dust the landing upstairs, and she shook it out of the window. Somebody in the village was watching at the same time every day. I knew Cyril Maude's father, because we were on the stage together.

We had an anonymous letter through the door, saying why had we taken so many black children – I must have been in bed with a black man. I never had. It's something I missed.

My husband being a Tory – he's been a Tory all his life – he should never have married me. He had a hell of a life with me, he really did. Everyone said, 'That poor Rod – that awful woman that he married!' We had to bring up those kids. I had thirty-four of them – not all black, some of them just because their mother was in trouble, and so on. I had all sorts of kids. I had my own school: one of our houses we made over as a school. One of the biggest problems I had was to get a black qualified teacher. Eventually I found one. She couldn't get a job. She was selling stamps in the post office in Acton. Having black as well as white children, I wanted to have a black teacher as well. But I only had French house-mothers so that the kids were bilingual.

They all learned horse-riding, shorthand typing, and the little ones learned to write. They've never been out of a job. One came to see me the other day with his white wife. He's got a black son and two white daughters! He taught diving in Saudi Arabia.

I didn't agree with Dora Russell's ideas, because I think lack of discipline is wrong. You've got to find a way of discipline that isn't noticeable to them. I didn't agree that you could let them do what they like when they like, with no feeling about the other person attached to it. They didn't want religion or anything, they wanted a bit of nous in their minds: it's going to hurt somebody – why do I want to hurt that person? If only the teachers could have had discussions, it's amazing how much you could understand them. Rod financed all that.

AS: Did Rod believe in what you were doing?
T: I'm never quite sure [*Turns to Rod.*] Did you believe in what I was doing?
Rod: Yes, why not?

The school developed really when I couldn't dance any more, and I started teaching. I've got an enormous barn converted into a theatre. Sokolova from the Diaghilev ballet was with me down there. During the war. I taught eurhythmics and she taught the ballet. Her daughter was here too. She committed suicide, and I think that killed Lydia in the end. Somebody should write a book about Lydia. I could tell you stories that have never been told. Somebody should put that in a book.

The schools I went to were useless. If you gave me a long-division sum now I couldn't do it. I never needed arithmetic – the men that fell in love with me had plenty of money! I always had the best seats at the theatre or the opera. The biggest lesson I've learned is that the most uncommon thing is commonsense. Just ordinary commonsense. And the more religion they pump into people, the less commonsense they'll have.

What is so extraordinary to me – I've discussed this with my brother too, he thinks he's got an answer to it. I haven't. How is it that you get people with very good brains – scientific – and yet they've got a religion bug which is just like the Berlin Wall, it shuts off part of their brain. My brother says it is true that they are steeped in that when they are children. But wouldn't you think – with the other part of your brain working? Isn't it a fear of dying, and when you're dead you'll be something else? Some of them think they'll come back as something. I shall probably come back as a cabbage. I'm going to heaven and I'm going to convert the angels to Women for World Disarmament.

Today they've been talking a lot on TV about the jobs, people out of jobs. My father spent his life inventing things so that people wouldn't work their guts out if machines could do it. When you think people need only work a few hours a day, with all this technology, and the money's there just the same ... what's stopping it? It's capitalism. I think until we've got rid of religion and capitalism we've got no hope at all. The two work together, just like that. It's why we've got all the different religions in the different countries: it keeps the people quiet. It's so obvious isn't it? I can't imagine myself being tied down to something like religion. Of course, never having had it I don't know what I've missed!

There are words that don't mean anything any more. It depends which side you're on how you interpret it. Democracy – what is democracy? Freedom is even worse: freedom to do what? Freedom to exploit each other, or freedom to stop people from doing that? Peace – I had a letter from Mrs Thatcher when I wrote to her about it, and she says she wants peace just the same as I do. Well, so what does peace mean any more? Her idea of peace and mine are two different things entirely. When you're writing to people you've got to be very careful about the words you use.

AS: So much that you do is to make the world a better place, isn't it?

T: Because God doesn't do it – somebody's got to do it!

AS: Why has somebody got to do it?

T: I think – I can't sit around and see people suffer and not do something about it. It's impossible for me anyhow.

That's why I took those black children. What sort of lives would they have had? Now, they've never been out of a job. They're marvellous. None of them has got a religion, but they help people. So what? Isn't that better than letting them all turn into thugs?

I never had any trouble with them. They learnt cooking, they learnt the three Rs, and on Thursdays when all the staff went out they could ask me any questions and I could ask them. They always had a leader, which they planned beforehand, and we all sat round and discussed things. That was a wonderful time for me, because I learnt so much of what was in their little brains, their problems and things.

But all that's like another life. It's so totally different. I became involved in the Peace Movement in 1950 and started a new life. It was just by accident really, because I'd had three operations on my hip. I went to lecture on eurhythmics in Bradford. While I was there, staying with friends, there was a newspaper on the breakfast table and it said something about a conference on peace in Sheffield. I said to my friends, 'D'you know, I'd like to go and hear that.' 'Well let's go!' I wasn't allowed in. I hadn't got a pass. It was in the Town Hall. I waited outside. People were being turned away. Priests in their black hats from Bulgaria and so on. The doors opened and I saw Picasso on the platform. I thought, 'Good gracious me!' So I got a piece of paper out of my handbag and I wrote a letter on an old envelope. I said, 'Tacchi's outside. Please can she come in?' I gave it to a policeman and said, 'Would you take that to Picasso?' He said, 'Who's Picasso?' I said, 'He's the second on the left.' Picasso said, 'Of course, bring her in!' So I went in and found myself on the platform, and that was the beginning.

Hardly any women there at all, and I thought, 'This is funny' – the place was packed with people; well-known people, writers, all sorts of people. It was terrific. I said to Picasso, 'Why aren't the women in this as well?' He said, 'Well *do* something about it', and I said 'All right, I will.' He said, 'Promise you will?' I said, 'Yes.' He said, 'Well you know, I can't go to Warsaw. We're asked to shift the whole thing to Warsaw and I can't go to Warsaw. Will you go there for me?' I said, 'I've got ten shillings in my pocket' – I'd been shopping you see, up there – and I thought that would be enough for a cup of coffee on the way home. I'd got my return ticket anyway. So I didn't go home. I sent a telegram to my husband, 'I'm going to Warsaw.' He sent one back saying, 'I take a dim view of this', but I didn't take any notice, I just went.

So that was the beginning of it. I'd never been behind the so-called Iron Curtain. Then you see, Picasso couldn't go, and to represent him at an occasion like that – I became something straight away. I've still got the card signed by Joliot-Curie, so I belonged to the Peace Council straight away.

I went to Moscow with Dora Russell at one time, too. I'll tell you this, people who are really working all out for peace go on longer than those people who are religious and waiting for God to take them. It's really true. I don't put make-up on and I don't put creams on. You see, it's like exercising any other part of your body; if you exercise your brain it keeps going longer.

The doctor says my heart goes too fast. And do you know, the women in the hospital, no more than sixty-odd years most of them, all looking stupid (the men were worse than the women) and I said to them, 'What were you before?' 'Oh, I was a pianist. I used to teach piano.' 'Well, why don't you do it now?' 'Oh well, you know, my age. . .'. I said, 'Oh, to *hell* with your age. That doesn't matter. Get your *brain* young!'

The husband of the Queen of Holland had an aunt who spoke umpteen languages. She heard about me and Women for World Disarmament, and she said, 'You've got what we should be working for.' She got me to Düsseldorf. I travelled with her right down to the Rhine. We stopped at different places, picked up different women, more and more until we got to Strasbourg. There I was asked by the priest – the one that was the head of the cathedral there – and they got me to talk on television, to speak in the Strasbourg court; they got all the nuns there – what a thing! Well now, I thought a lot would come out of that, but it didn't, but what it did do was to get the West German women with us. The very fact that the old girl came with me sort of got them together. Then, what I thought put them off a bit . . . they had a reception for me in Strasbourg. I was invited to the cathedral on the Sunday morning. There were crowds there, waiting to see Princess whoever she was, and they had a contraption inside the cathedral, which was trundled out for

people to see every Sunday, with the virgin coming out doing
this and God coming out doing that, and, you know – bells rang
and all the rest of it. The priest said, 'Isn't that wonderful? God
does this every Sunday morning!' – you see, so I looked at him
and said, *'God* does it?' He said yes, so I was really bold: 'May I
look at the back of this thing?' He said, 'No, nobody's allowed
in there.' I said, 'But I want to see what's at the back.' There was
all this machinery you see. I said, 'Who made the machinery?
God?' He said, 'Aren't you religious?' I said, 'I don't know what
I am – I'm only trying to find out what this is about. I said, 'Don't
you let the people see at the back there, and see what's *really*
doing it?' He said, 'No, it's not allowed.' I said, 'Well, I think
that's absolutely disgusting.' That night it was the reception. I
seemed to have caused such a to-do in this place. They were all
saying, 'Who is this woman?'

The Princess was grand. She had thick woollen stockings on.
She had a black hat and a costume ... beautifully made
everything – made in the year dot I should imagine. Very old-
fashioned. Real old Victorian I don't know what. Oh she was a
sweetie! We got on awfully well together.

I don't think I've ever been unhappy. I never sat down and cried
about anything, except when Mum died and Pop died. They
meant so much to me. They were both such sensible people. The
way Mother coped when there was very little money.

Although I reacted to injustices at various times, I lived in an
ivory tower. I gave hospitality to the anti-Nazi refugees and
offered homes to the unwanted children fathered by the soldiers
out of a sense of humanity. The war hardly touched us at all.

When I saw the ruins of Warsaw and heard the story of their
suffering and the heroic struggle against the Nazi occupation, I
knew that the rest of my life would be devoted to the struggle
for peace.

Bessie Brennan

8

Bessie Brennan

'I feel like carrying on, you know, because if you sit down and think, you've had it. You think of all the hard times you've had, and how you've struggled on with your own ten fingers.'

Bessie Brennan was born in 1902 in Niddrie, Edinburgh. Her father was a miner, her mother had been a mill-worker; she had six brothers and four sisters. Bessie left school in 1915 and went briefly into domestic service, then to field-work. When she was fifteen she started work in a confectioner's in Musselburgh, where her family had moved while she was still a child. She was married to a coal-miner in 1923, and had three children. Her husband died when he was thirty-nine, and Bessie went out to work from then on, mainly as a waitress. She retired in 1972.

I wrote an article for the *Scotsman* about how we used to be released from school for two weeks every year for the potato harvest, and what it was like. Shortly afterwards I wrote another article about how without realizing it I must have become middle-class, because I could not immediately find an octogenarian working-class woman among my friends. Bessie's granddaughter, Faye, wrote to me about her own memories of potato-picking, and mentioned in passing that if I was looking for a working woman in her eighties, her granny would be ideal, 'Though I doubt very much she'd take kindly to a person from the *Scotsman*. She'd think you were a Tory and you'd never get inside her house.' Her granny, Faye said, was 'not known to be diplomatic'.

I established my credentials, Bessie was persuaded to meet me, but the problem was that her daughter and her daughter's husband and son live with her, so that in order to interview her in peace I would have to meet her at Faye's house, and Bessie is not one for making visits: she had never been in Faye's house.

Eventually Bessie agreed to this as well. She arrived at Faye's house dressed in her best coat and frock and wearing her crystal necklace; nervously co-operative and, it turned out, quite deaf.

Listening to the tapes of my interviews with Bessie is an entertainment in itself. I would shout a question two or three times and finally receive the answer to another question altogether, perhaps one that I had asked ten minutes before. The questions that would lead better-educated, more articulate interviewees into long passages of exposition would be answered with innocent monosyllables, as when, after Bessie had described some of her working life, I asked, 'Did you ever think to yourself, why am I doing this?' She replied, 'Too true.' When I asked her, 'Do you ever think to yourself, why are we here – what are we doing here?', she said, 'True enough ...', thought, and added, '... yet some sail along, no bother.' This fairly put me in my place. The more I thought of it, the more I realized they were perfect answers to unanswerable questions.

I visited her in her own house the day after our first interview, with a photographer. Bessie's living-room took me back to my childhood. There was a miner's fire burning extravagantly in the grate; her grandson, who is a nurse, sat watching morning television; the room had photos here and there of Bessie's family, and the odd little seaside souvenir. It was cosy and homely.

Bessie wore the apron she had on on all my subsequent visits. Straight away she offered me tea and biscuits. She used the biscuit-tin lid as a tray for the tea, and kept urging me to have more.

Since the light indoors was poor, the photographer suggested she take Bessie's photo outside. Rising to get ready, Bessie said, 'I won't need to dress up, for I'm not going anywhere. I'll just put on my coat I wear for the messages.' She kept her slippers on. Outside, she stood meek as a lamb wherever she was directed, allowing herself to be photographed without the slightest sign of self-consciousness. She was not at all interested in seeing copies of the photos we took. She was equally co-operative about my tape-recorder. Where other interviewees had been nervous of it, or asked me to switch it off when they were about to make some intimate revelations, Bessie just ignored it. She is very much her own woman.

Her facial expressions are a study in themselves, they are so various and so telling. When she is not pleased, she has an eye like a gimlet. Sometimes as she sat thinking back, her hands folded under her breast and the front of her home-made apron poutered up, she reminded me of a little black grouse on its nest. She is comfortable sitting silent, with just the occasional sigh to let you know she is still with you. When something strikes her sense of humour she has a high, husky laugh.

Bessie does all the cooking, washing, and cleaning in her house; her daughter goes out to work. When I asked her if this was not too much for her, she said, 'You want to keep going, and there's nothing for it but to toddle on.' There is no ruling passion in her life, unless you can describe survival as a ruling passion. But Bessie loves to talk about politics, and she has some scandalous theories about Mrs Thatcher – Faye told me that once when Mrs Thatcher appeared on television during the election campaign, Bessie commented acidly, 'Look at her. If this set wasnae rented I'd put my foot through it.'

Every time I visited Bessie she would first of all run through a list of friends and relatives who had died since I saw her last, with grim relish. She was not morbid, nor was she particularly gloating about her own survival: she was facing the facts of life, and chronicling them. Nothing conveys the mystery of life quite so poignantly as the way Bessie records death.

Very reluctantly, because a lot is lost in the process, I have anglicized Bessie's conversation. She has a deep voice and speaks with a strong Scottish accent, very emphatically.

THE INTERVIEW

My first memory is of a laddie who was drowned. We were playing together, and he just wandered away and was drowned. . . .

. . . I was one that never bothered with anybody – never bothered with chums or anything like that. I was always in the house with my mother. I used to go with her for the messages every Friday, and blacklead the grate on a Friday night.

I had six brothers and four sisters. Three died in Niddrie before we shifted to Musselburgh. We used to eat off a table that ran right up the middle of the room – kale, chappit tatties [mashed potatoes], and turnips; a big chunk of beef cut, you know? And they enjoyed it. There was no fish and chips and carry-on then. All good substantial food. The laddies used to work in the paper-mill. They'd say, 'Put a bit of that beef in Ma', for their piece, for their breakfast, and then they'd get home for their dinner.

We had no cooker; it was all done on the fire, and it was smashing. One of yon frying-pans you hang on the hook, and an oven that was heated from the fire. My mother made scones on a Saturday night, and they were all laid out on a clean white sheet – treacle scones and girdle scones and ... my mother was a rare baker. She made her own bread. It was a good oven she had, you see, off the fire. If she was here today she wouldn't give it house-room, the bread. One or two bakers were good then; they baked French halves, you could eat one all to yourself, and Jenny Lind halves.

My mother used to get a sheep's head and a lump of meat and make a pot of soup, and if there was a dog about the place, it got the bones.

My mother was thin, and always on the alert – always happy. She never took drink or anything, my mother. My father could make up for her though. Mind, he didn't do it through the week – he was always night-shift – but by God he made up for it on the Saturday – but it was always draught beer; he never got sooey [blind] drunk. And oh, you daren't blow your breath wrong when they're on the night-shift! He used to walk from Musselburgh to the Preston Grange pit.

We played at rounders and jumping-ropes. You jumped the shoes off your feet and you were going to get your lugs rattled [ears smacked]. The laddies played too. On the ground round the houses where we lived there were some lovely singers. At home we'd all sit round a big roaring fire and sing.

But from the time you were any age at all, there was never much enjoyment, it was all work in the house. You never got away from the grindstone from you were nine years old, because there was a good lot of old folk stayed on our stair, and I did a turn for them, cleaning. Then when the war was beginning to take shape you came home from school and had to go out and work in the fields at night.

I was brought up in the Scotch religion. There used to be a mission at the foot of our street and I used to go in there. They

used to sing, 'Tattie Tylant'. I used to sing [*claps her hands*]
'Tattie Tylant, Tattie Tylant'. My mother said, 'Bring her out of
it' – I used to come home and sing and she'd say, 'Will you get
away to your bed!' . . . And the Salvation Army: 'My cup's full
and running over'.

AS: What's 'Tattie Tylant'?
BB. Oh, God knows. They were foreigners.

My Mum and Dad weren't church-goers. My Mum came off
Highland folk, and my Dad was brought up in Newcraighall.
There was about nine in his family.

I don't bother about the church, but I believe in it. There is a
God – there's somebody. He died on the cross for every religion,
didn't He? But then some of them forgets that. You often
wonder if half the young ones nowadays that's doing what
they're doing: do they think that that man died for them?

You've often said to yourself, 'Thank God that this is done
and the next thing's done', and you always fall back on that
'Thank God', don't you? Aye.

My mother used to always say, 'The Lord sits high and He
looks low, and He judges everybody accordingly.' And my
mother was a hard-working woman. She had to go out to the
fields when the First World War started. She had twenty-seven
shillings a week money from the government.

All my family were in the army during the wars, you know? I
had a brother died in 1970 – he was all through the last war.
And there was one died in 1942 – he was in the First World War.
And my father was in the First World War, and my father-in-
law, and I had a brother-in-law killed in the First World War.

There was eleven in my family and I'm the only one left. The
youngest one of the family, my brother, I got [found] him lying
dead when I went to waken him for his work. Twenty-six years
old. My brother. He lived with me. My mother died with me.
There was Tam, Alec, Meg, Andrew, Annie, and Mary, all older
than me. Yon was my brother killed at Niddrie pit bing [slag-
heap] forty-eight years ago. Took another man's place because
his wife was ill, and he was killed – knocked right out into the
ashes and suffocated. . . .

. . . I had a good teacher at school when I was a bairn. She
came from Edinburgh. A Miss Spence. She was getting gey old.

I used to take her shoes off and put her slippers on; put her shoes back on at night and tie them; put her coat on and chum her to the tram. She was quite the thing; she was fair away with herself. I liked the school. I liked knitting and sewing. We used to knit wee squares and sew pillow-slips, sewing bags, and these things, you know?

We had a schoolmaster, and I never set eyes on him till I left school. I was widowed with three bairns and they were all up, and he was the first man that I met in the North British Hotel, getting a feed. I was waitressing. Know what he done? That brother that died in 1970, he had done something he shouldn't at school ... this man had him on the table and he was laying into his backside with this belt. Some of the laddies came to me and said, 'Here, you'd better get in there or he's going to have your brother Jock killed.' I went in and said, 'What's your game?', see. He says, 'Get out or I'll do the same to you!' I gave him a shove and said, 'Come down, John.' John came off the table. I went home and told my father; my father went down to him. And do you know, he would have given my father anything so's that he wouldn't report him. My father says, 'I'm not wanting anything off you', he says. 'You'll keep your hands off my bairns. That's what I want you to do.'

... When I left school there was a Dr Millar, and she wanted a housemaid, and I went there. After her man died she gave up and I went to the field-work. I enjoyed all my work. I never wanted to be anything else. I started in the fields at six o'clock in the morning – weeding turnips, tattie-lifting. I worked with Lowe of Musselburgh, the great man for the leeks.

In the fields there was nothing with machinery, it was all hand work; it was your own hands that you done the work with, no machinery. We used to shove the tatties into a bag and tie them up, and tie the leeks up ... shaw [cut off the leaves and stalks from] the turnips. We finished at five at night. We'd an hour for our dinner. Then when the summertime came you'd to go back and work on till nine o'clock.

It was awful hard work. When I came fourteen, I shifted away from the field-work and started as a sugar-boiler in the confectioner's. I was there up to I got married. And two sisters was there, and a brother. Fred used to make snowballs. John worked with me, but he didn't fancy it and left and went to the paper-mill. He was in the paper-mill till he was cried up [called up] during the Second World War.

When I was in the confectioner's we used to work from half-past seven in the morning till twelve o'clock dinner, back at one and finished at five, and the boss would come at five and say, 'You'll have to work late and get this batch of stuff out.' We'd work till nine o'clock for threepence extra.

I liked working there. We used to get a big bag like that, full of chocolates, for a shilling, the workers. I'll guarantee you there were about two pound of chocolates for a shilling. And you used to get two pound of sugar for sevenpence ... a tin of syrup, tins of Nestlé's Milk – you used all that, you see – treacle ... and the workers got all that cheap. Them I worked to, the boss's granddaughter is married on my grandson.

The boss and I got on well, but one of his sons ... he came along one morning; we had a sweetie-can we used to make a fly cup of tea, and I used to hide it. I was just hiding it this day and he was watching through from the other room. He said, 'Get the can out of there and get that tea stopped.' I said, 'So you've been watching?' and I argued with him, then I said, 'Well, that's me finished.' I had a heavy job at the time, don't forget.

Next day, he must have spoken about it when the old boss was there, for he said to him, 'Since you've been so damn' smart about the cup of tea carry-on, get telling her sister to get Bessie to come out to her work', he said, '– Do you know that that lassie's lifting fifty-six pound o' sugar and making toffee? There's not a man in the boiling-shop lifting a pot with fifty-six pound in it.' He didn't half tell him. Of course, I wasn't going to go back, but my mother said, 'Get back. Let him see you're determined.' So I went back, and he apologized. I said, 'Take your apologies with you, I'm not here just to be made an idiot of.'

Aye, fifty-six pound a time, don't forget, lifting this big pot with two handles, and pouring it on to a slab to make toffee. I was like a rake. I was only seven stone something. We started at six o'clock, and at nine the men used to say, 'C'mon Bessie, put the can on for the tea', but I never gave the men away. When he said, 'Who told you to make the tea?' I never let on. I said, 'Me.'

Well, the boss had a ball for the workers. Oh, they were all going in velvets and everything. I was seventeen. I got a velvet dress done with gold. It was lovely: mauve violet, and a white fox fur tippet, white gloves and shoes, and I was the belle of the ball. That son of the boss's was the first one that came over. He said, 'Are you coming up for a dance?' I said, 'No.'

He had a sister, she was going with this man – she'd went for years with him – and he had taken a good bucket, you know, and something had happened to her, you see. Well after the bairn was born they wouldn't let her have anything to do with him – they put him out. Well, she never bothered anybody else. She bade in a wee house. I used to see her when I had a daft notion to go for a walk. She would blether on about olden times. . . .

Another brother, he was a bitter one. 'Can you not shut the doors', he said, 'when you're going out and coming in?' 'Are *you* doing anything?' I said. 'No.' 'Ah well *you* shut them', I said. That's just what I said to him. He was a twerp. My mother said, 'How did you get on today?' I said, 'Oh, the Wullie yin was getting his rip going', and I told her what I said. She near fell through the floor laughing.

Oh, in the summer in the confectioner's, the heat . . . you were swarmed with wasps; you were walking over the top of them. It was terrible. They just used to all flock together. The summertime used to be murder. The heat takes it out of you. I was the thinnest of the family. Our next-door neighbour used to say, 'No wonder you're so damn skinny, you never sit down on your arse.'

Once it was slack, they weren't getting much orders. I went up to a confectioner's in Edinburgh, and the manager phoned up my boss. The old boy himself answered and he said, 'Yes', he said, 'she's a grand worker. We're very sorry that the place is so slack.' So I got started there. I wasn't in the boiling-room, I was at the chocolate-dipping: macaroon bars – sitting all day dipping sweeties. I never got fed up, no. Because, you see, when you're a chocolate-dipper you've got to keep your chocolate to a certain heat, you've got to keep it soft, and you can't leave it. I was a confectioner for seven years. I handed over my pay the way I got it and I got a shilling a week pocket-money.

Hard work keeps me going – plenty hard work. It was just a case of work, get to your bed a wee while, then up and work again, that was the way of it. Nowadays they get everything handed on a plate for them, and they turn round and tell you to your face what do they want to work for when they can get money without work. That's what's wrong. They get too much nowadays. But then, who's paying for it? The likes of us. My rent's going up again, about another couple of pound a week here. That'll make this rent over fifty pound a fortnight. It used to be eight and sevenpence a week. And now they're talking about poll-tax. Where are they going to get it? I've paid taxes all the sixty-five years I've been married, and *I'm paying no more*. Because I couldn't. I've only got the pension.

The whole thing is, every politician who's gotten in hasn't been genuine. That Callaghan wasn't a genuine prime minister. He was pee-heein' [trying to ingratiate himself] with them and pee-heein' with the next one – no, he wasn't the right thing at all.

... It was saying in the paper about Marilyn Monroe's blouse being sold for so many thousands. Do you know what Reagan told another lassie? To put up her knickers and try and get the same. Sell her knickers. She said, 'I don't wear any.' Oh, they're dirty, filthy, bad-minded folk! And that's the president for you. And do you know, three Tory MPs have been divorced. *Three* of them.

When I was young, I never heard of lassies getting pregnant without being married. There was one, that was young, and the time the soldiers was billeted on the racecourse ... she had been pestering the men, and they took and they tarred her, that was what they done, the officials, to get rid of her. The soldiers couldn't get peace for her. She was wild. I never came across any who were right wild in our young time. Never. Where I lived anyway.

My mother didn't tell me the facts of life. She used to say, 'Now remember, you're going out, and *look after yourself*. Watch what you're going about.' She gave us good sound advice, she did. You heard all the wee bits at your work. You picked up from there.

My mother-in-law was a Catholic. She had affairs with three different men that my man never knew about. How can the Catholics go and confess to just an ordinary man? A priest I knew hooked away with the housekeeper. The biggest half of that crowd that goes to be priests is all homosexuals. Oh, it's terrible. The world's upside-down. You never heard of such a thing.

There has been a big change. A big, big change. The generation that's come up have ruined the world, and they've ruined the music too. It's only a lot of rubbish. It's not the world, it's the generation that's in it.

I don't smoke and I don't drink. I just take a drink of lemonade. I used to go to the Old Time class – you know, the Old Time dancing? The doctor told me to try and keep going, but it's impossible.

We used to have a good Labour Hall in Musselburgh. It was sold after the war finished. The floor was all Canadian pine. There was a band from Edinburgh. The man that had the band used to work the car – you know, the tram-cars. Many a good night we had there. Lord Wheatley used to come to the Labour Hall, and Attlee and his wife. I've met them, and served them all.

I remember one night there was a pipe band in Musselburgh Town Hall and I landed there. I was only about sixteen. The oldest sister came home and told my mother where I was and I got a skelp on the lug [a smack on the ear]: 'I'll dancin' ye!' And the best of it was, my mother and father went to the dancing themselves. Aye, they were dancers themselves!

I was twenty-one when I got married. He was five years older than me. I met him in my auntie's house. My mother's sister was married on my father-in-law's brother. There were seven daughters and so many sons, in a house in a row of cotton-mill houses. I was fifteen when I met my man. I had no other boyfriends, never bothered no other chaps.

I met him in my auntie's house, and he started coming home with me. The best of it was, my mother never knew. But one that stayed on the same stair as us told my mother that I was going with a fella. My mother says, 'I'll *fella* her when she comes in.' And when my mother gave you a biff, mind, it was a biff you got. When I came in she says, 'Who's the chap you're going with?' So I says to him, 'You'd better come over and tell her.' So he came over to the house and that was it. Never stopped. We was quite happy.

We was quite happy. . . . We only fell out when he was taking too much booze. Because I never drank. And I see a lot of it, out working. Mind you, some women can make a mess of themselves. I had a customer at the North British, she used to come in every Sunday, and she'd over with two glass of whisky, and two Bass bottles of beer, and her man sitting with lemonade.

I had a brother twenty-six years old when he died, four months after my mother, and every time there was a dancing competition our Jim lifted the prize – he were a good dancer. Well, my man shifted from Musselburgh and went to stay in Fife and get a job there, and I used to hop away with my brother, you see, to the dancing. My man found out when I came back: 'Who was you at the dancing with?'

There was a huge big square in Mitchell Street where we were all staying. One of Musselburgh's greatest councillors was born and brought up there too, Mrs Hyde. She was brought up there. Well, there was a huge big square, and they used to get their accordions and their harmonicas and they used to dance like fury. And I was there among them, of course. My mother used to up with the toilet window: 'He's comin'. You'd better get into the house.' [*Laughs.*] He was in Fife you see – but *I* didn't know what *he* was doing in Fife. I wasn't going to sit in the house. Although I never run with no other chaps – I never run with nobody except him.

My man was a Catholic. He was hammered and made to go to the Catholic school by the father, but after we got married he never bothered with it. Now look, between you and me, there's nobody under the sun could live up to it. If they were being faithful to their religion the IRA wouldn't be doing what they're doing.

My man's mother was an old weed. She had three fancy-men the father knew nothing about. After I got married I stayed in his mother's room, because there were no houses to be got then, and I used to take my washing over to my mother's and do my mother's washing too, in the sink. My brother used to carry my basket of clothes back for me. My mother-in-law told my man that there was another man bringing me home. It was just I was a different type from her. She liked the loose life but I didn't. And she knew I knew all about her.

I'll never forget the day, the father-in-law came back from his work – and don't forget, this could drink; she could swallow it – and somebody down the street had told him about her. She'd been down the street just with her vest on, slippers and a coat. The policeman said, 'Up the stairs or you'll go to jail.' (She had a brother carried on the same way with women.)

... This day the father came home. He just took the table and wheeched everything about her. He battered her with jam and milk and sugar. I never went through. I stayed where I was. I said, 'Let her get it.'

After that we got a single-end away from it. The best of it was, her daughter in Fife knew nothing about it. She thought there was nobody like her mother.... Never sober, never sober. It's an awful thing, drink.

My man started in the pit when he was thirteen. He worked from six in the morning till three in the afternoon for eight and six a shift, often up to the waist in water. It was slavery. And they'd put them into a seam that there was no money to be made in. They used to lie on their stomachs hewing the coal. My man was all scratched and torn. And there was no baths in those days. They worked for contractors, and it was the contractors who made the money, not the miners.

Bob Brennan was a worker, like myself. A good worker too. He could do *anything* in the house: paper, paint, joiner – anything at all – boot-mending. He used to mend the bairns' shoes. He used to buy the leather. He was in the pit from thirteen years old, and he died at thirty-nine. He and his brothers used to come in from their work and hand over their dig-money, and their mother was never sober.

I didn't want a big family. My mother had eleven and her sister had thirteen. My older sister had eight, and another sister had six. One of my brothers' wives had ten bairns. My brother that was killed at the bing had three, and my brother that died during the war had three, and the other two brothers wasn't married. My own daughter had ten.

We used to go to the Empire every week, my man and me. The Empire and the Theatre Royal, time about. Oh, he wouldn't go to the dancing – oh no. He didn't like the dancing.

Near the confectioner's where I worked there was a whisky bond. They used to get a pint at seven and six. My man ended up at Smeaton Colliery. There was a brake came from there every Saturday, and that was where they went, to get their whisky, the miners.

My first baby was born nine and a half months after I was married. It was before its time, and it lived a month. Next time I was pregnant I went up to the Labour Exchange with my cards, for my man wouldn't hear of me working, and I fell downstairs coming out and the police had to get an ambulance straight away. They put my arm in plaster for about six weeks. I got the plaster off on the Saturday and the bairn was born on the Sunday.... I went downstairs to the shop to get cigarettes for my man, came back up and the pains started. That one died too. Nobody knows how you feel.

It was in the month of April that that wee bairn was taken away with instruments and everything. The following June I had John, my son; the following July I had a daughter, Isa, and she was two when I was carted in and had an operation for ulcers and kidney trouble. There was four years till my next. When she was two years old I was taken in again. I had been haemorrhaging for seven weeks. I couldn't see, hear, nor talk. I was nearly thirty-five. It was a hysterectomy I had. The doctor was very neglective. He kept on saying, 'I'll get you into hospital.' Then the father jumped at him; he says, 'If you're not going to get my wife away I'll get her away.' After that operation it was touch and go. I was very thin. I'm slim-made. I've come through the mill, never worry. And I didn't get any time between them. Nobody knows ...

I had no chloroform with my three. I had them in the house. There was no money for hospitals. My second bairn was born during the first miners' strike, in 1926. They were out nine months then. My mother was good to us with meat, and she gave my man his cigarettes.

The whole thing with miners is that they've never had union leaders to stand by them. Arthur Scargill tells the truth – there's truth in him, and he's fighting and carrying on, and a lot of them could slap him in the mouth.

I walked from Musselburgh to Portobello Laundry every day during the strike, and my man looked after the bairns. I walked up and I walked down for I hadn't the car-fare. I ironed.

The wages weren't big in the pit then, and what you had you put on your bairns, kept them respectable. You got nothing yourself. You just had to do away with the clothes that you had.

But you always saw that your bairns were kept clean and kept respectable. I did anyway.

To begin with, losing your family was a break, a big break. I had a good mother. She was sixty-two when she died. My father dropped dead in the pit in 1932. He dropped dead after his shift was finished. He was sixty-four. The Saturday before he had been away seeing about his pension. He went to his shift on the Sunday, and he was up the lie [railway siding in the mine], giving the horse two slices of toast he always took from the house for it, and he came down and collapsed. This man said to him, 'What's wrong wi' you? Are you not well Jimmy?' He never got any answer. My father was away. And my father-in-law was away on Hogmanay, just eight days before him. My mother died in 1934. Two years. When one goes the other follows. My mother never done a day's good after my father died.

When he told my ma he'd been to see about his pension, she said, 'Aye well, you can get your sleeves up and do some work in the house then.' 'Oh', he says, 'I can wash.' He was in the army in the war you see. He was wee and stout and smart.

Off his pocket-money that he used to have on the Saturday, the old boy, he'd have four pennies in his pocket, and he kept these for my bairns, and my man used to say, 'There's the bairns' pocket-money from their grandfather.' Well, when he died and they brought home his clothes from the pit, the bairns' pocket-money was in his trousers. You sit and think about it, mind, eh?

After they brought home his things from the pit, my ma never done a day's good. She only rallied a year and ten month after my father died. She had shingles, and she just sort of lost her balance after he went. She died with me.

. . . I remember once my father and mother went through to Blackburn. My uncle and his wife had a restaurant and dance-hall there. The next day after they left, when I came home from my work, my mother was back. 'I like my ain bed', she said. My father was mad at her!

. . . Four months after my mother died my brother died, twenty-six years old. It never stopped. Then my man died on the fourth of January 1939, two days after another brother was killed at the pit. Silicosis. Weather like this: it was windy and snowing, and he came home from his work. He used a bike, and he was cycling home and he got soaking wet, and he lay a week. Two days after that, my brother was killed at the bing. It never stopped for two year for us – never stopped.

My mother's sister's son was got lying dead in bed, fifty-seven. A fortnight after it, her other son died, and a fortnight later the daughter died. She had thirteen of a family that auntie. She's only got four left. It just never stopped.

When my man died I got five shillings for the laddie and three shillings each for the lassies, a week. Twenty-one shillings for the four of us. My pension-book didn't come through and I went to the parish office to ask about the money. The man said, 'Get a job – you're a young woman – go and get a job.' I said to him, 'And who's going to look after my bairns if I get a job?' (My mother looked after the bairns. I just stayed across the road and it was handy.)

I worked all the time. The housing factor came and he said, 'Now you put in for a rent rebate', he says, '– see if you can get a rebate.' I had my youngest brother living with me then, but he hadn't a big wage. I got a pound a week from him. I put in for the rebate. Back came the letter: one and six. My brother says, 'You take that letter down and tell them you can live without their one and six.' So I took it down and telt them!

After that I started getting work myself. My son John was about thirteen, and he got started in the pithead in Niddrie, and my daughter who came thirteen months after him, then my daughter who's living with me now, got started. When my older daughter started working, five shillings came for the daughter left in the house. Her birthday was on the Monday, and I went down and drew my pension on the Tuesday, fifteen shillings: ten shillings for me and five shillings for her. The next week I went they took the five shillings off me, and handed me only five shillings, because I'd drawn it the week before. After that it was work all the time.

I wasn't waiting then. I was a waitress, but whenever the time came round that you could get a job you had to take it. Anything I could get my hands on, I had to take. Field-work, tattie-lifting ... until I got back to the waiting.

I had no bother with the bairns. They say, they need a father at their back ... well, I had no bother. They were just told they had to behave themselves, and that was all that was needed, because I led a clean quiet life, and so did they. That's what's wrong nowadays. Half the bairns is just getting to fly here and fly there and let their mother out to have a good time. That's not bringing up a bairn. You feel sorry for some bairns, so you do. You get all those bits of bairns that's in shelters. It's a scandal. Wherever I went my bairns went with me. The father used to take the two lasses, and the laddie would be away to the football, and they were no bother.

That was one thing; he wasn't an unfaithful man, he was a faithful man. He was all for his bairns. That's what's wrong these days: they just shove from one man to another man, one woman to another woman, and the bairns are all forgotten about.

Getting married again was the least of my thoughts. I had enough the first time. You're better single. But I was happy enough married.

I had a pal, her man walked out and left her. She was a Catholic, but her man was a Protestant, and her sister's married on a Protestant. Her other sister's married on an Englishman. This one that I knocked about with, married her man and got him to turn his coat. Her mother flung her out because she was going with him. Now no woman would do that who had any love for her family. But her mother did. There were ten years of difference between her age and his, because nobody would take her. It's funny, none of their own kind married into one another – do you notice? Eh?

Well that one: I gave her pots, pans, a beautiful big double wardrobe, sheets, pillow-slips, bedcover ... I fed her and her daughter and the daughter passed by there, and never came to me to say her mother was dead. I was too bloomin' good.

There was another pal that used to go to the Old Time dancing with me. We were sitting one night and – I knew this wee man's father, and he says, 'You don't drink, Bessie?' 'Not me – I never took drink in my life. Nor', I says, 'I don't smoke either. Not that I'm against anybody else doing it.' And he sat and he paid for seven – *seven* – glasses of whisky that my friend had. And she couped it over [knocked it back] and when we came out, we were standing waiting for the bus – she was twice

married too – this other lass came out. I knew her fine. We had
worked in the confectioner's together. She said, 'Are you
waiting for the bus, Bessie?' I said, 'Aye.' She walked over to the
other woman and said, 'You. I've seen what I want to see and
you can take him with you if you want him.' It was her own
cousin's man my friend had taken up with. And he ended up
with her. He's with her yet. I said, 'Now, that's me finished.'
When they start with their fancy-men and everything, I'm not in
it. They're deceitful. No, I've not come through the world
without knowing them ...

What I liked about the waiting, you got all different meals;
some want this and some want that, and you had to remember
what they wanted. Now they get books for to write it down, but
we got no books.

I've been at Elgin, St Boswell's, Inverness, Braemar,
Carnoustie – I've been all over the country. The only place I
haven't been is England and America. The train you went to
Inverness in, you could have come out and shoved it quicker.
And it was bucketing rain. It was murder. It's a thankless job,
but as long as you enjoy it yourself ... I was two years catering
at the Highland Show, and I was up to here in muck. They sent
me umpteen letters but no, I wouldn't go back there.

I was fifteen years in the City Chambers in Edinburgh. I
travelled back and forward there every day. When you was
there, they were wanting you to pay your own taxi home, but it
couldn't be done, because you was depending on what they gave
you. So then I shifted from there and went to Harwell's of
Colinton. I was six years with them, and I travelled all round
the country, as First Woman of the waitresses.

Then Mr Harwell was attacked, robbed, and beat up in his
house, and he never done a day's good after it.

I went from there to the Shelbourne Hotel in Edinburgh. You
used to get Johnny Dankworth and them all with bands there.
Then I shifted from there when she got slack, and I went to the
North British Hotel – and you talk about chefs? There's one in
that North British could learn them all! What a smashing man
he is. I was on with the head waiter, Mr Valotte. And I was
shifted from there to the Caledonian.

We had black and white uniforms at the City Chambers: you

had to buy it yourself too. They gave you the white gloves for serving royalty. I've served every one of them, from auld Queen Mary to auld Geordie. The Queen Mother, and the Queen, and her husband, and Margaret.

At one of the golf tournaments, I served the ex-King Leopold of Belgium. His first wife was killed in a car crash. Can you remember that? After she died, he must have fell in with this other woman, and they got married, and she was just like me or you, skirt and jumper and a headsquare. We had a marquee and everything. The meal was quite simple – Scotch egg and chips and a sweet and soup. He gave me two pound of a tip. He said, 'You people in Scotland will be making me too fat.' I said, 'You could do with some fat.' He was getting his kill [killing himself laughing]. He said, 'It's been lovely, thank you very much', and his purser came back and gave me a tip.

They've all been very nice. Only Margaret was a bit ... you know. There was one encounter with her. The manageress says, 'You can put the coffee through.' If she had said she didn't want coffee, but she didn't. She let me fill it out and then she said, 'I don't want any coffee. I don't like coffee.' Well, when I came down the aisle the manageress said, 'What was she talking about?' I said, 'Oh, she didn't want coffee.' She said, 'What did you do?' I said, 'I let the damn thing lie of course.' She says, 'And you done the right damn thing', she says, ' – *let* it lie.' I could have hit her.

I was away at Falkirk. They were opening up a skating-rink there. The Queen and the Duke of Edinburgh were there. You know you've to put the chair in for them and pull it out when they're getting up to go out ... aye, you have to do all these things ... and here when he got up, the Queen walked up the aisle and – she never speaks: none of them – you're not allowed to speak to them. She never speaks, neither do none of them. Well, the Duke got his chair back. He says to me, 'I wonder if I could have that other glass of beer?' I says, 'Certainly, your Royal Highness.' So I filled out the beer. The Queen turned round – if she didn't sink him with a look! [*Laughs.*] You could write a book about them.

... This is some carry-on in the papers about Charles, eh? You know, they can't turn. And the fella's done nothing out of place. I'll tell you though, Charles is a bit down in the dumps. If his mother would abdicate and let him on the throne. Because I read about him, and they say he's fed up with not having a right job. See what I mean? But she'll not abdicate. She'll be another Queen Vic-tory – another Queen Vic-tory ...

Anne has her work cut out there. But the Margaret one, I don't know what *she* does for her money.

The Queen Mother had a sister; she was married on an Elphinstone. She stayed not far from where I'm biding: just up the brae. She was very nice. And I'll tell you another nice one of the Royal Family, Princess May, auld Queen Mary's daughter. She married on Lascelles. I looked after Lady Elphinstone's daughter during the war, when I was working in Eden Hall Hospital. She was a nurse there. I was doing bedpans, a'thing and everything.

There were some sore sights when I was at Eden Hall then. There was a man sat outside all day, and they had to lift him into bed at night. Couldn't do nothing for himself. Terrible ... some with legs off, some with arms off.

But when I was there, there was a man that roamed about in the fields, from the Poor's House. I was scared from that man, coming home. I shifted to Musselburgh Maternity. I was thirteen months there. There was a nasty, nasty sister – oh, she was a besom! You had to be there dead on the dot and your uniform spotless clean...

When I worked in the North British there was a wee Jap there. He was a waiter. Mr Valotte put me up at the top table: 'You go up there and keep an eye on these buggers', he says. So I went. I had sixteen golfers. They went round with the plate and the head one said, 'That's for you.' There were a ten-shilling note in it. And here I came down the aisle, and left the plate lying, and the ten-shilling note. When I went back, here the wee Jap had scooted up the aisle and lifted the ten shillings off the plate. So I looked at him. I let him come right down to me. I took him by the lapels; I says, 'Now give me that ten shillings before I put you through the wall, see?' 'What ten shillings? What ten shillings?' I said, 'Now *give me the ten shillings.*'

Mr Valotte came along. He said, 'What's wrong, Bessie?' I said, 'This one's after lifting ten shillings.' Well, you didn't get it to yourself. You had to hand it in. You had to put it on a chit how much you got and your initials. I said to him, 'C'mon, fork it out', and he handed the ten shillings up. Valotte said, 'Do that again and I'll knock your so-and-so head off.'

Well, the Jap was coming out to go away, and he shoved a chicken up his jacket. I ran after him: 'Put the chicken back.' He said, 'Chicken?' I says, 'Take the chicken out of there', and I took the chicken out of his jacket. Valotte said, 'I'll knock the head off that one if he comes back' – but it wasn't 'knock the *head* off', believe me! Eh, you get them. Oh, you meet some dandies mind. Don't think you don't. But the Queen is very nice and so is the Queen Mother, and King George was a right gentleman.

I've always been a Labour voter from the day I had a vote, because I've had to labour, hard and sore.

I'll tell you something: your Queen's Tory. They're all Tories, the lot of them. When you're like that you daren't speak; you daren't say what you are, because it would be a rammy.

Politics is one fighting against the other, and that's how it goes on, all the time. Don't you forget that Labour were the men that was the cause of the Family Allowance, and that was a big, big mistake, because they're getting it now and their bairns isn't getting looked after. When in my life did I ever see so many bairns getting put into homes, into care, and murdered, and neglected? Never. You could be poor, but you were looked after, and you were kept clean. But not now. I don't understand them.

... Once I had sixteen at a table, and they were all coloured, and you'll know what they were like – they demolished three loaves. And one woman clapped her hands at me, and I never let on I heard her, and she did it again, and I went over and said, 'Is there something you want?' She said, 'Yes, we want more bread.' I said, 'Well, you're not getting it', I said, 'You've had three loaves on this table, and that's your ration.' These coloured folk are awful greedy!

There was another occasion. I had the table all set, all the food out ready for the meal, and this man pops up, whistling to me. I never let on I heard him. He'd had a good drink. He shouted. I went over to him: 'Is there something you want Mr Lowe?' He said, 'Oh, you know me?' I said, 'Aye, I come from Musselburgh too', and his eyes nearly fell out on to the plate. His friend the doctor just looked at him as if to say, 'Well, that's one up *your* shirt!' Oh, you had to be ready for them, or they took a rise out of you ...

Once when I was working I had served two men with their meal, and the boss told me to get something out of the fridge. As I went to do it this big guy comes walloping down the stairs and gripped me by the neck. The two I'd been serving had robbed a man's house and took his clothes and put them on, and taken his money. And this was them sitting getting fed! Of course, I could have claimed against the detective – it was, 'Out the road, this is a hold-up!' By jings, he didn't half give me a neck. It was black and blue and mauve for ages, the way he gripped me with his thumb. It's hurted the bone of my neck, and when I go to sleep and get up, it's murder.

Once I broke my pelvis, and it's affected my hip. It was in 1973. I was papering the ceiling and I just had it about finished when the ladder gave way and walloped me right against the wall, and then fell on me you see. My daughter and her husband were away at a dance, but my grandson was in the house. I had to crawl on my hands and knees, and he helped me up. I went to my bed and when the doctor came in next morning he said, 'The Infirmary immediately.' I was taken in and they gave me exercise eventually, to try to walk up a wee stairs. They gave me tablets and I came on fine after that. The leg was fine.

... The Co-operative has a set price for funerals, seven hundred pounds. But look what they take for breaking the ground now. I've got my own ground up there, right enough. My brother was buried in it, and my man ...

I feel like carrying on, you know, because if you sit down and think, you've had it. You think of all the hard times you've had, and how you've struggled with your own ten fingers. You want to keep going and there's nothing for it but to toddle on. If you're fit to toddle on you're not so bad.

Afterword

The last time I saw Bessie she had accepted the inevitability of the poll tax. Tacchi has finally set up the Tacchi-Morris Trust to promote international relationships by providing a centre where young people from all over the world can meet. No one has as yet benefited from the Trust, but Tacchi lives a life of extreme frugality in order to save enough to keep it going once it starts. She worries that people may be out to cheat her in her helpless old age, and finds it difficult to sleep at night for thinking of all that is still to do.

Josephine is still concerned with exhibitions of her father's work. Mary Coull is as full of the joy of living as she was when I met her first: her latest venture was to organize a bus trip to Perth for her fellow-pensioners in Peterhead. I have had no further communication with Miss X, who was for me the strangest of interviewees, inasmuch as her life seemed to run along classic lines and to have a significance that is social rather than personal.

Hers is the story I brood on most. On the surface, it is the easiest to analyse; the perfectly conventional life of an Edwardian spinster, an unemancipated woman with her Freudian papa; but a life lived back to front in many ways, with all the intimate duties, responsibilities, and pleasures at the beginning and all the freedom at the end. With her Guides, her old school ties and her commitment to committees, Miss X stirs up faint, elusive memories in me. More than any of the other women I interviewed, she makes me realize how dramatically the world has been changed by war. If I brood on her life long enough, I begin to feel that everything since 1914 might be the nightmare of some sensational writer of science fiction. What a price we paid for democracy, for emancipation! But it was worth it. I imagine what Mary and Erica might have done had they been born fifty years later, and I am sure of that.

Erica died quickly and peacefully in April after contracting a virus in the nursing home. Alice died in March. Her daughter's letter telling me this went to an old address and I did not find out until I telephoned the home where Alice had been staying. She had had a stroke and was given only a few hours to live, but she struggled on for a week.

I am glad to have known all the women in this book. Knowing them has changed me: altered my perspective on my own life, connected me up better to the continuity of my own sex, and given me examples to follow when my own inner lights failed me. I saw serenity in Alice; wild romanticism in Erica; a glorious contrariness in Enid; self-discipline and the world that failed in Miss X; innocence, courage, and genuine joy in Mary; a fine honest intelligence and a beautifully poetic sensibility in Josephine; gaiety in Tacchi, and the female courage that endures in Bessie.

I am grateful to every one of them, but to Bessie and Mary I owe a particular and personal gratitude, for they restored my lost faith in my own class. They above all are their own women; they above all fought for their independence every inch of the way. I humbly dedicate this book to them.